Loyal Subversion?

Caricatures from the Personal Union between England and Hanover (1714 – 1837)

Edited by
Anorthe Kremers and Elisabeth Reich

Vandenhoeck & Ruprecht

This publication was supported by the Volkswagen Foundation, Hanover.

VolkswagenStiftung

With 95 illustrations

Bibliographic information published by the Deutsche Nationalbibliothek

The Deutsche Nationalbibliothek lists this publication in the Deutsche Nationalbibliografie;
detailed bibliographic data available online: http://dnb.d-nb.de.

ISBN 978-3-525-30167-8
ISBN 978-3-647-30167-9 (e-book)

Cover illustration: James Gillray: A Connoisseur Examining a Cooper, 1792,
etching, BM 1868,0808.6215 © Trustees of the British Museum

Typesetting by: SchwabScantechnik, Göttingen

Coordination and editing: Anorthe Kremers
Project Management: Anorthe Kremers, Elisabeth Reich, Vanessa Spitau
Copy-editing: Catherine Atkinson

Printed in Germany by Memminger MedienCentrum, Memmingen

Printed on non-aging paper.

Contents

Introduction

In 2014, 300 years after the ascension of a Hanoverian monarch to the British throne, the Lower Saxony State Exhibition entitled 'The Hanoverians on Britain's Throne 1714–1837' celebrates the period of 123 years when England and Hanover were united under one monarch. The exhibition is on display in five different locations in Hanover and Celle. As a preview to the tercentenary, the Volkswagen Foundation, Hanover, organized a symposium clustered thematically around the aforementioned exhibition and highlighting one of its subtopics. This symposium, 'Loyal Subversion? – Caricatures from the Personal Union between England and Hanover (1714–1837)', was held in the rebuilt Herrenhausen Palace in Hanover on February 21–23 2013, organized in cooperation with the Wilhelm Busch – Deutsches Museum für Karikatur und Zeichenkunst, Hanover. The present miscellany assembles nine of the twelve papers of the symposium.

The 'Hanoverian dimension', which for a long time has been somewhat neglected by historiography, played an important role in eighteenth century British domestic and foreign policy and for the rise of civil society. During the last few years research has thus focused more and more on the Personal Union as a space of communication and interaction rather than just on the political and territorial dimension that was constituted by the coronation of a 'foreign' monarch.[1] Transfer of goods and cultural transfer between the monarch's two different territories were part of everyday business. Caricature is a brilliant example of this. Although the form of the Personal Union was not uncommon in history, it became a determining factor and was in itself a historical condition for the emergence and development of caricatures in England after the Glorious Revolution. As a political weapon of the opposition and as an institution of public opinion, the caricatures affected the establishment: on the one hand, their visual potential was a threat to the sovereign, on the other they helped to stabilize his leadership. When, after the death of Queen Anne in 1714, the reign of the Stuarts ended and the Hanoverians ascended the throne, they were strangers to the English; they hardly spoke the language and were limited in their power by a parliamentary system. George II's frequent absences in Hanover began to cause friction. The arrival in London of his mistress Amalie von Wallmoden added further fuel to the opposition. His son William

1 As in the Ph.D. research project 'The Personal Union of Great Britain and Hanover, 1714–1837. An International Space of Communication and Interaction' at the University of Göttingen.

Augustus swiftly became the butt of satire after his cruel suppression of the Scottish highlanders. When George III came to the throne in 1760, he and his favoured minister were castigated for assuming too much power in relation to parliament; the campaign against their plans to end the Seven Years' War gave rise to one of the great eighteenth century outpourings of satire. By the end of the century, the art of graphic satire was at its height in Britain. The culmination came with attacks on George IV's extreme extravagance. At the time of the American Revolution and during the Napoleonic wars, caricature became the most critical medium on the level of political communication in Britain and was later brought to the continent. Compared to England, freedom of press was very restricted in the rest of Europe. Therefore, British caricatures were able to define themselves as an instance of criticism, playing with different social levels. Caricatures at that time can be likened to an experimental laboratory for the democratic process in the long eighteenth century. From the French Revolution to the industrial revolution, they are an invaluable source from the perspective of cultural history, the history of mentalities and politics and last but not least they are masterly artworks.

The miscellany is arranged in four parts. The first section deals with the king as a central figure of the Personal Union. Werner Busch's essay 'The king falls into the hands of caricature – Hanoverians in England' analyses how the royal family became the caricaturists' favorite prey. Sheila O'Connell focuses on how the Hanoverians were exposed by caricaturists in her essay 'Attacks on the House of Hanover in Satirical Prints'. In 'Gillray and Royalty: The Politics of High and Low in Eighteenth-Century Art', Christina Oberstebrink concentrates on the artist and reconsiders the work of the caricaturist James Gillray. James Baker then turns his attention to the actual subjects, especially to George IV in 'The Royal Brat: Making Fun of George Augustus Frederick', giving an example of how the public nature of the Prince of Wales's indiscretions proved an irresistible commercial opportunity, seized upon by those London businessmen who printed and sold satirical prints.

Two essays deal with the topic of images. Karl Janke's paper on 'Counter-Image, Anathema, Vision of Terror. Republic and popular Rule in English Caricature of the Eighteenth Century' closely examines four revolutions that influenced the image of the republic in English caricature: the two English ones of the seventeenth century, the American Revolution, and finally by the French Revolution. In the debate on the 'right' image, the loyalist political caricature either refers to the basics of political perception or to the narrative conducted in contemporary forms of media and art with a view to changing republican views. This is the beginning of a conflict between loyalty and a growing republican self-confidence. In her essay 'In Bad Taste? Slavery and the African presence in the Subversive Mockery of Royalty', Temitope Odumosu takes a closer look at the representations of Africans in caricatures. Caricaturists illustrated Africans who were pushed out of social life – they pointed out the negative impact of the booming slave trade at that time.

The production and sale of caricatures is the central topic of Timothy Clayton's essay, 'The London Printsellers and the Export of English Graphic Prints'. Closely connected at first with the trade in political and topical pamphlets, caricature later became very fashionable, and the location of caricature print shops shifted to the expensive residential areas of Bond Street, St James's Street and Piccadilly, while images became larger, more ambitious, brightly colored, and increasingly expensive. Understanding caricatures often required intimate familiarity with political and social conditions in London, so it could be expected that this factor might repel foreigners. Yet there does appear to have been substantial foreign interest in British caricature.

In 'The Satirical Image – Politics and Periodicals 1820–1837', Brian Maidment concentrates on the history of the caricature as a print commodity and the emergence of seriality as a widespread mode of publishing. The rapid development of magazines and other modes of serial publication and the increasing familiarity with both wood engraving and lithography as reprographic media allowed political and social caricature to be developed and adapted to serial publication.

The last part leaves the field of caricature: In 'Politics Beyond Caricature: Practices of the Artistic Field' Sune Schlitte investigates the interaction between political pamphlets and caricatures. In a further step he analyses the practice of critiques of the newly developing exhibition scene as a political fight. Thus caricatures developed in interaction with many other media in the artistic field of the long eighteenth century.

There were three more papers given at the symposium that are not published in this miscellany. Christian Deuling's essay 'The Reception of English and French Caricatures in the German Journal 'London und Paris' (1798–1815)' was already published in 2012 in a more extended version.[2] In his paper, Deuling traced the path taken by certain exemplary caricatures from the streets of London and Paris to the journal 'London und Paris', edited in Weimar during the Napoleonic era, which was an important medium for the cultural transfer of images, especially English and French caricatures. 'London und Paris' provided the German public with a large quantity of prints, about half of them caricatures, which enriched the supply of English and French prints in the hands of bourgeois and noble collectors.

Ian Haywood's paper 'Milton's Monsters: Monarchy and Iconoclasm' will form part of his forthcoming book on 'Romanticism and Caricature. Visions of Excess, Fantasies of Power'.[3] In his presentation Haywood re-considered the impact of Milton's allegory of 'Satan, Sin and Death' on the culture of caricature in the Romantic period. The primary point of reference was Gillray's astonishingly 'rude' print, 'Sin, Death and the Devil' (1792), published only weeks after a royal proclamation against 'seditious' publications – the beginning of the 'white terror' of Pitt's counter-revolu-

2 Christian Deuling: Aesthetics and Politics in the Journal *London und Paris* (1798–1815), in: Maike Oergel (ed.), (Re-)Writing the Radical. Enlightenment, Revolution and Cultural Transfer in 1790s Germany, Britain and France (Berlin, 2012), pp. 102–118.

3 Ian Haywood, Romanticism and Caricature. Visions of Excess, Fantasies of Power (Cambridge University Press, forthcoming).

tionary cultural offensive. Gillray's print illustrated Milton's original. Haywood considered how the print exploited and disseminated a powerful iconoclastic tradition that can be traced back to the Reformation roots of political cartoon. His argument was that caricature reflected the satirical composition of Milton's allegory, a theme overlooked in the more famous sublime depictions of the scene by Romantic artists and illustrators. Gillray's unparalleled success in ridiculing the image of the ruling classes established a new aesthetic and imaginative standard for caricature.

With 'Johann Heinrich Ramberg (1763–1840) – Painter, Borderliner and Contemporary of the nascent Hanover Kingdom', Thomas Schwark glanced aside to view a German caricaturist of the time. Ramberg was born in Hanover just when the Seven Years' War ended and Britain emerged as 'ruler of the world' – with the Hanoverians on the throne. In 1781, Ramberg had the opportunity to study at the Royal Academy in London for the next seven years, instructed by Benjamin West. After this, he visited Leipzig, Dresden, Vienna, Rome and Naples. Back home in Hanover in 1793, he was witness to both Baron Knigge and his enlightened ideas and to the occupation by Napoleonic troops as well as their defeat. As a painter at court he established a new residential culture in Hanover. Apart from his official paintings, theatre decorations, illuminations, vedutas, and portraits he produced numerous illustrations for books by more than 50 contemporary poets (e.g. Hoffmann, Kleist, Goethe). But in fact, he was passionate about drawing, caricature, satire, and bawdy pictures – influenced by Bunbury, Rowlandson, and Gillray, whom he had met in London during the 1780s. The targets of his later caricatures were the members of higher society, social climbers, and the councillors at court.

The editors would like to thank the excellent speakers of the symposium as well as the audience, who listened to the presentations and discussed the papers with great interest. Dr Wilhelm Krull, Secretary General of the Volkswagen Foundation, has made the symposium and this miscellany possible. Dr Gisela Vetter-Liebenow, director of the Museum Wilhelm Busch, put forward the idea of the symposium to the Volkswagen Foundation. Our deepest thanks is to all contributors to this miscellany: thanks to their willingness to re-write the papers we are able to present this book and thus illustrate the fruitful exchange between England and Hanover – be it in 1714 and the years that followed, or in 2013/2014.

Hanover, January 2014 Anorthe Kremers and Elisabeth Reich

Werner Busch

The King Falls into the Hands of Caricature. Hanoverians in England

Durch die Hinrichtung Karls I. auf Veranlassung Cromwells im Jahr 1649 wurde das Gottesgnadentum des Königs ein erstes Mal in Frage gestellt. Als nach dem Tod von Queen Anne 1714 die Hannoveraner auf den englischen Thron kamen, galten diese den Engländern als Fremdlinge. 1760 wurde mit Georg III. zudem ein psychisch labiler, später geisteskranker König Regent. Als 1792 der französische König Ludwig XVI. inhaftiert und später hingerichtet wurde, musste das Königtum generell um seinen Fortbestand fürchten. In dieser Situation bemächtigte sich die englische Karikatur endgültig auch der königlichen Person. Wie es schrittweise dazu kam und welche Rolle dies für das königliche Porträt gespielt hat, wird in diesem Beitrag zu zeigen sein.

If I were to ask you how you would define the genre of caricature, then you would perhaps answer, after brief reflection that Caricature is basically a drawing reproduced in newspapers or magazines that comments ironically on political or social events in narrative form and both satirises the protagonists shown there by exaggerating their features and body shapes on the one hand and by reducing them at the same time to a few typical characteristics on the other hand characterising them unmistakably. Perhaps you would then add that the few typical characteristics of well-known people become binding stereotypes in the course of time and as such are sufficient to let the person become instantly recognisable. I think one could reach a consensus on such a definition. This form of caricature appears, however, at a very late stage in its history. In 1820/30 printing machines were invented that permitted text and image to be reproduced in one single printing process. Before this the illustrations had to be printed in a separate process and mostly on pages inserted into books and magazines. That was laborious work and expensive and was not worthwhile for newspapers, which were intended for consumption. So the newspaper caricature, which influences our view of caricature today, only started to exist from this point on. At the same time the first caricature newspapers came into existence, such as *La Caricature,* in 1830 or *Le Charivari* in 1832. Before this, printed caricatures were solely caricatures on single sheets or leaflets, sold by caricature shops, whose owners were printers and publishers; the caricaturists worked for them. In London in the second half of the 18th century, these shops were to be found around St. Paul's and near Parliament. The caricatures sold here would certainly fit into our definition, with the exception of the fact that they did not appear in newspapers or magazines. However, this type of single sheet caricature is also a relatively new development. They only start to appear around 1750, namely from the synthesis of two hitherto separate genres. One of these genres is the satirical image, which, in contrast to the caricature as we defined it, knows nothing of caricaturising individual portraits, arguing rather by means of allegory and often in the context of quite long printed explanations. It sketches out scenes. The second genre is that of the drawn, caricatured, individual portrait and this alone; it was not intended to be reproduced.

Around 1750 the caricatured, individual single portrait is inserted into the satirical image.[1] Interestingly, it was amateurs who brought about this synthesis. Their drawings, which staged the caricatured people in a certain context or scene, or at least hinted at one, were reproduced by publishers; they were not engraved or etched by the amateurs themselves. The most famous amateur caricaturist – and the most important for the origin of the genre – was the field marshal and member of Parliament, George Townshend, whom one can call the inventor of modern political caricature. His main sheet, *The Recruiting Serjeant* (Illustration 1), appeared in 1757. Its topic is a political occasion important at the time. The Duke of Cumberland, to whom homage is being paid here in a temple, had undermined the government of Prime Minister Pitt, and now Henry Fox is lining up with parliamentary colleagues to inherit his position. The duke, with his fat cheek falling down to his neck, needs no further facial features to be instantly recognisable.[2] This head shape became a cipher and reminds us immediately of Louis Philippe's pear-shaped head, which was formed by Philipon in the circle of artists around Daumier and was adopted for the German chancellor Helmut Kohl by the caricaturists Mulatier and Alex. Henry Fox, in contrast, is shown as a fox – something that also continues for quite a long time. The allegory of humans as animals derives from satires of the Reformation period. With the exception of the last figure, all those shown are depicted in profile; this comes from the drawn individual portrait caricature, as we will see in a moment. The last figure is shown from behind – something that Townshend knew from the drawn Venetian caricatures of the 18th century, the most characteristic examples having been produced by Giovanni Battista Tiepolo. This type was not conceivable before the 18th century, for it presumes certain insights into perceptual psychology. A figure seen from behind can also be unmistakeable in its contours; if we recognise it, we imagine its face. So we should note that in this early period, political caricature only knew en face, profile and rear views; all three forms revert back to a figure developed on a surface, a sort

1 Werner Busch, Die englische Karikatur in der zweiten Hälfte des 18. Jahrhunderts. Ansätze zu einer Entwicklungsgeschichte, in: *Zeitschrift für Kunstgeschichte* 40, 1977, pp. 227–244; on the pre- and early history of English caricature: Jürgen Döring, Eine Kunstgeschichte der frühen englischen Karikatur (Hildesheim, 1991).

2 Herbert M. Atherton, George Townshend Caricaturist, in: Eighteenth Century Studies 4, 1971, pp. 437–446; Eileen Harris, The Townshend Album, National Portrait Gallery (London, 1974); Döring, op.cit., pp. 199–202, Ill. 149; Diana Donald, The Age of Caricature. Satirical Prints in the Reign of George III (New Haven and London, 1996), pp. 47–50.

Illustration 1: George Townshend, *The Recruiting Serjeant or Brittanniais Happy Prospect*, April 1757, etching, BM 1868,0808.4057 © Trustees of the British Museum

of ornamental outline that, once studied, is easily repeatable. Townshend amused his parliamentary colleagues greatly with his caricatures and used his drawings to slander his political opponents. This in turn was only possible in the English context of the constitutional monarchy, in which political parties, the Whigs and Tories, competed with one another. In this context, the caricature was well suited as an argument for disparagement and derision.

We should take a look at the origin of the two components of the genre because it is only by understanding how they arose that we can actually gain access to our topic, which deals with how the king managed to fall into the hands of caricature. In terms of chronology, the satirical image is the older component of the political scenic caricature of the 18th century. One finds the earliest examples in the late 15th century, but the genre gains its actual function as a weapon in the struggles of the Reformation. Famous examples such as the pope as a donkey, the monk-calf or Pope Alexander VI as a diabolical monster with bird's talons show clearly that the animal allegory appeared to be the most appropriate weapon.[3] It should be empha-

3 Eduard Fuchs, Die Karikatur der europäischen Völker, vol. 1, Vom Altertum bis zum Jahr 1848, (4th ed. Munich, 1921), pp. 42–77; Konrad Hoffmann, Typologie, Exemplarik und reformatorische Bildsatire, in: Josef Nolte, Hella Tompert and Christof Winhorst (eds), Spätmittelalter und frühe Neuzeit. Kontinuität und Umbruch. Tübinger Beiträge zur Geschichtsforschung, vol. 2 (Stuttgart, 1978), pp. 189–210; ibid., Die reformatorische Volksbewegung im Bilderkampf, in: Exh. cat. Martin Luther und die Reformation in Deutschland, Germanisches Nationalmuseum Nürnberg, (Frankfurt a. M., 1983), pp. 219–254; Peter-Klaus Schuster, Abstraktion, Agitation und Einfühlung.

sised that the satirical image of the Reformation did not yet know the distortion of the individual portrait. The second component of modern caricature, the drawn and not reproduced, caricatured representation of an individual person emerged in the 1580s and 90s in the circle around the Carracci, a Bolognese artist family (Illustration 2). In this circle, which was also organised as a small academy, there were discussions with scholars, especially with church dignitaries, about art and its possibilities. This is easily explained. Since 1545, in reaction to the Reformation, the Council of Trent had been taking place as part of the Counter-Reformation, and during the last session in 1563, judgement was passed on the question of art, with a clear tendency. When dealing with biblical topics the artists should stick closely to the text of the Bible, not embellish the scenes as they chose and expressly avoid lewd topics; but a certain powerful urgency – for example in depicting scenes of martyrdom – would do no harm, in order to touch the emotions of the faithful. This was still couched in relatively general terms, so it was the task of the official interpreters of the Tridentine Edicts to deliver binding and detailed guidelines. And the main interpreters, the later canonised Carlo Borromeo, and Gabriele Paleotti, both resided in Milan resp. Bologna as archbishops. It was a question of exploring the possibilities and limits of art, and this was exactly what was being discussed in the Carracci workshop: as artists they were sounding out the limits. Regarding caricature, they asked themselves: How far can I distort a face and still guarantee a recognisable likeness? The Carracci conducted a whole number of experiments that opened up new means of expression in their intellectual circle of art. It was the legitimacy of the means of expression that was being discussed in this Counter-Reformation debate. Contrary to the assumptions of researchers, the question remains unsettled whether the caricatures created by Agostino Carracci, the actual inventor of the genre, and his brother Annibale were already of particular people or whether through experimenting on paper caricatures of particular types were being made. At any rate it is certain that the drawn, caricatured portrait of individual people emerged from these beginnings.[4]

It is astounding – and cannot be emphasised enough – that the history of this genre evolved, from about 1600 to about 1750, almost exclusively at the papal court. Just about all papal court artists drew caricatures – from Guercino and Domenichino, through Bernini, perhaps the most ingenious caricature draughtsman of all times, who also introduced the genre at the court of Louis XIV, down to Pier Leone Ghezzi, who particularly liked caricaturing the English travellers on the Grand Tour.[5]

Formen protestantischer Kunst im 16. Jahrhundert, in: Exh. cat. Luther und die Folgen für die Kunst, ed. Werner Hofmann, Hamburger Kunsthalle (Munich, 1983), pp. 115–125 and subsequent catalogue nos.

4 Anthony Blunt, Artistic Theory in Italy 1450–1600, (6th ed. Oxford, 1966), pp. 103–136; Donald Posner, Annibale Carracci. A Study in the Reform of Italian Painting around 1590, 2 vols. (London, 1971).

5 The literature on Italian caricature continues to be completely inadequate, cf. at least Exh. cat. Guercino Drawings in The Art Museum Princeton (Princeton, 1969); Irvin Lavin, High and Low

Illustration 2: Agostino Carracci, *Grotesque Heads and Caricatures,* 1594

His caricatures were so popular that the travellers went to him to let themselves be caricatured as they would to an official portrait session. This suggests to us that in the first 150 years of their existence there was something very exclusive about drawn caricatures, they were not made public, they remained at the papal court or in closed aristocratic circles, serving to amuse them – an amusement that this circle could afford; they were laughing at themselves and were not being scoffed at by a public audience. Such circles were able to enjoy the caricature as an intellectual experiment and understood caricature as the dialectic counterpart to fine art, to the official portrait. Just as caricature makes something appear ugly, the official portrait enhances one's appearance – the artistic process of careful deviation is more or less identical – even Winckelmann still defined caricature in this way. Bernini preferred profile and en-face depictions and developed an amazingly convincing method of abbreviation, which sketched memorable two-dimensional figures. We are fortunate to possess a

before their Time: Bernini and the Art of Social Satire, in: Kirk Varnedoe and Adam Gopnik (eds), Modern Art and Popular Culture: Readings in High and Low (New York, 1990), pp. 19–50; Anne Thurmann-Jajes, Pier Leone Ghezzi und die Karikatur, phil. Diss. Bochum 1993 (Bremen 1998); Werner Busch, Guercino und Rembrandt. Eine Begegnung der besonderen Art, in: Rembrandt – Wissenschaft auf der Suche. Beiträge des Internationalen Symposiums Berlin. 4. und 5. November 2006, ed. Holm Bevers i.a. [Beiheft des Jahrbuchs der Berliner Museen, N.F. 51, 2009] (Berlin, 2009), pp. 87–95.

caricature and an official bust of one and the same person, both by Bernini: of Cardinal Scipione Borghese (Illustrations 3 and 4). The bust shows the stout, but very lively cardinal, who was one of Bernini's most important clients, in a transitory moment unusual for a sculpture. The cardinal seems to be speaking, at the same time thinking and reacting to someone facing him. Such a strategy for bringing somebody to life is typical of Bernini, though it was not undisputed in the context of the demands made on classical art – which was supposed to capture a lasting impression rather than a fleeting moment. The caricature reduces Scipione Borghese's appearance to its cogent features and arranges them in a remarkably ornamental figure – one that works with symmetrical correspondences. The fat cheeks, the goatee beard, the bulbous nose, the eyes sunk in rolls of fat, the broad, fleshy shoulders, each marked with strongly simplified strokes: once one has seen this, one cannot forget it again and will imagine it even when looking at the official bust. The cardinal is stuck with this image – and this demonstrates the power of caricature right from the start. In Bernini's case this may have been something enjoyed by an insider – something that will have amused the cardinal, too – but beware the moment something like this becomes public.[6]

A first step into the public eye was taken by the aristocratic Englishmen on the Grand Tour in Rome, without actually aiming at a specific public. If they had themselves caricatured by Pier Leone Ghezzi, took these caricatures with them to England, showed them to friends as a form of evening entertainment, this then broadening out to become a fashion, then it is only a short step to wanting to have them reproduced, in order to give them to friends and acquaintances as gifts. But then it is no longer possible to limit their circulation. The first Ghezzi caricatures were being reproduced in England in about 1730, for example by Arthur Pond, who went into serial production of such pictures.[7] In Germany Matthias Oesterreich undertook something similar around 1750. The reception of Italian caricature in England was very close to the origins of amateur caricature and must be seen as its precondition. But before tracing the professionalising of caricature, we need to look at the further path of satirical image as a political weapon, since this is where people were thinking about the image of the king.

The obvious examples to use for this are the satires of Louis XIV, who not only had propagandist imagery programmes designed in Versailles, but also staged his whole existence as a scenic production. Hundreds of programmatic medallions swamped Europe and set out the image of the sun king, who saw himself as a second Apollo. Thus, in the Versailles fresco, his court artist Charles Lebrun places him in a sun chariot and has him rule over the stars and peoples. This exaggerated claim could not but

6 Werner Busch, Die Autonomie der Kunst, in: ibid. and Peter Schmoock (eds), Kunst. Die Geschichte ihrer Funktionen (Weinheim and Berlin, 1987), pp. 192–199.

7 Henry M. Hake, Pond's and Knapton's Imitations of Drawings, in: Print Collector's Quarterly 9, 1922, pp. 325 ff.; Louise Lippincott, Selling Art in Georgian London. The Rise of Arthur Pond, (New Haven and London, 1983).

Illustration 3: Gianlorenzo Bernini, Caricature of Cardinal Scipione Borghese, drawing
© Rome, Vatican Library
Illustration 4: Gianlorenzo Bernini, Bust of Cardinal Scipione Borghese, 1632, marble
© Rome, Galleria Borghese

provoke furious reactions among his opponents. It was obvious to imagine the sun chariot crashing down, thereby replacing the allusion to Apollo with one to Phaeton, who was not capable of steering the horses harnessed to the sun chariot, was thrown off his course and plummeted down to Orcus. This scene is to be found on numerous counter-medallions, though one should note that while the sun king does meet with an evil end, the imagery remains within the allegorical tradition and the king's features are not distorted.[8] This is also confirmed, ultimately, by the pamphlet propaganda directed at Louis that swamped France from Holland. If Louis XIV is represented directly in satirical images or in pamphlet literature, it remains an undistorted portrait, as a German etching of 1702 entitled *The Hawker of Versailles* (Illustration 5) demonstrates, which recognisably follows Hyacinthe Rigaud's often repeated official state portrait of Louis XIV of 1701. Romeyn de Hooghe's illustration of his *Aesopus in Europa* (Illustration 6) is from the same time, 1701/02, and is more interesting inasmuch as it develops the Phaeton iconography further and the defamation of Louis as a person increases. Even if his features are still not really caricatured, he does nevertheless become a ridiculous figure. His seat in the sun chariot, from which he has risen with some difficulty, is shaped like a toilet stool, he is using crutches and is try-

8 Hendrik Ziegler, Der Sonnenkönig und seine Feinde. Die Bildpropaganda Ludwig XIV. in der Kritik (Petersberg, 2010), pp. 21–74; Fuchs, op.cit., pp. 78–88.

Illustration 5: Anonymus, *The Hawker of Versailles,* 1702, etching, © Bibliothèque nationale de France

Illustration 6: Romeyn de Hooghe, Louis XIV as Phaeton, aus: Aesopus in Europa, 1701/02, etching

ing in vain to follow his mistress Mme de Maintenon, who has taken over steering the horses harnessed to the chariot and has completely failed in this task, also when influenced by Louis's opponents from the Grand Alliance of 1701. Even though Louis may still be surrounded by the sun's splendour, his fall, like that of Phaeton, who was incapable of steering, seems to lie directly ahead. So, with the following example of Louis XIV, the point has been made why the king, despite all the attacks, was not subject to individual caricaturing. The English author William Thackeray, who was also a good draughtsman, published a travel account in 1840 with the title *The Paris Sketch Book.* The frontispiece, designed by himself, shows Louis XIV as a threefold figure, as it were (Illustration 7). The first one is called 'Rex' and shows the royal robes together with the wig arranged on a coat stand, as was already generally familiar from Rigaud's state portrait of 1701. The second figure, called 'Ludovicus', shows the wigless Louis, a sad, puny person walking with a stick in private clothes, who can hardly stand on his skinny legs. Then, in the third figure, the synthesis takes place of the first and second appearance, now sub-titled 'Ludovicus Rex'. Clothes make the man. What is concealed behind this was expressed by Ernst Kantorowicz in a famous book title in 1957: *The King's Two Bodies.* According to medieval doctrine, the king possesses two bodies, one of which stands for the body politic – 'L'état c'est moi', as Louis XIV is said to have expressed it – the other is his body natural. Since the king is anointed by God's grace and merges with the body politic, he is inviolable. This

Illustration 7: William Thackeray, *Louis XIV. A Historical Study. Rex – Ludovicus – Ludovicus Rex,* Frontispiece in the *Paris Sketch Book,* 1840, etching, BM 1961,1012.335 © Trustees of the British Museum

taboo was maintained as far as the 18th century and was thus valid for caricaturists, too. It would be sacrilegious to distort the king's features.[9]

But to be able to understand how the caricaturists' struggle to gain control over the king was fought out at the time of the French Revolution, one still needs to mention an important development in English history. In 1688 the Glorious Revolution took place with the bloodless expulsion of the Stuart King James II, thereby ringing in the end of the Catholic dynasty. To avoid a Catholic succession with the support of either party Parliament had called for William III of Orange, who defeated the Catholic Jacobites in Ireland and triggered off James II's flight. That led, in 1689, to the Bill of Rights, i. e. to a separation of powers into legislative and executive and to the guarantee of freedom and of private property. Since this point in time, England has had a

9 Eva Horn, Vom Porträt des Königs zum Antlitz des Führers. Zur Struktur des modernen Herrscherbildes, in: Alexander Honold and Ralf Simon (eds), Das erzählende und das erzählte Bild (Munich, 2010), pp. 131–141, based on: Louis Marin, Das Porträt des Königs (Berlin, 2005) and ibid., Le corps glorieux du Roi et son portrait, in: ibid., La parole mangée (Paris, 1986), esp. pp. 219–225; Ernst Kantorowicz, Die zwei Körper des Königs. Eine Studie zur politischen Theologie des Mittelalters (reprint Munich, 1990).

constitutional monarchy, which firmly curtails the power of the monarchy, reducing it for the most part to representative duties. This is also of great importance inasmuch as the king's divine right was thereby dropped. The monarch can style himself 'The father of the people', as George III was to do, but his actions are no longer sacrosanct; they are publicly controlled. This makes it easier, so to speak, for the caricaturists to get the king into their clutches, though one also has to state that, as far as the individual portrait is concerned, the king still enjoyed a period of grace for quite a long time, and it was not until the events of the French Revolution that the last scruples were removed. In England, getting closer to the king's face was a step taken via the Princes of Wales. That needs to be explained briefly. After the death of Queen Anne in 1714, the rule of the Hanoverians began in accordance with the Act of Settlement. The first two Georges hardly spoke a word of English, the second did at least understand it; they were a foreign body in the country, George II also on account of his German mistresses blessed with English titles of nobility. The first George was the first to quarrel fiercely with his son, the Prince of Wales – thus pushing him politically into opposition. From then onwards each Prince of Wales established something like a counter-court, gathering opposition politicians around him and waiting for his chance to inherit his father. Furthermore, the first George preferred to be in Hanover, making it easier for the Prince to scheme against him. Robert Walpole sided with the King and particularly with the Queen, thereby coming to power and managing to stay in the position of prime minister with the support of the Queen, even after the death of George I in 1727. George II was just as stubborn as his father, but very much more caught up in political business, just as was his much more intelligent wife, Caroline, who betted on Sir Robert Walpole – something that brought England, despite all the corruption of the latter's ministry, a decided period of peace up to Walpole's resignation in 1742. In his desire for peace Walpole did however lose touch more and more with international politics. Clashes with France began, above all over supremacy in the colonies, which finally led to the Seven Years' War from 1756 to 1763. George II had problems with his son, the next Prince of Wales, from an early stage, who began to gather the forces of opposition around him in the early 1730s. Just like his father as the Crown Prince, Frederick Louis rented Leicester House, which became the centre of the opposition; in fact it was a second or alternative court right up to the death of George II in 1760. This was despite the fact that the Prince of Wales died unexpectedly in 1751; but his wife continued the opposition politics, knowing that her son would one day become king. She had William Pitt the Elder on her side, a gifted orator, who was more than a match for the royal ministry, thereby strengthening the opposition. Pitt pleaded for war with France, knowing that he had the backing of the aspiring middle-class, which grasped the fact that mercantile interests were involved. At the end of George II's life, Pitt and the opposition had achieved their goal. When George III came to the throne in 1760 he was barely 22 years old, extremely insecure and in search of a father figure for the whole of his life, which he repeatedly looked for among the influential politicians, who ultimately pursued their own interests. At first he was committed to the Earl of Bute. After a first fit of madness in 1765 he turned away from Bute and brought Pitt back to power. The international unrest, the clashes in America and domestic problems were too much for the king. The attacks of an increasingly independent press grew in number, in particular those made by the left-wing political gambler John Wilkes in his newspaper *The North Briton,* especially as Wilkes was devoted to the notion of freedom, which on the one hand strengthened parliamentary power and which on the other hand was understood by the strong entrepreneurs in the early Industrial Revolution as economic freedom, particularly by those from the country. No wonder that the events in France were welcomed in their circles, especially in the early phase of the French Revolution. The weakening of the monarchy was their item on the agenda, even to the point of wishing to abolish the monarchy. However, the king began to defend himself, insisted on his inherited rights, swore to uphold the constitution strictly; he recognised the threat from the newly rich, who were engaged in international business. The opposition, particularly in the shape of Charles Fox, made mistakes by attacking the monarchy as an institution. After all the attacks he had had to bear from all sides, this gradually brought the people on the side of the king. Above all he refused to give up the right of appointing ministers. The opposition forces fought tooth and nail to change this. Without royal consent, no minister could be pushed through; eventually he was in a position to dismiss the whole government. Which is what he did do to bring William Pitt the Younger to power. The people were wary of accepting Fox's anti-monarchical extremist position and saw in Pitt the more moderate political party; thus the king and Pitt won the elections of 1784.

But in October 1788 the king again relapsed into insanity. It was not only the political events, but above all family problems that probably triggered this off. George II was a family man, even though he did perform the marriage with Charlotte of Mecklenburg-Strelitz for reasons of state and she really was extremely ugly, which – as we shall see – did not escape the caricaturists; nevertheless, he was really devoted to the woman who bore him 15 children and he was clearly an affectionate father – for which his sons in particular did not thank him in the least. George III, modest and full of a sense of duty, to the point of being completely stubborn in this respect, had sons who lived extravagantly and ran up huge debts, which even led to crises of state, since Parliament was involved in settling the debts. And the worst was without doubt the Prince of Wales: a charming, unrestrained bon viveur, who was truly opposed to his father and in 1788, when his father was taken ill, already believed that he would soon be able to inherit him. He sided with his father's arch-enemy, Charles Fox, and so it has been said, rightly, that the Prince of Wales, with Fox, his unofficial prime minister, became the monarch of the reform-oriented Whigs. Even his sympathies for the events in France were clearly revealed. In 1785 he married his mistress Mrs Fitzherbert, which appeared particularly scandalous, as she was a convinced Catholic. That was too much for the king, sworn as he was to the constitution; he resorted to all possible measures against his son, despite being fond of him as his father. The king's insanity appeared incurable; he had to be forced into a strait-jacket. Yet hardly half a year later, in February 1789 – incidentally, one should note that the Bastille was stormed in July – the king came to his senses again and was able to take up his official duties again, though to a reduced extent. His struggle touched the public, he became a popular figure, his loyalty to England and the constitution became all the more significant, when the events of the French Revolution passed over into the phase of terror, when the September murders of the Swiss Guard and the clergy took place in 1792, when the French king was arrested, executed in January 1793, just as Queen Marie-Antoinette was subsequently, and when the Dauphin, the heir to the throne and still a child, was killed. The fear that the Revolution might spread to England grew continuously, which strengthened the king and weakened the opposition; it was not just caricature that made of Charles Fox a bloodthirsty sans-culotte. The Prince of Wales continued to devote himself to his excesses and was in the public's bad books. And although the king's health became worse and worse, until he finally went insane for ever in 1811, as the embodiment of the institution of monarchy he continued to represent the state. In 1812 the Prince of Wales became Prince Regent until his father's death in 1820.[10]

In this tendency towards a power vacuum it was no longer possible to hold caricature in check, all the more so since some of its proponents, especially James Gillray, took on an extremely anti-French attitude. It has already been said that the amateur caricatures of the late 1750s had brought about the synthesis of drawn individual caricature with satirical image, the latter acting with the help of allegory, thereby establishing the scenic modern caricature as a genre. It was only after 1770 that the first professional caricaturists came onto the scene, in particular the aforementioned James Gillray, born in 1757, and Thomas Rowlandson, born one year earlier. George II, who died in 1760, managed to escape the true professional caricature. The amateur caricaturists were concerned with the members of Parliament, for the most part excluding the king. One exception was George Bickham, who had the king appear on his pages in the 1740s, oscillating between satire and caricature. But it is precisely his example that demonstrates what problems he had in caricaturing the royal physiognomy. In a caricature of 1742, Walpole and George II, accompanied by their mistresses, are playing shuttlecock with the Duke of Argyll (Illustration 8). One or other of the textual allusions may be obscene, the physiognomies are not distorted, it is only the king's happy smile that does not conform with etiquette. One can recognise a certain tendency towards exaggerating typical features: the pointed nose, the large, somewhat piercing, bulging eyes, yet these are not yet really the features of a caricature. If the features are distorted – and, to stress it once again, this is definitely the exception – then this is a conscious approximation to an animal. George II can become a bird, his

10 A still convincing portrayal of the historical and political development in 18th-century England and the role of the kings: J.H. Plumb, The First Four Georges (3rd ed. Manchester, 1967); from the perspective of caricature: Donald, op.cit.

Illustration 8: George Bickham, *The Court Shittle Cock,* 1740, etching, BM 1868,0808.3679 © Trustees of the British Museum

basic physiognomy can suggest this tendency towards allegorisation. This is at best on the border to caricature.

The same can be said of a caricature called *The Queen of Hungary's Whetstone* (Illustration 9) of 1744. It is certainly obscene. Maria-Theresa has gathered up her skirts with her legs wide apart and is pissing on the whetstone to cool it. A weapon against France and Prussia, whose invalid soldiers appear on the right, is being sharpened, and George II is happily turning the whetstone. Yet neither Maria-Theresa nor George II is really being caricatured. Scatological matter often turns up in early satire, since the satire of the Reformation it has been part of the basic repertoire of the satirical image. Nevertheless, it does not represent a real attack on the individual body of the queen or king.[11]

The royal princes first have to stand in for that. In James Gillray's caricature of 21 April 1786 (Illustration 10) the problem that George III had with his sons is expressed succinctly. The king is coming from the royal treasury with Queen Charlotte; they are carrying off endless amounts of money in order to settle the national debt. That is paradox in a two-fold sense, not only because the national debt could hardly be settled from the state reserves, but also because George and Charlotte were extremely niggardly, as the caricaturists often accused them of being. Pitt, who has also helped himself, and is thereby declared to be open to bribery, is handing the king

11 On Bickham cf. esp. Döring, op.cit., passim (cf. Index) and Ill. 71, 81 und 82.

Illustration 9: George Bickham, *The Queen of Hungary's Whetstone,* approx. 1744, etching, BM 1868,0808.376 © Trustees of the British Museum

Illustration 10: James Gillray, *A new way to pay the National-Debt,* 21 April 1786, etching, BM 1868,0808.12472 © Trustees of the British Museum

a further bulging sack of money, but on the right appears a completely tattered Prince of Wales. An elegantly dressed man, who can be identified as the Duc d'Orléans – a note on the wall of the treasury shows two intertwined hands, a classical friendship symbol with Orléans written on it – and indeed the duke is offering the prince to settle his horrendous debts.[12] The friendship between these two, irritating enough with all the tension between France and England, was to take on an explosive form, for the Duc d'Orléans, not called Philippe Egalité in vain, had voted for the death of his cousin, King Louis XVI of France, and thus there is a caricature by Isaac Cruikshank that shows Philippe Egalité alongside the guillotine holding Louis XVI's head, struck off and dripping with blood, in his hand. The print was created less than four weeks after the event.[13] The duke's sympathies for the radical path of the Revolution are thus transferred via the Prince of Wales to his political entourage and to Charles Fox in particular. The English supporters of the revolution during its first phase had hoped that a sort of second Glorious Revolution would take place in France and that the French would adopt the English system of a constitutional monarchy. The belief was upheld until 1792. For a while the English still supported the moderate Girondists and basically they also delineated the position of the circle surrounding the Prince of Wales. But the English anti-French propaganda quickly turned Fox into a Jacobin and a sans-culotte, bloodthirsty, a dagger hidden in his cloak and thus a potential king's murderer.[14] In a caricature by Gillray from 5 April 1788, the Prince of Wales is shown after his wedding night with Mrs Fitzherbert, with whom he was living in a morganatic marriage. The date of the caricature is irritating; the event, which is supposed to have taken place in France after the prince's flight with his mistress, already lay two years back. It can only be explained by the fact that the English relationship to France was particularly tense, just as was the relationship of George III to his son. The Prince of Wales, with his sympathies for France, must have appeared like a traitor. But even on such an occasion the prince's physiognomy is not really distorted.[15] During the Revolution itself the boundaries between caricature and serious portrait were finally no longer clear-cut. The pair of opposites portrayed by Gillray on 2 July 1792 is a famous one, showing on the one page the Prince of Wales's meal (Illustration 11) and on the other that of his parents, King George and Queen Charlotte (Illustration 12).[16] And although Gillray basically stands more for the position

12 Donald, op.cit., p. 69 and Ill. 72; M. Dorothy George, English Political Caricature. A Study of Opinion and Propaganda, vol. 1, To 1792 (Oxford, 1959), pp. 189 f.

13 David Bindman, The Shadow of the Guillotine. Britain and the French Revolution, The British Museum, London 1989, Cat. no. 109, pp. 136 f.

14 Donald, op.cit., pp. 162 f. and Ill. 175.

15 Ibid., p. 69 and Ill. 71; Vic Gatrell, City of Laughter. Sex and Satire in Eighteenth-Century London (London, 2007), pp. 324 f. and Ill. 142.

16 Ibid., pp. 100 f. and Ill. 110; coloured illustration of both graphics: Exh. cat. James Gillray 1757–1815. Meisterwerke der Karikatur, Wilhelm-Busch-Museum Hannover; Staatsgalerie Stuttgart; Museum für Kunst und Gewerbe, Hamburg (Stuttgart, 1986), cat. nos 35a und b, p. 201 and Ill. pp. 70 and 71; Gatrell op.cit., pp. 215–218 and Ill. 90.

Illustration 11: James Gillray, *A Voluptuary under the Horrors of Digestion,* 2 July 1792, etching, BM 1868,0808.6219 © Trustees of the British Museum

of the king and Pitt, by being contrasted both parties come out it equally badly. The prince's stomach is dangerously stretched, he has already wolfed down mountains of meat, the bones are lying on his plate, the chamber pot behind him has already had to accommodate the puked up contents of his gluttony, now he is poking around in his teeth with a fork – for someone of princely lineage a faux pas of the first order.

Illustration 12: James Gillray, *Temperance Enjoying a Frugal Meal,* 2 Juli 1792, etching, BM 1868,0808.6224 © Trustees of the British Museum

Above him, like the commentary of a picture within a picture, as Hogarth before him particularly liked to use it, there is a portrait of Luigi Cornaro, who wrote an autobiographical treatise entitled *Discourses on the sober life* more or less at the end of his life. Truly, a *memento mori* for the prince. If one looks out of the window, then one learns that the prince is not only a slave to his appetite for food, games and lust, he also has a craving for erecting buildings. Unfinished colonnades are to be seen –

here, too, incidentally a quote from Hogarth's *Marriage à la Mode,* scene 1. His face is still not really distorted. However scandalous the prince's behaviour may be and however much public offence it may cause, he remains the potential king. A revealing detail shows well that the intention to portrait the prince is stronger than that of caricaturing him. As long as the facial features are depicted in detail, as long as the fleshy forms appear carefully dotted – this contradicts the caricature's principles of reducing and simplifying as far as possible.

It is no different in the royal counterpart. Here, thrift is being practised; the king's and queen's miserliness was proverbial, the king is eating boiled eggs, the queen salad. To take good care of the royal armchair, they have not even removed the protective covering. They are drinking water rather than alcohol, bottles of which the prince was consuming. Here, too, the behaviour of the royal couple is commented upon on the wall. The figure of 'munificence', generosity, standing on the mantelpiece, is holding two huge horns of plenty, empty unfortunately. And above the king there is an empty picture frame. But the title of the picture that has been removed is named on the frame: 'The Triumph of Benevolence'. Now, the niggardly royal figures are truly not benefactors. But the allusion actually goes further here, for the picture title refers to a poem by Samuel Jackson Pratt of 1786, in which the good deeds of the prison reformer, John Howard, are praised, and Gillray himself had executed a serious etching of this in 1788, celebrating the benefactor Howard as a redeemer.[17] Above the empty frame there is enough to see of an oval frame to recognise the inscription 'Epicure'. Clearly this is the counterpart to the portrait of Cornaro with his appeal for restraint in the image of the Prince of Wales, for Epicure was, as is well-known, in contrast a pleasure-seeker, and one really cannot say that of poor George III.

Another late example is showing the Prince of Wales. He had hardly mended his ways, he eventually married Caroline of Brunswick for reasons of state and dutifully sired an heir, only to continue indulging himself in his customary excesses. How he behaves towards his wife, who is sitting on the sofa and shyly clasping the baby, is made clear in an anonymous caricature of 31 May 1796, which can probably be ascribed to Isaac Cruikshank (Illustration 13). The prince is losing his temper and kicking over the tea-table, behind him the cuckolded husband of Lady Jersey, who is lying sprawled on her sofa in an obscenely welcoming posture, is opening the door and is even offering his good lady to the Prince of Wales. The motive with the tea-table kicked over again derives from Hogarth, taken here from scene 2 of *A Harlot's Progress* from 1732. Once one has realised the origin, the Prince of Wales becomes even more of a lecher. The prince has not only got a map of Jersey in his pocket, he is also holding a text called 'Thoughts on Despotism' in his hand. So even when portraying a domestic scene, the political dimension is not far off; he was still regarded as a supporter of the revolution, who would like to transplant French conditions to

17 Werner Busch, Romneys 'Howard'. Revolution und Abstraktion, in: Städel-Jahrbuch, N.F. 16, 1997, pp. 289–332, esp. pp. 296–300.

Illustration 13: Isaac Cruikshank (?), *Future Prospects or Symptoms of Love in High Life,* 31 May 1796, etching © Trustees of the British Museum

England.[18] The fear of a French invasion remained alive in England for a long time. However, even here the Prince of Wales is portrayed elegantly. Gillray, who was given a state pension by the government loyal to the king at the end of 1797, now only speaks in the name of the government, leaving out Pitt for example, whom he had previously enjoyed caricaturing, from all criticism and dealing with the king very much more cautiously, especially in the Napoleonic times. It was Swift's *Gulliver* that supplied the model for *Little Boney.* In a famous caricature by Gillray, dated 1803, Napoleon is being observed through a telescope by George III, the latter astonished by the fuss he is kicking up, despite being balanced on the palm of the king's hand.[19]

In February 1791 the first volume of Thomas Paine's *The Rights of Man* was published, thereby supplying the revolutionary counterpart to Edmund Burke's *Reflexions on the Revolution in France* of November 1790. It was enhanced by the second volume, added in February 1792. Thus the loyalists and the supporters of revolution had their pieces of writing with which to identify. An anonymous caricature of 26 May 1791 describes how the readers of Tom Paine's treatise were split into groups (Illustration 14).[20] With Paine's treatise, the French seed seemed to have sprouted in England.

18 Donald, op.cit., p. 101 and Ill. 111; Gatrell, op.cit., pp. 327 f. and Ill. 145.

19 Exh. cat. James Gillray, op.cit., Cat. no. 147, pp. 239 f. and Ill. p. 161.

20 Bindman, op.cit., Cat. no. 51, p. 108.

The fear that the revolution might spill over into England was particularly great at this time. On 16 August 1792, after the events of 10 August, when the French king was removed from power, Richard Newton depicted the reaction of the English king to the alarming news in a caricature as grandiose as it was striking. The horrified Pitt is informing the thunderstruck king, and Queen Charlotte is hoarding money as a precaution, in case flight becomes necessary.[21] The dethronement of Louis is likened to hell breaking loose in Paris. The caricature of the reading of Paine's treatise is more moderate, but the different sympathies are clear – and again the king and queen are involved. The couple is characterised wonderfully: Burke is raving, Fox is greatly satisfied, the king cannot believe it, Baron Hawkesbury is reading with pleasure, the queen is rolling her eyes, Hannah More, the philanthropist, is enjoying what she reads, and Pitt is losing his temper, which Sheridan cannot understand. The texts attached, which will not be discussed here, make clear the different reactions. But then, on receipt of another piece of shocking news, which Pitt brings the royal couple (Illustration 15) – it concerns the murder of the Swedish king – Gillray loses all moderation, and the king and queen are unmasked in a most wicked manner and caricatured.[22] The page is dated to 11 April 1792; disaster is coming closer and closer. As a result of the fright, the king and queen are relieving themselves on a double shit-stool. In the true sense of the word they have lost all control of their reactions. The reversal thereby performed is really cynical. The king has let his trousers down and come clean: an English sans-culotte from the opposite camp. The king's gobbledygook exposes him even more. This royal physiognomy can no longer pass for a mere portrait; caricature has now taken over control. The thin Pitt, the simple king, the nasty queen – they are all of a kind.

Gillray can still retract here, Richard Newton cannot; he belongs, alongside Isaac Cruikshank, to those supporters of the revolution that do not change their opinion even after the execution of the French king in January 1793. And his publisher William Holland was in total agreement with him, which led to the publisher having to end up in Newgate prison in 1793 on the charge of circulating inflammatory literature. One should realise that censure applied to book publishing, whilst there was an amazing amount of freedom for graphic art. Richard Newton made no secret of his opinion of the king. In a small caricature of 1798 (Illustration 16), by which time Gillray had long been bought over by the government, John Bull, the embodiment of England, is taking pleasure in farting at a poster of the king, with Pitt loudly declaring this to be treason. At the same time Newton lets the people's sun rise. His sympathies are clear, and the king is simply left with a blank look of incomprehension.[23] Newton behaves in a similar way after the September murders of 1792, which, as mentioned, had also led to a massacre among the clergy. Some of those who managed to escape emigrated to England, and now the king and queen, with collecting boxes, are trying

21 Ibid., Cat. no. 47, p. 106.
22 Donald, op.cit., p. 146 and Ill. 157.
23 Ibid., pp. 161 f. and Ill. 173; Gatrell, op.cit., p. 483 and Ill. 235.

Illustration 14: Anonymus, *Contrasted Opinions of Paine's Pamphlet,* 26 May 1791, etching © Fitzwilliam Museum, Cambridge

Illustration 15: James Gillray, *Taking Physick; -or- The News of Shooting the King of Sweden!,* 11 April 1792, etching, BM 1868,0808.6181 © Trustees of the British Museum

Illustration 16: Richard Newton, *Treason!!!*, 19 March 1798, etching, BM 1868,0808.6712 © Trustees of the British Museum

to take care of their support – which, knowing their miserliness, in itself makes an unintentionally humorous impression (Illustration 17). But the caricaturing of the royal couple, particularly of Charlotte, stops at nothing, not even rank. Newton is in the position to create unmistakeable figures using very few features. The king has found a particularly expressive pose; the butler in *Dinner for One* could not have presented a better one.[24] Step by step the significance of the monarchy is being undermined; the king no longer needs to be executed.

What remains of him after being dismantled in this way? In spite of everything he can still become idealised, as was the old, ailing George III. He is still suitable for trashy magazines, he can socialise on the same level with the stars and starlets, he can become a legend of what used to be, or he can, as was the case more recently, simply abdicate and become a private person. For the private aspect of his person is no longer really cloaked by his representative persona. The king now only has one body. With his resignation as pope, Joseph Ratzinger has abandoned the last bastion of the doctrine of the Two Bodies.

24 Bindman, op.cit., Cat. no. 218 and Ill. p. 208 (wrongly called no. 219).

Illustration 17: Richard Newton, *Sturdy Beggars collecting for the Emigrant French Clergy,* September 1792, etching © Trustees of the British Museum

Sheila O'Connell

Attacks on the House of Hanover in Satirical Prints

Dieser Aufsatz beschäftigt sich mit den satirischen Drucken, in denen die Karikaturisten die hannoverschen Könige Englands angriffen, sowie mit den Methoden, die die Künstler benutzten, damit ihre Botschaften von den Betrachtern verstanden wurden. Ähnliche Kompositionen erscheinen wiederholt in unterschiedlichem Kontext als visuelle Kurzschrift und mit dem Ziel, durch den Bezug auf zurückliegende Ereignisse oder auf vertraute Bilder bestimmte Aspekte hervorzuheben. Der hannoversche Schimmel symbolisiert den König; der Wandschirm, der den Blick auf königliches Fehlverhalten zur Zeit der Südsee-Spekulationsblase (South Sea Bubble) im Jahr 1721 versperrte, erscheint wieder in Drucken der späten 1730er Jahre und weist auf die versteckte Korruption Georgs II. und insbesondere seines Ministers Robert Walpole hin; eine auf Drucken aus der Zeit des Jakobitischen Aufstandes von 1745 dargestellte Kutsche, welche die mühsam errungenen Freiheiten niederwalzt, geht zurück auf einen anti-Jakobitischen Druck, der kurz vor der Thronbesteigung Georgs I. 1714 herausgegeben wurde. Die sich 1782 in Opposition zu Georg III. stellenden Politiker werden so abgebildet, dass sich der Betrachter an die Schießpulververschwörung aus dem Jahre 1605 erinnert fühlt; Georg IV. beleidigt seine Untertanen, indem er auf dieselbe Weise furzt wie einst Georg II. in einem Druck der 1730er Jahre und die Art wie Wilhelm IV. von seiner Frau geschlagen wird, ist schließlich der Wiederhall auf pornographische Drucke der Zeit.

British satirical prints attacking the House of Hanover were inspired by artists' anger or by their sense of humour, or by a mixture of both. What made the British angry about the Hanoverian kings were in many ways the same things that make us angry or make us laugh about our current leaders. We, like our 18th- and 19th-century predecessors, get angry with greedy or incompetent politicians and we get angry when we see our taxes being wasted. The British still find many of the same things funny as they did in the 18th century, particularly bodily functions and anything to do with sex. We also still have an unfortunate tendency to laugh at foreigners and their ways. All these tendencies are evident in satirical prints concerned with the House of Hanover. But attitudes revealed in prints can also surprise and there are clear indications of how our predecessors differed from us: we are less comfortable at making fun of people's religious beliefs than were the Georgians, who respected no faith other than the Church of England, and present day leaders are urged to make peace rather than war, while George II and, especially, George III were mocked for their reluctance to pursue military activities.

This paper will look at the subjects of anti-Hanoverian satire, but also at the motifs that artists used in order to get their messages across to their audience. Similar compositions appear over and over again in different contexts as visual shorthand and to reinforce points by referring back to previous events or to familiar images. The white horse of Hanover is used throughout the period to stand for the king; the screen that hides royal wrong-doing at the time of the South Sea Bubble in 1721 appears again in prints of the late 1730s pointing to hidden corruption by George II and more particularly his minister, Robert Walpole; a carriage mowing down hard-won liberties in prints produced at the time of the Jacobite rebellion of 1745 is derived from an anti-Jacobite print published just before the accession of George I in 1714; politicians opposed to George III in 1782 are depicted in a way that would have reminded viewers of the Gunpowder Plot of 1605; George IV insults his subjects by breaking wind in the same way as George II in a print of the 1730s; William IV is beaten by his wife in an echo of a pornographic print.

The Hanoverian dynasty was largely welcomed in Protestant Britain when George I's coronation followed swiftly on the death of Queen Anne in 1714. Jacobites who supported the claim to the throne of the Roman Catholic James Stuart would no doubt have treasured portraits of James and his family and displayed them to show their allegiance, but there was no concerted campaign of satirical prints attacking George I until 1721. We can sympathise in the light of the current financial crisis with the anger provoked in that year by the failure of John Law's Mississippi Scheme in Paris and the South Sea Scheme in London. The South Sea Scheme was particularly problematic because it had involved the British government and an attempt to disguise the national debt by converting it to South Sea Company stock. Moreover, the royal family and close associates had been bribed with South Sea stock at a time when its value was rising. When the 'South Sea Bubble' burst, Robert Walpole, then an ambitious young minister, devised ways of hiding royal involvement in order to avoid devastating scandal. This is illustrated symbolically in *A True Picture of the Famous Skreen* (Illustration 1),[1] a composition that appeared in many versions. A folding screen decorated with scenes of the punishment of criminals blocks from view a number of people who can be glimpsed beyond either as shadows or reflections in a mirror. There are politicians who were involved in, and profited from, dealings with the South Sea Company. Three women are also present: Melusine von der Schulenburg, the king's mistress, and Sophia von Kielmansegg, his half-sister, who was assumed by the British also to be his mistress, each of whom had been given £15,000 worth of South Sea stock, and Henrietta Howard, mistress of the future George II, who had received £11,500 worth of South Sea stock.

1 See F. G. Stephens and M. D. George, Catalogue of Political and Personal Satires in the British Museum (London, 1870–1954), II, pp. 579–80, No. 1710. The print, and all the others referred to in this paper, are described and reproduced on the British Museum website. Descriptions of satirical prints up to 1750 have been revised on-line by Rosemary Baker.

Illustration 1: Attributed to Bernard Picart, *A True Picture of the Famous Skreen,* 1721, etching © Trustees of the British Museum

Satirical prints of the early 18th century were largely emblematic and accompanied by a good deal of explanatory text. The great flowering of graphic satire did not occur until the end of the century, and most of the printmakers and publishers who attacked George I and George II are little known today. Their work is often difficult to interpret for the modern viewer and would have been aimed at a narrow audience of those involved in political affairs. *The Festival of the Golden Rump,*[2] published in 1737 (Illustration 2), has an immediate shock effect but its meaning requires reference to an article in *Common Sense,* an opposition journal. George II takes centre stage in the print and beside him stands Robert Walpole, who by then had led parliament for nearly two decades. Walpole felt threatened by satirical performances in London theatres and was manoeuvring to introduce censorship. The print illustrates a scene

2 Stephens and George, op.cit., III, pp. 223–37, No. 2327.

Illustration 2: Anonymous, *The Festival of the Golden Rump*, 1737, etching © Trustees of the British Museum

from a farcical play, in which the king, represented as a goat-legged satyr, responded to the approach of his courtiers by breaking wind. Not surprisingly, the king was disgusted at being depicted in this way, and Walpole was able to bring in the theatrical censorship that he wanted. It seems, in fact, that the play had been written at Walpole's instigation, deliberately to shock the king – a clever trick by a devious politician.

The satyr-king in the *Golden Rump* is kicking out with his left leg. George II apparently had the habit of kicking out when he was angry. He was particularly liable to kick his hat as shown in *Solomon in his Glory,*[3] where he sits embracing his mistress Amalie von Wallmoden, who had arrived from Hanover after the death of Queen Caroline in 1738.

In *The Screen*[4] of 1742 George II is accused of complicity with Robert Walpole's notoriously corrupt practices, a deliberate reminder of the *Famous Skreen* of 1721 and thus of George I and Walpole's involvement in the South Sea scandal. Hidden behind a large screen George II sits beneath a huge crown selling offices of state and military

3 Stephens and George, op.cit., III, pp. 247–48, No. 2348.
4 Stephens and George, op.cit., III, pp. 424–46, No. 2539.

commissions, while Walpole stands at a table behind him dressed as the comic character Punch, handing out bags of money to supporters. Walpole had just defeated a call in parliament for a committee of inquiry into corruption, but opposition politicians were still determined to remove him from power: breaking through the screen to reveal Walpole's wrongdoing is his powerful opponent the Duke of Argyll.

The British taxpayer was angered by what was seen as George II's greater care for Hanover than for Britain. In a clever piece of trompe l'oeil draughtsmanship, *An Actual Survey of the Electorate,*[5] he is identified with his German state. Viewed horizontally we see a (not very accurate) topographical view of Hanover with the Herrenhausen Palace and gardens, the River Leine and so on, but viewed vertically the image becomes a profile of George II. There was particular public anger at the king's concern to protect the electorate during the War of Austrian Succession. George II famously led his troops at the battle of Dettingen, but it was believed that he failed to follow through initial success in order to protect his Hanoverian army and, furthermore, that he neglected British soldiers. In *The Hanoverian Confectioner General,*[6] George II is shown as the white horse of Hanover riding a starving British lion. The enfeebled lion was fed, like British soldiers, on bread fit only for horses. General von Ilten hides behind a tree saying that he must take care of the Hanoverians, while in the background, the brave British troops are eager to pursue the French as they gallop off in retreat.

Moving on to 1745 we find a military threat to Britain itself in the form of the Jacobite Rebellion led by Charles Edward Stuart, the 'Young Pretender', who invaded Scotland with the promise of French support. *The Invasion or Perkins Triumph*[7] is one of several versions of the same composition showing the event in emblematic form. The Young Pretender rides through London in a carriage driven by Louis XV with the pope as postilion and a devil on the footboard. A figure representing British liberty is mown down and conventional anti-Roman Catholic images are shown in the background – Protestants burned at the stake or hanging from gallows, and monks kneeling before a large cross erected in front of St James's Palace. The composition was based on *Needs must when the Devil drives,*[8] published in 1710 shortly before the death of Queen Anne when the Hanoverian succession was expected, and when an earlier generation of Jacobites were seen as a threat to moderation, toleration, liberty and property.

By 1745 such emblematic imagery was becoming out-dated. Visual satire was beginning to take over and there was less reliance on text. An easy shorthand for the satirist was to stereotype his target and, as the Stuarts were a Scottish dynasty, the Jacobite threat could be identified with the Scots, readily recognised in their tradi-

5 Stephens and George, op.cit., III, p. 467, No. 2587.

6 Stephens and George, op.cit., III, p. 465, No. 2584. The title is a pun on General von Ilten's alleged determination to 'conserve' the Hanoverian soldiers.

7 Stephens and George, op.cit., III, pp. 510–11, No. 2636; see also, pp. 511–12, No. 2637 and 2638. 'Perkin' is a reference to Perkin Warbeck, a 15th-century pretender to the throne.

8 Stephens and George, op.cit., II, pp. 275–76, No. 1496.

tional dress of tartan. *Sawney in the Boghouse*[9] belittles the enemy by showing the highland Scot as an uncouth, almost savage, creature who did not even know how to use a lavatory. The humour of disgust, of scatology, is used to reduce fear of a dangerous opponent. We will see an even greater enemy – Napoleon Bonaparte – literally belittled in a later satirical print.

George II's son William, Duke of Cumberland, was given credit for defeating the Jacobites at the battle of Culloden in April 1746. In *Tandem Triumphans*[10] the Young Pretender and his general John William O'Sullivan ride away from the battle leaving their foot-soldiers to be slaughtered. Cumberland enters on a white horse, representing the triumph of the Hanoverian dynasty over the Stuarts. But Cumberland's moment of triumph was marred by the cruelty with which the Scottish highlanders were subdued. Within a month a satirical newspaper announced that he was to be made a freeman of the Worshipful Company of Butchers. At the end of the year he was portrayed as *The Butcher*[11] in a print that follows the tradition of showing tradesmen and women as figures made up of the tools of their trade. Here the butcher is a bull with a meat tray as a breast-plate, behind which can be seen the Duke's star of the Order of the Garter. In the background a house is in flames and two grenadiers stand outside to prevent the residents from escaping.

By 1749 Cumberland had become a figure of fun. As so often, the satirists exploited royal sexual adventures. Cumberland had fallen for the charms of a Savoyard street musician and there are many prints of the grossly overweight Duke adoring this simple girl. In *John of Gant in Love, or Mars on his knees* (Illustration 3)[12] his grotesque form is echoed by an advertisement for a gigantic pig which is on show in a nearby building. A Scotsman shrugs his shoulders in disgust saying: 'No swines for me'.

Publication of satirical prints clustered around particular events or personalities. The latter were as often senior ministers as members of the royal family. Twenty years after the fall of Robert Walpole, Lord Bute, Prime Minister at the beginning of George III's reign, became a focus of attack when the young king succeeded his grandfather. While George I and George II had come in for criticism for absences in Hanover, George III was attacked for trying too strongly to assert his role as king at home in Britain. His moves to end the Seven Years' War with France were particularly unpopular. However in *The Times Plate I*[13] of 1762 William Hogarth supports the king's attempts at peace-making – he was one of very few printmakers to do so. Fire-fighters pumping water on a flaming globe wear badges on their sleeves lettered 'GR' for *Georgius Rex;* they are assisted by men in tartan indicating that they are followers of Bute, who was a Scot and thus suspect to those who recalled the Jacobite

9 Stephens and George, op.cit., III, pp. 539–30, No. 2678.
10 Stephens and George, op.cit., III, pp. 597–98, No. 2788.
11 Stephens and George, op.cit., III, pp. 633–34, No. 2843.
12 Stephens and George, op.cit., III, pp. 350–51, No. 3037.
13 Stephens and George, op.cit., IV, pp. 188–92, No. 3970; Ronald Paulson, Hogarth's Graphic Works (3rd ed., London, 1989), pp. 179–80, No. 211.

Illustration 3: Anonymous, *John of Gant in love, or Mars on his knees,* 15 July 1749, hand-coloured etching © Trustees of the British Museum

Rebellion; King Henry VIII, raised up on stilts and surrounded by City of London aldermen, encourages the flames of war by pumping with bellows. Henry stands for William Pitt the elder, the minister who did most to promote the war and was supported in his policies by the City of London, then as now the financial and mercantile centre of the country. The City had prospered from gains won during the war – especially in the Caribbean islands and India. City merchants did not want a peace treaty that might lose profitable territories.

More typical of political prints of the period is *John A Boot's Asses*[14], a far simpler composition in which the young George III is attacked, together with his mother Princess Augusta and his ministers Lord Bute and Henry Fox. Bute is shown riding an ass, which represents the widowed princess – sexual accusations were a major part of the campaign against Bute. He leads another ass, representing the king, which is ridden by Henry Fox (shown as a fox). Bute's supporters are again dressed in tartan. This print was part of a vicious series of attacks on Bute and the king. There were stories of real life processions similar to this scene: Horace Walpole described a pageant in the west of England in which the mob 'dressed up a figure in Scotch plaid, with a blue riband, to represent the favourite [that is Bute], and this figure seemed to lead

14 Stephens and George, op.cit., IV, p. 208, No. 3979.

by the nose an ass royally crowned.'[15] Bute resigned after less than two years as Prime Minister and the young king, too, must have been deeply affected.

Having been criticised for trying to play an active role as a monarch in his early days, George III was frequently accused in the following decades of paying too little attention to affairs of state. In *Farmer George Studying the Wind & Weather,*[16] an illustration to the *Oxford Magazine* in 1771, he is shown looking out of a window through the wrong end of a telescope while some of his many children play unheeded. The oldest prince, the future George IV, rides a rocking horse that bears a strong resemblance to the white horse of Hanover. Lord Bute looks down from a portrait resting his hand on a table on which lies a crown: the implication – completely untrue by this time – is that Bute remains the power behind the throne. A letter in the magazine complains that 'a certain young farmer' neglects his farm and his flock 'while he is observing the fickleness of the wind or making a curious button …'. George III's unusual hobby of button-making was alluded to eight years later in *The Botching Taylor.*[17] He is shown sitting on a tailor's bench cutting cloth to cover buttons. The discarded scraps of cloth are lettered with the names of matters to which he should be paying greater attention: 'Bill of Rights', 'Magna Carta', 'Africa', 'West Indies', 'North America'. Furthermore, he appears about to cut the connection between Ireland and Great Britain, while retaining Hanover. The king is shown as still acting under the direction of Lord Bute (identified by his Scottish tartan clothing) and he is watched over by the pope and the Young Pretender. In fact, George III was vehemently anti-Catholic so any accusation that he might pay attention to the pope was clearly false. A picture hanging on the wall titled 'Flight into Egypt' shows the king and queen and their children setting off for Hanover. In this case, the satirist is not complaining about royal absence in the electorate (George III never visited Hanover): he is suggesting that Britain would be glad if the king were to leave the country. Broadsides pasted to the wall are even more menacing, one mock medical advertisement is topped by crossed axes and lettered, 'Dr Cromwell's effectual and only remedy for the King's-evil',[18] an ominous – even traitorous – reminder that the parliamentarians under Oliver Cromwell had rid the country of monarchy in 1649 by beheading King Charles I.

In *Guy Vaux,*[19] published in 1782, George III is again shown ignoring his duties: he has the head of an ass and wears a fool's cap as he dozes on a throne under which is a barrel of gunpowder; his wrists are tied and the orb and presumably the crown

15 Henry Walpole, Memoirs of George III, I, p. 280, quoted by John Brewer, The Misfortunes of Lord Bute: a case-study in eighteenth-century political argument and public opinion, *The Historical Journal* XVI, no. 1 (1973), p. 7.

16 Stephens and George, op.cit., V, p. 27, No. 4883.

17 Stephens and George, op.cit., V, pp. 344–45, No. 5573.

18 'King's Evil' was a common name for scrofula, a tuberculous infection of the lymph nodes in the neck. Monarchs before the Hanoverians were believed to be able to cure the disease by touching the patient.

19 Stephens and George, op.cit., V, p. 596, No. 6007.

are ignored in a sack on the floor beside him. Through the door enter members of the newly elected liberal Whig government bringing more gunpowder. Their leader is a man with the head of a fox who holds a lantern. This is Charles James Fox. In this early representation of the man who was probably the fiercest radical to hold high office, he is represented, as his father Henry Fox had been, by the cunning animal whose name he bears. There is also another pun in the print and another reference back to a familiar image – the satirist reinforcing a topical message by echoing an older one: Fox's surname sounds very like that of Guy Fawkes, who was the most famous member of the Gunpowder Plot of 1605 to blow up the king in parliament. Many prints of Guy Fawkes show him carrying a lantern as he entered a vault below the House of Lords and so this print draws an immediate parallel between the radical Charles James Fox and the potential destroyer of both monarchy and parliament.

Guy Vaux was made by the young James Gillray, the greatest of all satirical printmakers. Gillray drew on all the means of attacking his targets that earlier satirists had used, but his wit, his brilliant draughtsmanship and his skill as a caricaturist[20] meant that his message was instant and devastating. His prints need far less explaining than earlier text-heavy, emblematic satires, and they are almost as accessible to us as to contemporaries. The title of *Monstrous Craws,* (Illustration 4)[21] a print of 1787 refers to the current exhibition in London of three South Americans with enormous goitres (or 'craws') growing on their necks. Gillray could not resist drawing a parallel with the monstrous greed of the royal family. He shows the King, Queen and Prince of Wales (the future George IV) spooning gold coins into their mouths so that money-bags taking the place of goitres swell to huge sizes. Parliament had just voted the vast sum of £161,000 to pay the debts of the prince, plus £20,000 for the completion of his rebuilding of Carlton House, and at the same time increasing his annual income from £50,000 to £60,000. A skilled craftsman in the 1780s would expect to earn just £50 a year.

Before long the royal family had more to worry about than the extravagance of the eldest son: the French Revolution of 1789 soon became a matter of high anxiety among British conservatives. In May 1792 'tumultuous meetings and seditious writings' were banned. *A Bugaboo* (Illustration 5)[22] published on 2 June of that year shows Prime Minister William Pitt the younger riding on the back of a heavily caricatured George III, who opens his mouth to announce the creation of 'Bastilles' in major British cities, as well as 'Dungeons, Racks, Tortures, No Mercy' – all the dreaded instruments of authoritarian monarchy. The artist is Richard Newton, a brilliant young man who might have challenged Gillray if he had not died in 1798 at the age of 21. Three weeks

20 Caricature, the exaggeration of features for comic or satirical effect, was introduced to British political prints in the 1750s by admirers of the work of caricaturists like Pier Leone Ghezzi whom they had commissioned to make humorous likenesses while on the Grand Tour in Italy.

21 Stephens and George, op.cit., VI, p. 417, No. 7166.

22 Stephens and George, op.cit., VI, pp. 913–14, No. 8102; David Alexander, Richard Newton and English Caricature in the 1790s (Manchester, 1998), p. 117, No. 7 and p. 143, No. 49.

Illustration 4: James Gillray, *Monstrous Craws, at a New Coalition Feast,* 29 May 1787, hand-coloured etching with aquatint © Trustees of the British Museum

after *A Bugaboo,* Newton showed the situation in Britain from four varied points of view: in *Content and Discontent*[23] George III hides up to his neck in a bag of seven million gold coins, a clergyman sings the national anthem while reading a paper offering lucrative positions in the church, a butcher complains that trade is bad because people are not buying meat, and a starving man reads about the high cost of food.

Like Walpole and Bute before him, Pitt, as prime minister at a time of national ferment, takes his place with the monarch as target for the satirists. In another print by Newton, *Louis dethron'd; or Hell broke loose in Paris!!!,*[24] Pitt, in his nightshirt, breaks the news to the king of the assault on the Tuilleries on 10 August 1792. Although full of mocking satire, Newton's portrayal of the two panic-stricken men, only six days after the event in Paris, has an element of pathos. However, Queen Charlotte, portrayed by the satirists as thinking only of her money and jewels, hides bags of coins in the lavatory.

---

23 Alexander, op.cit., pp. 117–18, No. 8 and p. 144, No. 53.

24 Alexander, op.cit., p. 144, No. 59. Richard Newton, *Louis dethron'd; or Hell broke loose in Paris!!!,* 16 August 1792, hand-coloured etching (see paper of Werner Busch in this volume).

Illustration 5: Richard Newton, *A Bugaboo!!!,* 2 June 1792, hand-coloured etching © Trustees of the British Museum

There is no sympathy for the royal couple in Newton's *The Inexhaustible Mine*[25] of 1797, where John Bull, the British everyman – here specifically the taxpayer – is viciously robbed by the king and queen, Pitt and Henry Dundas, the minister in charge of pursuing war with France. Each character is identified in an economical fashion. Dundas, a Scot, is easily recognised by his tartan dress. Pitt's long neck, receding chin and turned-up nose are exaggerated. The Queen's distinguishing feature is her greed for jewellery and she feels around Bull's genitals saying, 'I wonder if he has any Jewels or Precious Stones'. George III is identified most briefly of all: only his hands are shown as he pulls strings of coins from Bull's ear, but he speaks in the king's characteristic repetitive manner: 'What what …'

Gillray's *The Royal Bull-Fight*[26] of 1795 is another attack on repressive government measures. Pitt is riding again. This time his mount is the white horse of Hanover and he is a toreador attacking John Bull. The message is clear but it is reinforced by the text below the image describing how the bull 'appeared to be extremely peaceable till opposed by a desperado … who by numberless wounds provok'd the animal to the

25 Stephens and George, op.cit., VII, p. 357, No. 9025; Alexander, op.cit., p. 157, No. 259.
26 Stephens and George, op.cit., VII, pp. 203–04, No. 8691.

Illustration 6: James Gillray, *Presages of the Millenium,* 4 June 1795, hand-coloured etching
© Trustees of the British Museum

utmost pitch of Fury'. Pitt is also on horseback in *Presages of the Millenium* (Illustration 6),[27] another print of 1795 that is one of Gillray's masterpieces. In a shocking image, the naked, emaciated Pitt appears as 'Death on a Pale Horse'[28] bringing about the end of the world. The white horse of Hanover tramples his opponents – Charles James Fox, now caricatured with bushy black eyebrows and an unshaven chin, has been kicked in the face by the horse's outstretched hind leg, and a herd of pigs (the 'swinish multitude' so described by Edmund Burke in *Reflections on the Revolution in France,* 1790) flees before the horse and Pitt's flaming sword. The Prince of Wales clings on behind the Prime Minister clutching a paper lettered '£125,000 pr ann' – the increased sum he was claiming as necessary since he was now married.

27 Stephens and George, op.cit., VII, pp. 179–80, No. 8655.
28 One of the four horsemen of the Apocalypse: 'I looked and behold a pale horse; and his name that sat on him was Death' (Book of Revelation, vi, 8).

Illustration 7: James Gillray after Thomas Braddyll, *The King of Brobdingnag, and Gulliver,* 26 June 1803, hand-coloured etching © Trustees of the British Museum

Earlier in 1795 Gillray had produced a print on the prince's forthcoming marriage. *The Lover's Dream*[29] appeared while Caroline of Brunswick was en route from Hanover. The prince is shown asleep in bed dreaming of a beautiful bride and of an increased

29 Stephens and George, op.cit., VII, pp. 151–52, No. 8610.

allowance – a bulging sack labelled '£150,000 Pr Ann' is held out to him by his father, George III. The prince's friend Charles James Fox and several former mistresses recoil in horror at the suggestion that the prince might reform the profligate habits that they all shared. Of course, he did not reform his ways, and, of course, the marriage was a disaster. Four years later Gillray warned him of the effects of his lifestyle in *Duke William's Ghost.*[30] The prince is again in bed. This time he is in a drunken stupor dreaming of his horribly fat great uncle, the Duke of Cumberland, whom we have seen as the Butcher of Culloden and as the lover of the Savoyard girl. The naked Cumberland holds out an hour-glass whose sand has nearly run out: a reminder that the Duke himself had died at the age of 44 after a life of indulgence.

Satirists commonly attempt to reduce perceived threats by belittling opponents. We saw the Scottish Jacobites portrayed as uncouth country people as their rebel army made its way across the border and into England: Napoleon Bonaparte became a diminutive figure of fun in prints produced in 1803 when the British feared invasion across the English Channel. In fact, Napoleon was of average height but he has remained a small man in collective memory. Gillray shows him standing on George III's hand in *The King of Brobdingnag and Gulliver* (Illustration 7),[31] a reference to Jonathan Swift's highly popular *Gulliver's Travels* (1726), where the traveller appears tiny in comparison with the giants of a land across the sea. The print was based on a design by Thomas Braddyll, an amateur caricaturist, but Gillray undercuts the ostensibly triumphalist message by portraying the king as puzzled and anxious as he peers through his telescope at the little general.

By the last years of his reign George III was old and sick and in 1811 parliament, with some misgivings, appointed the prince of Wales as Regent. Gillray, near the end of his life, was no longer working and the leading satirical printmaker was George Cruikshank. In *Loyal address's & radical petetions* (Illustration 8)[32] of 1819 the Prince Regent is showing what he thinks of Radical petitioners by breaking wind in their faces. Cruikshank is echoing *The Festival of the Golden Rump,* where George II was shown insulting his courtiers in the same way. This was a period of post-war economic depression and great hardship for the population. Governmental reforms were desperately needed, but the Regent is shown as paying attention only to 'loyal addresses' by conservatives. In *A Radical Reformer,*[33] also of 1819, Cruikshank produced a reminder of the French Revolution by bringing a guillotine to life to pursue the government. The Regent is shown fleeing faster than anyone else so that he is only recognizable by his gouty leg and his wig flying through the air as he disappears to the right of the print.

The Prince Regent became King George IV in 1820. His estranged wife Caroline of Brunswick returned from exile demanding to be recognized as Queen. Her cause

30 Stephens and George, op.cit., VII, p. 550, No. 9381.
31 Stephens and George, op.cit., VIII, pp. 157–58, No. 10019.
32 Stephens and George, op.cit., IX, pp. 935–36, No. 13280.
33 Stephens and George, op.cit., IX, pp. 926–27, No. 13271.

Illustration 8: George Cruikshank, *Loyal address's & radical petetions,* 4 December 1819, hand-coloured etching © Trustees of the British Museum

became a rallying cry for the political opposition. In *The Royal Extinguisher*[34] Cruikshank illustrates emblematically a moment in the period leading up to the coronation when Caroline had accepted a parliamentary grant of £50,000 a year, thus losing much credibility among the Radicals. The Queen and her supporters are shown as tiny figures on a table about to be extinguished by a large candle-snuffer held by the giant 'King of Brobdingnag'.

George IV reigned until 1830. His only child by Queen Caroline had died and he was succeeded by his brother William IV, the last Hanoverian king. As a younger brother, William had been less prominent in public life, but his private life was of interest to the satirists. He had a long relationship with the popular actress Dorothy Jordan, with whom he had ten children and lived a conventional domestic life, although as a royal prince he could not marry someone of such low status. In *The Devil to Pay*[35] of 1791 Gillray had depicted the couple happily in bed, but alluded to the inevitable end of their liaison by quoting from one of Jordan's famous roles as the poor mistress of a wealthy man; six years later in *La Promenade en Famille*[36] he showed them out walking with three of their children. The anticipated separation took place in 1811 and

34 Stephens and George, op.cit., X, pp. 204–05, No. 14145.
35 Stephens and George, op.cit., VI, pp. 820–21, No. 7908.
36 Stephens and George, op.cit., VII, p. 348, No. 9009.

Illustration 9: Anonymous, *A German governess; or, a rump and dozen,* May 1832, woodcut © Trustees of the British Museum

William sought out a suitable bride, naturally looking among German royal families. In 1818 he married Princess Adelaide of Saxe-Meiningen.

Adelaide did not come to the attention of satirical printmakers until twelve years later when William came to the throne. By then campaigning for parliamentary reform was reaching a crescendo and the conservatively minded queen was attacked in prints. In John Lewis Marks's *The Bull in a Rage*[37] she is shown riding a bull (John Bull, the British everyman again). The bull has broken its collar, lettered 'Slavery', and is kicking out at King William; both king and queen have lost their crowns. Adelaide was thought to have too much influence on her husband, and in *Under Petticoat Government*[38] Marks shows the king hidden under her skirts while she speaks in an exaggerated German accent saying that she will let Johnny Bull have his bill – the Great Reform Bill finally passed through parliament in 1832. She holds a broom to identify her with the German girls who sold brooms in British streets at this time.

37 Stephens and George, op.cit., XI, p. 623, No. 17071.
38 Stephens and George, op.cit., XI, pp. 628–29, No. 17083.

Even more insulting was the depiction of the queen beating her husband with a birch rod: *A German governess; or, a rump and dozen.* (Illustration 9)[39] The queen wears breeches under her dress, suggesting that, in reference to a familiar phrase, she 'wears the trousers' as the dominant partner in the marriage. The print is a cheap woodcut based on a higher quality etching which itself derives from pornographic flagellation prints – adding an extra insult to this representation of the last Hanoverian king.

It was the role of satirical printmakers to attack those in power. For favourable images of members of the Hanoverian dynasty we must look to portraits where the artist's role was to flatter – the anxious and confused George III looks perfectly in control when portrayed by Allan Ramsay, Queen Charlotte's jewellery is much in evidence in Johann Zoffany's portrait but she is a dignified and caring mother, while even the grotesquely obese George IV appears elegant in the hands of Thomas Lawrence.[40] Both types of depiction, the loyal and the subversive, can tell us about attitudes of the time if we examine them with care.

39 Stephens and George, op.cit., XI, p. 634, No. 17099.

40 Paintings in the Royal Collection, RCIN 405307, 400146 and 405918.

Christina Oberstebrink

Gillray and Royalty.
The Politics of High and Low in Eighteenth-Century Art

Die Karikaturen James Gillrays sind oft beißende Kommentare über das Königtum in England des achtzehnten Jahrhunderts. Besonders George III. und Königin Charlotte oder ihre Söhne – und gelegentlich auch ihre Töchter – sind dabei die bevorzugten Themen. Als Sujet bietet das Königtum nützliche Paradigmen, um Gillrays Arbeitsmethoden und seine Denkweise zu untersuchen: Es repräsentiert die oberste Schicht in der Gesellschaft, verlangt aber in der Kunsttheorie in der Regel nach einem höherstehenden Modus der Darstellung als die Karikatur es ist. Der vorliegende Beitrag wird die oft komplexen Konstruktionen von ‚hoch' und ‚niedrig' in Gillrays Karikaturen erörtern, von denen einige einen fast manifestartigen Charakter in Bezug auf die visuelle Satire haben. Zudem geht es um die Positionierung Gillrays zwischen ‚Alten' und ‚Modernen'.

James Gillray's caricatures very often contain biting remarks about the English royalty in the eighteenth and early nineteenth centuries. His preferred topics were King George and Queen Charlotte or their sons, but occasionally the princesses were taken on, too. Gillray's depiction of royalty in satirical compositions provides useful paradigms for analysing the artist's approach to caricature and its multi-faceted nature, not only because kings, queens, princes and princesses represented the uppermost stratum of society, but also, seen from the perspective of art theory, they stood for a subject that normally demanded more elevated genres of depiction than that of caricature. In reviews of his work, Gillray's art was often considered primitive and base, and, according to the patterns of reception at the time, accounts of his life and person mostly mirrored these traits. Thus, as a person, the caricaturist was described as having lowly inclinations and as being uneducated too – and not intellectually capable of meeting the demands of the elevated genre of the Grand Manner.[1] But in fact Gillray's art is often very complex and the criticism of his caricatures we find voiced in the decades after his decease in no way does justice to their multi-faceted nature. In a mode of art

1 For example, in Anonymous, 'James Gillray, and His Caricatures', *The Athenæum, Journal of English and Foreign Literature, Science, and the Fine Arts,* London, no. 24 (Sept. 1831), 634: 'He [i. e. Gillray] had a plain straight-forward practical understanding, which never rose above the comprehension of the crowd – he never desired to veil his satire in subtleties, nor hide it in thoughts far-fetched and profound.' And on p. 633: 'Works of this kind suit the ignorance and hurry of the mob: they express, by visible and familiar signs, feelings congenial to a large portion of the vulgar part of mankind.'

that, in the 18th century, one can no longer really call caricature, Gillray's visual satire embraces not only the combination of text and image, it also frequently references the entire spectrum of early modern art, from paintings of Royal Academy artists to those of George Morland, from William Hogarth to Guido Reni, and Antiquity.[2]

Against this background I would like to take a brief look at Gillray's portrayals of royalty as a starting point for exploring his often complex handling and juxtaposition of the high and low in caricature. From there I will proceed to Gillray's famous print, *Shakespeare Sacrificed,* and examine its virtually manifesto-like character in relation to visual satire, staking out the caricaturist's position in the battle of the Ancients and the Moderns and between high and low art. But first I will take a look at what royalty thought of James Gillray and what this reveals about contemporary responses to his art. Allegedly George III once spoke of the satiric 'artist' and, on another occasion, even granted him an audience. In the accounts of the meeting and of what the king said about the caricaturist we are able to view James Gillray from the vantage point of his contemporaries – at least from the angle of the official apparatus embracing academic norms for art and criticism – so the king's comments are ultimately relevant to art theory. My subsequent analysis of *Shakespeare Sacrificed* will serve to uncover subversive mechanisms that challenge the accepted categories of art criticism of the time, seeking to uncover how the protagonists of 18th-century English visual satire rated their genre in relation to the art scene, how they comprehended a genre that did not find validation in the form of a published treatise, at least not for the visual arts.[3]

In 1828, the first volume of Henry Angelo's *Reminiscences* was published. Here he related how George III praised James Gillray's aptitude in catching a likeness and rated the caricaturist in the art of portraiture even higher than Sir Joshua Reynolds – at least seemingly. King George is alleged to have said of Reynolds's *Portrait of Charles James Fox* that 'it was very like. Sir Joshua's picture is finely painted – but Gillray is the better limner [i. e. 'painter'].'[4] However, the king's comment was probably intended to diminish Reynolds's abilities rather than to praise those of Gillray. The king would not have been amused by the President of the Royal Academy having painted the portrait of the prominent Whig statesman. After all, Charles Fox was highly vocal and articulate in his support of the French Revolution and in seeking to restrict the power of the Crown in Parliament. But Charles Fox too was a very likely target of George III's remarks. Gillray's biting satires of the radical Whig were many, so the king would certainly have enjoyed the caricaturist's unfavourable renderings of Fox much more

2 Gillray obviously based his *Confederated Coalition – Or – The Giants Storming Heaven* (1804) on Bartolomeo Coriolano's print of *The Fall of the Giants* (1638) after Guido Reni. Gillray adeptly applied Hogarth's visual vocabulary in *Morning After Marriage – Or – A Scene on the Continent* (1788) or in his own version of *The Rake's Progress At the University.*

3 For example Francis Grose published his *Rules for Drawing Caricatures* in 1788. In it he focuses on the original sense of caricature as a form of portraiture that distorts the features of its sitters. It provides very little insight, however, into the kind of pictorial satire we find in Gillray's work.

4 Henry Angelo, *Reminiscences* (London, 1828) vol. 1, p. 363.

than a prestigious portrait of the prominent politician painted by the Royal Academy president. Additionally, the king's comment was very probably drawing on the lowly social status and vulgar manners ascribed to an artist working in the genre of caricature to give weight to his comment. In making Gillray the ideal portrait artist for painting Charles Fox, the king put both of them on one level. After all, not only Fox's political views would have met with George III's disapproval, but his reputation of being a rake, too. Henry Angelo continued his documentation of George III's art critique in this vein: 'Nobody hits off Mr. Fox like him – Gillray is the man – *for the man of the people*'.[5] The emphasis on the last phrase insinuates that the famous statesman not only supported revolutionary ideas but also had habits unbefitting of his station. What we must not forget is that by the time Henry Angelo recorded these lines, which were published in 1828, biographical descriptions of the caricaturist never failed to mention his wayward habits. Henry Angelo's readers would not have had to be acquainted with the details of Gillray's biography to understand the analogy. Low artists were traditionally and generically comprehended as having correspondingly low habits – they were very often reputed to spend much of their time in inns with people of dubious reputation and to consume alcoholic beverages in immoderate quantities. Such characteristics were not only thought to apply to caricaturists. The same behavioural pattern was shared by artists who painted after nature without enhancing it, such as we find in the painter of animals and rustic scenes, George Morland, a contemporary of Gillray. The biographies of both artists are interchangeable as far as their careless and coarse social habits are concerned.[6] In terms of art theory, in both cases the biographies articulate fixed notions about the mode of life of the uneducated artist from lower walks of society. This is the image, as presented by the vocabulary of art criticism of the time, of artists who did not abide by the rules of academic art. Their biographical traits were largely trimmed to shape according to the historiography of the age, revealing how they fell short, in terms of character, of the ideals of the *pictor doctus* or educated artist. Artists' biographies, especially in the past, are largely a synthesis of artists' identities and art theory. They are topical rather than factual.[7] For example, in the biographical accounts of Gillray we find that, throughout the 19th century, nothing is said of his close friendship to Lord Batemen, which is, however, well-documented in the caricaturist's surviving correspondence.[8]

5 Angelo, op.cit., p. 363.

6 Henry Angelo even compares both artists in the context of their similar behaviour when spending an evening at the inn; see Angelo, op.cit., pp. 388–389.

7 My approach here is modeled on reading biographical narratives as literary topoi as first done in the seminal work of Ernst Kris and Otto Kurz, Legend, Myth and Magic in the Image of the Artist (New Haven and London, 1979), German original first published in 1934.

8 For example in a letter to Gillray written by Sir James Bateman from Nov. 1798, BM add. mss. 27, pp. 337 f., 39. Viscount Bateman was 'a genial favourite of George III' and patron of Thomas Gainsborough and John Opie. Gillray's correspondence reveals that he regularly visited Sir James Bateman at Shobdon Court in Herefordshire; see also Draper Hill, Mr. Gillray, The Caricaturist. A Biography (London, 1965), p. 81.

In another episode, recorded by Henry Angelo, in which James Gillray had a brush with the king, the caricaturist was granted an audience. Following his collaboration with Philip James de Loutherbourg for the painting *Siege of Valenciennes,* the two artists were invited to show their preparatory work for a commission to George III. Gillray had accompanied Loutherbourg to Valenciennes to make studies for the large-format battle painting. In the meeting between the caricaturist and George III, the king was much less inclined to be well-disposed toward Gillray than formerly in his praise for him as Charles Fox's portraitist. Perhaps the king was voicing his general irritation about the caricaturist due to the satirical attacks by the same on his own person. Henry Angelo wrote:

> 'Monsieur De Loutherbourg, and the British limner, were summoned to appear before the King, that his most gracious Majesty might have the gratification of turning over the *matériel* for his uncle-Toby-like campaign of the siege over again. The view of the ruined steeples and battered walls of the extensive fortifications, and the lines of circumvallation were faithful, and true to their prototype; but not so the portraits in the opinion of the royal connoisseur. The features of the generals were little more than incoherent scratches – mere technical memoranda, to be worked into form by their author – and certainly incomprehensible to any but an artist, and perhaps only the artist himself. De Loutherbourg was complimented; whilst the only reward obtained by Gillray was a look which seemed to express, Mr Gillray, you might as well have stayed at home; in short, his Majesty freely confessed, that he could not read the likenesses as he did not understand the *stenography* of the painter's art.'[9]

Gillray's surviving sketches for the project show that he not only made studies of the details of the apparel worn by the soldiers, officers, and generals, along with portrait and figure studies. Additionally, he executed relatively detailed drawings of the topography and terrain where the battle took place. And Gillray's physiognomic studies of soldiers, though rendered sketchily enough, can hardly be described as indecipherable. Later, in the Romantic spirit, William Hazlitt reversed this critique of the historical painting, stating that: 'One of the merits of the picture [i. e. *The Siege of Valenciennes*] is the portraits it contains,' which he attributed to Gillray, 'a man of talents […] and uncommonly apt at sketching a hasty likeness.'[10]

In keeping with the proverbial characteristics of a caricaturist at the time, Henry Angelo presented his account as if Gillray's tasks for the commission exclusively entailed his ability to catch a likeness with a few strokes of the pencil.[11] As the term 'scratches' reveals, his sketches were unmistakably comprehended as caricatures rather

9 Angelo, op.cit., pp. 382–383

10 See William Hazlitt, The Life of Thomas Holcroft, in: The Complete Works, Centenary Edition, ed. P.P. Howe (London, 1932), vol. 3, p. 185.

11 This he even states in his prelude to the affair, see Angelo, op.cit., p. 381.

than studies.[12] Hogarth too was notorious for his ability to sketch a likeness with 'a few scratches of the pen' as far as eighteenth-century art criticism was concerned.[13] He himself used the synonymous term 'scrawlings' in his print *The Bench* as the essence of caricature. Hogarth's subheading states the programme of the illustration in his print: *Of the different meaning of the Words Character, Caracatura and Outré in Painting and Drawing.* An excerpt from the text underneath explains:

> 'Now that which has, of late Years, got the name of *Caracatura,* is, or ought to be totally divested of every stroke that hath a tendency to good Drawing: it may be said to be a species of Lines that are produced by the hand of chance rather than Skill; for the early Scrawlings of a Child which do but barely hint an Idea of an Human Face, will always be found to be like some Person or other'.

According to the tenets of eighteenth-century art theory in England, caricature was comprehended as the absence of art rather than art. But did Gillray himself consider his interpretation of caricature as the absence of art, as something that could be defined in terms of being primitive scratches? Hogarth's definition certainly does not fit the bill, any more than scratches or scrawlings are adequate terms in which to describe Hogarth's comic mode of art, even though he too was often called a caricaturist himself. Likewise, the king's comment on not being able to read Gillray's scratches did not do justice at all to the artist's studies done on location. And later on in this chapter close scrutiny of one of Gillray's major prints, *Shakespeare Sacrificed,* will demonstrate that he by no means found the satiric mode of the visual arts a primitive and simple one.

Allegedly Gillray retaliated in answer to the king's disparaging remarks about his art with the print *A Connoisseur Examining a Cooper* (Illustration 1). If viewed within the context of Gillray's audience before the king, we could say that Gillray responded on the level of art theory by addressing the topic of catching a likeness. He portrayed the king in a mode of realism that emphasized the regent's ungainliness and paunchiness rather than seeking to render him in any way heroic. Gillray obviously enjoyed having a dig at the king by letting him admire, in the print, a portrait of Oliver Cromwell by the 17th-century miniaturist Samuel Cooper (1609–1672), surely not a favourite historical figure for a king and rather provocative too. But Gillray also belittles George III's connoisseurship in art. Seen from an academic perspective, portrait miniatures, although popular, did not occupy an outstanding position in the hierarchy of genres according to 18th-century academic notions of painting. And as far as George's

12 Samuel Johnson, Dictionary of the English Language, ed. Alexander Chalmers (London, 1843), defines 'scratch' as 'to write or draw awkwardly.'

13 See, for example, Anon., *Somerset House Gazette* VII (22nd Nov. 1823), p. 108: 'Hogarth's talent for catching a likeness was most remarkable; indeed, the study of his whole life was reading the human countenance; hence, he could sketch a character with a few scratches of his pen.'

Illustration 1: James Gillray: *A Connoisseur Examining a Cooper,*1792, etching, BM 1868,0808.6215 © Trustees of the British Museum

praise of 'catching a likeness' in the satiric print goes, this may have been important for the art of portraiture, but portraiture too, like caricature, was fighting a constant battle at the time to win academic acclaim.

Gillray's depictions of royalty in his so-called caricatures or visual satires were often very life-like and even complimentary about the appearance of the person in the print, although he often did exaggerate the features and abnormities of his victims. But in Gillray's art we seek in vain the primitive quality of caricature as defined by Hogarth. In another of Gillray's creations, *Fatigues of the Campaign in Flanders,* he illustrated Prince Frederick as a quite attractive, although somewhat corpulent man. (Illustration 2) This print too was inspired by the trip he undertook with Loutherbourg and contains a portrait-like representation of the Duke of York. However, most of the figures around the Duke can best be described as caricatures for some reason or other – either due to their extreme fatness or thinness or exaggerated features. In the case of the Duke, it is the circumstances in which he finds himself in the print that make him an object of derision, portraying him in a situation unbecoming for a prince. In his caricatures representing royalty, Gillray could often rely on incongruent situations or behaviour in relation to the elevated status of these persons to make them ridiculous – these means often made making caricatures of their persons redundant. But as the sheet *Monstrous Craws* shows, royalty was not immune to being portrayed by Gillray with the distortions of features associated with caricature. (Illustration 3)

The accounts of Gillray's brushes with George III reveal much about the conflation of artistic biography with eighteenth-century understanding of genres. But they hardly do justice to the complexities of the artist's work, revealing more about its status within the hierarchy of genres from the point of view of art theory than presenting reliable facts. Hogarth's definition of caricature is also very inadequate to describe the genre pursued by Gillray. In general, eighteenth-century art theory concentrates on the more elevated kinds of painting and neglects the profundity of the lower genres. The artists working in the latter modes, with the exception of Hogarth, were unfortunately not very vocal about the merits of their art. It is therefore sometimes very difficult to ascertain their theoretical angle and how artists such as Gillray thought about their own work. Focusing on one of his prints, *Shakespeare Sacrificed,* I would like now to explore this question in relation to Gillray and attempt to answer it.[14] (Illustration 4)

Gillray executed *Shakespeare Sacrificed* on the occasion of the Boydell Shakespeare Gallery, an exhibition of paintings illustrating Shakespeare's works. The exhi-

---

14 Other than my own, the two most extensive studies of the sheet to date are Caroline Buchartowski, Nachahmung und individuelle Ausdrucksform: Eine Untersuchung zu den Motiventlehnungen in der politischen Karikaturen James Gillrays im Zeitraum 1789 bis 1805 (Frankfurt/M., Peter Lang, 1994), 131–158, and Gerd Unverfehrt, 'John Boydell's Shakespeare Gallery in Gillray's Caricatures', in: The Boydell Shakspeare Gallery, eds Walter Pape and Frederick Burwick (Exh. cat. The Boydell Shakespeare Gallery, Museum Bochum and Armand Hammer Museum and Cultural Center, University of California, L.A.), (Bottrop, Essen, 1996), pp. 345–353. For my interpretations see footnote 17 below.

Illustration 2: James Gillray: *Fatigues of the Campaign in Flanders,* 1793, etching, BM 1851,0901.652 © Trustees of the British Museum

Illustration 3: James Gillray: *Monstrous Craws,* 1787, etching, BM 1878,0511.1365 © Trustees of the British Museum

Illustration 4: James Gillray: *Shakespeare Sacrificed Or the Offering to Avarice*, etching, 1789, BM 1851,0901.464 © Trustees of the British Museum

bition was opened in 1789 and organised by John Boydell. He commissioned artists to execute paintings for the show, which were to be reproduced as prints. Apparently Gillray had hoped for a commission as engraver for the project but was unsuccessful.[15] His print *Shakespeare Sacrificed* is hence often seen as the artist taking revenge, a motive befitting the vindictiveness typically ascribed to satiric writers and artists.[16] An important goal of the exhibition was to promote history painting in 18th-century England. I will narrow down my reading of Gillray's print here to his response to this aspect of the exhibition and how he ranks his genre in relation to it.[17]

The complex composition is structured in analogy to Hercules at the crossroads.[18] According to ancient sources, Hercules meets two women at a crossroads who personify Virtue and Pleasure. It was a popular subject in art at the time as an allegory for the two roads open to artists for their careers. Shaftesbury adopted the allegory in his treatise on history painting, *A Notion of the Historical Draught or Tablature of the Judgment of Hercules.*[19] An illustration of Hercules at the crossroads between Virtue and Pleasure was included in the publication. The text outlines the virtues of the artist of the Grand Manner and implicitly the vices of those who deviate from such aspirations, providing a blueprint for understanding neoclassical models of artistic identity and their relationship to the artist's preferred genre. In art theory, Hercules at the crossroads is an allegory of the artist, who must follow classical ideals, learning from the ancients and old masters, that is, pursue the laborious path of the true history painter. The alternative is the allegedly mercenary, easy way of the lower genres. The artist had to choose between a hard life of dedication to learning and a sybaritic life of pleasure and vice. Shaftesbury, basing his ideas about history painting on poetry and painting as sister arts and on neoclassical notions of art, wrote that for 'the real History-Painter the same knowledge, the same study, and views are required, as in a real Poet.'[20] Both should not depict history as a sequence of events like the historian, but, in keeping with Aristotle's three unities, 'only describe a single action'.[21] Characteristic for the Grand Manner is 'credibility, probability, and seeming truth' and

15 See, e. g. Hill, op.cit., p. 27.

16 For an example see Unverfehrt, op.cit., p. 169.

17 See Christina Oberstebrink, James Gillray: Karikatur und Poetik (Berlin, 2005), pp. 234–286. The book is based on my PhD (2003) thesis.

18 Gerd Unverfehrt too sees the allegory of Hercules at the crossroads implied in the print but differs from this interpretation with regard to which details of the composition reference the motif. According to Unverfehrt, 'the motives arranged around the outside of the magic circle can be summarized in a programmatic statement: the arts and the artists whom Boydell has engaged are at the crossroads [i. e. Hercules myth] to success or disaster.' Unverfehrt, op.cit., p. 164.

19 First published in English in 1713, it was included in third volume of the posthumous, second, revised edition (author's revision): Earl of Shaftesbury, Anthony Ashley Cooper, Characteristicks of Men, Manners, Opinions, Times (London, 1715).

20 Shaftesbury, op.cit., vol. 3, p. 387.

21 Shaftesbury, op.cit., vol. 3, pp. 387–388.

'simplicity'.[22] In alignment with Horace's *Ars Poetica,* a history painting must be a real whole with the parts fitting naturally together.[23] The figures are to be represented in a manner befitting their status, gender, age and the action.[24] Humour is forbidden, as is also the enigmatic and mysterious, which would 'destroy its persuasive simplicity'.[25]

At a glance it is clear that both the individual detail and the overall concept of *Shakespeare Sacrificed* are the very opposite of what Shaftesbury calls for in a true history painting, despite the fact that it has adopted the basic structure of Hercules at the crossroads. In the satiric print the figure standing in the position of Hercules or the artist, a statue of Shakespeare, has disappeared behind a cloud of smoke. John Boydell is depicted in the role of Virtue adopting her typical declamatory pose, while the grotesque figure of Pleasure is depicted here as an outright caricature of avarice, the gnome grinning knowingly while clutching bags of money. Gillray's Virtue, as Boydell's gestures suggests, is as interested in the monetary aspects of the enterprise as Pleasure. The caricaturist has transformed Hercules at the crossroads to fit the print's subheading of 'Offering to Avarice' by illustrating a mercenary plot between Virtue and Pleasure with total disregard of the artist or playwright.[26]

Probably the most famous interpretation of Hercules at the crossroads at the time was Reynolds's rendition of it in his portrait *Garrick between Comedy and Tragedy.*[27] While obediently depicting Tragedy in a declamatory attitude as described by Shaftesbury, Reynolds turns the tables and has his 'Hercules', his friend and famous actor David Garrick, turn to Comedy and not, as prescribed, to Tragedy. Reynolds's departure from tradition reveals that tragedy's superiority was even being challenged within the Royal Academy, ultimately undermining neoclassical tenets, as tragedy was regarded as the poetological sibling of history painting.

The two portfolios of prints made after the paintings that were exhibited at Boydell's Shakespeare Gallery reveal that the subject of Hercules at the crossroads was addressed in the exhibition too. The prints taking up the allegory engage with the topic of Shakespeare's attitude or rather neglect of the 'Rules'. Executed after two paintings by Romney, there is a print of *The Infant Shakespeare attended by Nature and the Passions* in the catalogue of the large pictures and one of *Shakespeare nursed by Tragedy and*

22 Shaftesbury, op.cit., vol. 3, pp. 349, 381.

23 Shaftesbury, op.cit., vol. 3, pp. 388–389; see [John Oldham], 'Horace: His Art of Poetry, Imitated in English', in: Some New Pieces Never before Publisht. By the Author of the Satyrs upon the Jesuites (London, 1681), pp. 1–2.

24 Shaftesbury, op.cit., vol. 3, pp. 389–390.

25 Shaftesbury, op.cit., vol. 3, p. 381.

26 On Hercules at the crossroads in eighteenth-century British art see Ronald Paulson, Book and Painting. Shakespeare, Milton and the Bible: Literary Texts and the Emergence of English Painting (Knoxville, 1982), p. 85, and ibid., Breaking and Remaking: Aesthetic Practice in England 1700–1820 (New Brunswick, 1989), pp. 180 ff.

27 Edgar Wind; 'Borrowed Attitudes' in Reynolds and Hogarth, *Journal of the Warburg Institute* 2 (1938), pp. 182 and 184; Werner Busch, Hogarth's und Reynolds' Porträts des Schauspielers Garrick, *Zeitschrift für Kunstgeschichte* 47 (1984), pp. 177–192.

Comedy in the catalogue of the small prints. In a manner similar to Reynolds's portrait of Garrick, Tragedy does not take command in the case of Shakespeare, but has to coexist as Comedy's equal. The great playwright felt equally at home with comedy and tragedy and preferred to mix the two in tragicomedies or include comic scenes in tragedies. In light of Shaftesbury's treatise and the paintings by Reynolds and Romney, it is clear that the subject of Hercules at the crossroads had become established as an allegorical structure for addressing art theory issues.

It is at the level of the two poles of tragedy and comedy, of history painting and caricature, at which Gillray argues in *Shakespeare Sacrificed.* He points out that Shakespeare's plays and heroes did not meet the expectations of eighteenth-century classicism, which formed the basis of art theory at the Royal Academy and strongly coloured Shaftesbury's treatise. But in fact Gillray goes even further. In the language of the unities of time and place, verisimilitude and decorum, he turns academic norms upside down and paints satire as the overall winner. In the following I will attempt to show how he achieved this, making ample use of the allegory of Hercules at the crossroads as well as other configurations and especially by focusing on the issue of rules for kinds and genres. I wish to point out that Gillray's treatment of Hercules at the crossroads is, even more so than Reynolds's, profoundly indicative of a shift in views about art at the time.

In *Shakespeare Sacrificed,* the cloud of smoke blotting out Shakespeare forms a stage for the many references to the major – and some of the minor – paintings exhibited at the Shakespeare Gallery. By displaying various scenes from a number of different plays side by side, Gillray violates the three unities to the point of absurdity. Perhaps the most telling example of this is Gillray's placement of the scene of Lear banishing Cordelia directly next to the scene of him carrying her dead body towards the end of the play. Gillray references mostly pictures portraying Shakespeare's tragedies in *Shakespeare Sacrificed.* However, Henry Fuseli's *Midsummer Night's Dream* plays a prominent role in the print too, so that, together with one or two references to other 'comic' paintings, Shakespeare's comedies are also well represented in the print. In all Gillray borrowed three details from Fuseli's *Midsummer Night's Dream.* The two most interesting for the point in question are, firstly, the michelangelesque figure of Bottom with the ass's head, acting as an intermediary between the exhibition organiser and the 'borrowings' floating on the cloud of smoke. And secondly, an easily neglected detail in Fuseli's painting seems to play a likewise insignificant role in Gillray's print: a minute figure fights with an insect near the frame of the painting and, in the print, has been caught in a spider's web. By all appearances in both artworks it is a hero of antiquity, and, judging by his shield, very probably Perseus, now an absurdity condemned to fighting less significant monsters in the eighteenth century than in the ancient legends. (Illustration 5) If we take a closer look at the other details referenced by Gillray on the cloud of smoke in *Shakespeare Sacrificed,* we discover they all have one thing in common, regardless of whether from the great poet's comedies or tragedies. All of them have undergone a generic transformation

Illustration 5: Peter Simon after Henry Fuseli, *Midsummer Night's Dream,* Act IV, Scene I/ Shakespeare Gallery, 1796, print, BM Dd,6.21 © Trustees of the British Museum

so that they contradict the character they supposedly represent. Violating the rules of decorum and verisimilitude demanding that characters be represented befitting their station, gender, and the genre, Gillray has made a tragic figure of Bottom, who wipes away a tear, while the many tragic heroes have been made ridiculous in some way, either by lewdness, incongruity or absurdities. In operating in this way Gillray achieved two things. One is that he demonstrated his power over genre, that as a satirical artist he could play with the modes of genre in any way he pleased and thus enjoyed an unusual degree of artistic freedom for the time. The other is that, by mixing generic modes ad absurdum, Gillray points out that the requirements of history painting were not and could not be adequately fulfilled in the Shakespeare Gallery. He drew attention to the fact that Shakespeare blended the genres, for which the playwright was often criticized in the 18th century, and that his method clashed with the tenets of history painting.

Gillray's critique does not, however, appear to be aimed at the artists participating in the project. The tiny soldier or miniature ancient hero testifies to this. Both Fuseli and Gillray seem to argue on one level here, and both seem to say that, in the context of Shakespeare at least, ancient heroes have no place. Indeed, Shakespeare's heroes do not have the profoundly moral character of the neoclassical hero, they are not of 'the higher

Illustration 6: Jean Baptiste Michel after James Northcote, *The Third Part of King Henry the Sixth*/ Shakespeare Gallery, 1795, print, BM Dd,6.23 © Trustees of the British Museum

and nobler Species of Humanity'.[28] Fuseli has depicted the small Roman soldier as a parergon on the fringes of the composition at the far left, while Gillray has transformed the appropriated figure into an allegory based on a moral verse of Jacob Cats: 'As in the mesh spread by the Spider's skill / The weaker flies and gnats alone are caught, / While insects more robust of wing and will, / Break boldly through'.[29] Despite the factions that were critical of Shakespeare at the time, his greatness remained undisputed. Thus the 'small insect' caught in Gillray's spider's web is not the great playwright, but rather a warning to the artists exhibiting at the gallery: true artists, like Shakespeare, refuse to let their imaginations be confined by the 'Rules'. By all appearances Gillray goes a step further than Fuseli with the tiny ancient hero: he is saying that academic rules are passé.

As someone whose art essentially comprised breaking the 'Rules', Gillray is in fact elevating caricature onto a pedestal in *Shakespeare Sacrificed*. Such an interpretation is underscored by further details in the print that bring us back to Hercules at the crossroads. Gillray takes up the motif of Hercules at the crossroads several more times in the work besides its forming the aforementioned basic structure of the print. In one case it is a paraphrase of a paraphrase: Gillray references James Northcote's painting of *Henry VI*. Northcote in turn borrowed, for his two ladies-in-waiting to the left and the right of the queen, Reynolds's figures of Comedy and Tragedy from the aforementioned portrait of Garrick. Especially Northcote's 'Comedy' resembles that of Reynolds. (Illustration 6) Gillray treats Tragedy rudely here, having her turn away in disgust from the flatulent infant in the queen's arms. Obscenity is an unmistakable trademark of satire, and Gillray appears to be asserting his art as a viable alternative to academic rules. High art, represented by the figure resembling Reynolds's 'Tragedy', is being dismissed in no uncertain and gross terms. Another, admittedly somewhat veiled, reference to Hercules at the crossroads is in Gillray's appropriation from John Opie's painting, *A Winter's Tale*. (Illustration 7) In Gillray's print the hand of the king no longer points at the child in general, as it does in Opie's painting, but to the genitals of the baby girl. What at first seems sheer lewdness actually visually references an episode from Laurence Sterne's *Tristram Shandy*. There, Eugenius is party to a debate on comprehending the right meaning of the word 'crevice' when confronted with the dilemma of its ambiguity:

> 'Here are two senses, cried Eugenius, as we walk'd along, pointing with the fore finger of his right hand to the word Crevice, in the one hundred and seventy-eighth page of the first volume of this book of books,—here are two senses—quoth he.—And here are two roads, replied I, turning short upon him—a dirty and a clean one—which shall we take?—The clean, by all means, replied Eugenius.'[30]

---

28 Shaftesbury, op.cit., vol. 3, p. 389.

29 Jacob Cats and Robert Farlie, Moral Emblems: Aphorisms, Adages, and Proverbs of all Ages and Nations (London, 1860), p. 131.

30 Laurence Sterne, The Life and Opinions of Tristram Shandy, Gentleman (11th ed. New York et al., 1981) vol. III, chap. 31, p. 225

Illustration 7: Peter Simon after John Opie: *Winter's Tale,* Act II, Scene III/Shakespeare Gallery, print, BM Dd,6.38 © Trustees of the British Museum

Gillray's reference is anything but ambiguous, and again the path pointed out at the crossroads is that of satire. But at the same time the visual reference to the word 'Crevice' retains the meaning it has for *Tristram Shandy:* it is a signifier for duplicity of meaning and ambiguity. Again the position is diametrically opposed to one of the leading principles of history painting, of clarity, simplicity, of comprising a coherent whole. And a further aspect must be taken into consideration. A Eugenius figures likewise in the work of Laurence Sterne's predecessor, namely in John Dryden's *Essay on Dramatic Poetry.* There, Eugenius argues the case of the Moderns,[31] and with Dryden in mind, Gillray's reference could be arguing the case for the Moderns too, among whom he then would have counted himself, a Modern who was not restricted to building on the foundations of the Ancients.

Gillray's pictorial satires, as we can see in the case of *Shakespeare Sacrificed,* could be very complex and ambitious. The King's condescending attitude to the caricaturist, as passed on by Henry Angelo, has little to do with understanding the intricacies and the intellectual ambitions of Gillray's art and is anchored in notions of high and low art. But Gillray could sovereignly adapt the high and the low in multifarious ways in

31 John Dryden, An Essay of Dramatic Poesy, in Ibid. Essays, ed. William Paton Ker (Oxford, 1900), vol. 1, p. 33.

the genre of caricature or visual satire, which, like a sponge, could take up and adapt a myriad of visual and even literary forms, and only the subject matter of an individual work and the artist's interpretation thereof set the limits. Thus, in presenting the demise of history painting in *Shakespeare Sacrificed,* James Gillray could debunk the tenets of academic art using the same allegorical structures that the Grand Manner adopted to assert its elevated aspirations. Gillray's Hercules at the crossroads no longer chooses between comedy and tragedy or low and high art but argues for freedom of the imagination and against the 'Rules' of art. And no other genre fitted this description better than caricature at the time.

James Baker

The Royal Brat: Making Fun of George Augustus Frederick

Wenige der vielen Individuen, die Englands größte Metropole beherbergte, haben deren Einwohner derart überwältigend fasziniert wie die königlichen ‚Blagen', um Peter Pindar zu zitieren. Skandale, in die die Söhne von Georg III., William Henry, Duke of Clarence, (der spätere Wilhelm IV.), Frederick Augustus, Duke of York, und George Augustus Frederick, Prince of Wales (später Prince Regent und Georg IV.), verwickelt waren, trugen dazu bei, das Vertrauen nicht nur in Englands hannoversche Herrscher, sondern auch in seine sozialen Eliten zu untergraben. Es waren die Handlungen des Letztgenannten, die am auffälligsten Pindars Charakterisierung erfüllten: Der öffentliche Charakter der durch den Prince of Wales begangenen Indiskretionen erwies sich als unwiderstehliche kommerzielle Gelegenheit, die von jenen Londoner Geschäftsmännern aufgegriffen wurde, die satirische Blätter druckten und verkauften. Dieser Beitrag bespricht die Strategien, die Samuel Fores, ein von Piccadilly aus agierender Unternehmer, verwendete, um die Gerüchte der den britischen Thronfolger betreffenden Skandale gewinnbringend auszunutzen.

Of all the individuals to whom England's late-Georgian metropolis played host, few held the attention of her satirical scribblers, orators, and artists as overwhelmingly as, to quote John Wolcot's satirical nom de plume Peter Pindar, the royal 'brats'.[1] During the latter years of his reign, scandals involving George III's sons William Henry Duke of Clarence (later William IV), Frederick Augustus Duke of York, and George Augustus Frederick Prince of Wales (later Prince Regent and George IV) conspired to undermine confidence in not only England's Hanoverian rulers but also her social elites. Yet it was George Augustus Frederick as Prince of Wales whose actions most conspicuously fulfilled Pindar's characterisation. In response Hannah Humphrey's charge James Gillray famously cast the prince as profligate, greedy and arrogant in his infamous 1792 work, *A Voluptuary under the horrors of Digestion.*[2] The newspaper press were no less kind, visualising in allusive prose the errors of the future king. What is clear then is that the public nature of the prince's indiscretions was an irresistible commercial opportunity, one seized upon by a variety of London businessmen who

1 I am grateful to the audience at the Herrenhausen Symposium – in particular Tim Clayton, Ian Haywood, Brian Maidment and Sheila O'Connell – for their helpful and incisive comments on an early draft of this paper.

2 James Gillray, A Voluptuary under the horrors of Digestion (Hannah Humphrey, 2nd July 1792).

traded in words and representations, not least those who printed and sold satirical and caricature designs. And yet this was no simple game of reproducing every whisper doing the proverbial rounds, much nuance was required when censoring a man so powerful at a time of so acute revolutionary fears. With this dynamic of cautious commercialism in mind, what follows discusses the strategies used by Samuel Fores, a stationer, printer and entrepreneur who operated from Piccadilly, to exploit for profit the rumours of scandal involving the heir to the British throne. Using close object analysis, insights from science and technology studies and readings of and between satirical designs, I will explore how the complex, time consuming and costly processes involved in bringing satirical designs to the marketplace could shape and constrain how Fores' wares made fun of George Augustus Frederick.

Isaac Cruikshank, the artist-engraver to whom the print publisher Samuel Fores was to turn to most often for satirical plates during the 1790s, entered the discussion on Prince George's sexual indiscretions in December 1789. His *Grounds of FORTUNE TELLING or the PRINCELY Repast* (Illustration 1) published by the sometime Leicester Fields publisher James Aitken, speculated – in an ominous and prescient début – on the acrimonious domesticity of the Prince and Maria Fitzherbert. George's reckless pursuit of Fitzherbert was typically dramatic: beginning during the spring of 1785 with an aborted pursuit of her to France halted by intervention from both King and Prime Minister, and culminating in a vainglorious (and half-hearted) suicide attempt as a consequence of Fitzherbert's repeated rebuttals of his marriage proposals.[3] Fitzherbert, to her credit, had reason to be cautious. As a Catholic, no less than three statutes prevented her marriage to the heir apparent.[4] Moreover, abstract Catholicism remained a mortal foe of Englishmen: 'the nation', a concerned Charles James Fox wrote to the young prince on 10 December 1785, is 'full of its old prejudices against Catholics'.[5]

Despite these lawful impediments the pair married in secret five days later on 15 December 1785. Rumours of the nuptials quickly emerged, eventually reached the floor of the House of Commons in 1787, and yet even then London's writers declined to declare the marriage outright.[6] The perspective of London's satirical artist-engravers was little different: prints such as *Grounds of FORTUNE TELLING* would only allude to the marriage in the strongest possible terms – here through furniture emblazoned with the Prince's feathered motif and a chimney-piece adorned with a sexually sugges-

3 A. Aspinall (ed.), The Later Correspondence of George III, 5 vols. (Cambridge, 1962), i, p. 149.

4 These were the Act of Settlement (1701), the Act of Union (1707) and the Royal Marriages Act (1772).

5 Cited in Charles Langdale, Memoirs of Mrs. Fitzherbert (London, 1856), p. 16.

6 This caution was also found further afield; see Gloucestershire Archives, Gloucester, D2383/C6–8. The closest a newspaper came to declaring the marriage was on 10th December 1788, when *The Morning Post* suggested that the 'connection' between George and Maria was of a 'more *coercive* and *permanent* nature' than previously realised. Pamphleteers such as Philip Withers were less cautious, see John Wardroper, Kings, Lords and Wicked Libellers: Satire and Protest, 1760–1837 (London, 1973), pp. 130–37.

Illustration 1: Isaac Cruikshank, *Grounds of FORTUNE TELLING or the PRINCELY Repast* (James Aitken, 8th December 1789), BM 7564. All prints published in London unless stated otherwise

tive satyr's head. And yet Cruikshank's and Aitken's palpable caution was no impediment to the commercial appeal of the design, indeed a large print run from the plate is suggested by the poor inking and heavy colouring of surviving impressions. Nine days later Fores got in on the act. In his Cruikshank-designed print, the anticipated result of the hitherto heavily implied Fitzherbert-Wales union is played out. Central to the narrative of this print, entitled *THE NEW BIRTH,* is a warming-pan venting the princely motif as it enters the foot of Fitzherbert's bed.[7] Coded though it is, this device takes little unpicking, suggesting as it does that the prince is to father an illegitimate Catholic pretender, in doing so recalling the notorious birth, little more than a century earlier, of James Frances Edward Stuart.[8]

Five years after *THE NEW BIRTH,* as envisioned in *MY GRANDMOTHER; alias the Jersey Jig; alias the RIVAL WIDOWS* (Illustration 2), the Prince's attention had turned from Fitzherbert to the forty-one-year-old Frances Villiers, Countess of Jersey.[9] This

7 Isaak Cruikshank, THE NEW BIRTH (Samuel Fores, 17th December 1789) [BM 7565].

8 This was not the first time the Prince had been accused of fathering illegitimate children; Wardroper, op.cit., p. 118, p. 120.

9 Although Jersey was senior royal mistress for the next decade, Fitzherbert remained a Carlton House favourite, 'the only woman', argues Wardroper, 'who had the power, not to keep him faithful, for he was faithful to nobody, but to live in his memory even until he lay dying' (Wardroper,

Illustration 2: Isaac Cruikshank, MY GRANDMOTHER; alias the Jersey Jig; alias the RIVAL WIDOWS (26th August 1794, Samuel Fores), BM 8485 © The Trustees of the British Museum

design draws upon a rich contemporary vein of satire where artists and writers alike, in a collective act of charivari, had seized upon the nine-year age gap between the pair. Jersey is thus an ageing, snuff-taking crone. In a playful inversion she sits child-like on the Prince's knee, whilst her distraught counterpart Mrs Fitzherbert flees, discarded with only a £6,000 annual pension, her reputation reduced to a society moll.[10] Amidst the drama the Prince sings:

> I've kissed & I've prattled with fifty Grand dames
> And changed them as oft do ye see,
> But of all the Grand Mammys that dance on the Steine
> The widow of Jersey give me &c &c.

To reinforce this narrative of past and ongoing profligacy, a less topical comparison is made by Cruikshank between the Prince and Solomon, the biblical king of Israel,

---

op.cit., p. 177). Notably she invited Lady Louisa Ponsonby to a party on behalf of George in 1795 (York University, Borthwick Institute of Historical Research, HALIFAX/A1/2/22).

10 William Dent had done just that in 1786 by comparing Maria with the Shakespearean prostitute Doll Tearsheet; William Dent, *A Shakesperean Scene, as performed by the Brighton Company on a late occasion, to which was added the agreeable entertainment of the Mistake* (J Carter, 7th August 1786) [BM 6974].

through the portrait of a bearded George inscribed 'and Solomon had 300 Wives and 700 Concubines'. It would have been relatively commonplace knowledge in late-Georgian England that Solomon is threatened by God with the division of his kingdom for the multiplication of money, the ownership of many horses and polygamy – all acts forbidden of Kings – in the Bible.[11] In Cruikshank's design Solomon's polygamy offers more than a crude comparison and thereby becomes a veiled allusion to the unmentionable secret of the Prince's marriage to Fitzherbert and to the pair's mutual love of women: especially married foreign women who worshipped other Gods.[12] The parallel with Solomon then returns us to 1789 and Fitzherbert's spurious royal child: a sin for which the Georgians might pay, as Solomon did, with the destruction of their Kingdom. With George III, the popular and pious father of the nation compared to the biblical David in this narrative, the Prince's private life defines his character as an errant threat to the national unity his father had built.[13]

Familiar and comfortable as this type of analysis is, it is worth pausing to remind ourselves of how the designs I have been discussing came to market, of their status as technologies and of the agents who made them. Each design began with an artist, in most cases an artist-engraver, who worked up a copper plate from which the design they had developed could be reproduced. By purchasing tools and by spending their time working on plates, it was they who absorbed the first business risk in satirical print production: if their design was no good or failed to strike a chord with the public, their efforts would be wasted. Worse still, an inadequate design could hinder, constrain and curtail future commercial collaborations with London's print publishers. Returning to the process of making, not any copper plate would suffice for the task of bringing a satirical print to a publishable form: rather, the plate had to be of good quality, no more than 3 or 4 mm thick, and hammered and polished to a mirror finish to remove imperfections. Poorly prepared plates resulted in poorly finished prints: the irregular spread of black dots which mark surviving impressions of the Cruikshank-Fores *Legal Method of Thrashing out Grain* are indicative of this.[14] With the plate prepared, the design could then be transferred as a mirror image of the final impression. At this stage the softness and chemical properties of the copper were

11 The Holy Bible, 1 Kings 11.

12 John Barrell, The Spirit of Despotism: Invasions of Privacy in the 1790s (Oxford, 2006), p. 121. In a similar vein, comparisons were made between George and another infamous royal adulterer, Henry VIII.

13 A mock heraldry of George III, published 1785, similarly alludes to the heir: 'Supporters. The dexter, Solomon treading on his crown'; Anonymous, The Heraldry of Nature; or INSTRUCTIONS for the KING at ARMS: COMPRISING, The Arms, Supporters, Crests and Mottos, in Latin, and with a Translation, OF THE E_G_H PEERS. Blazoned from the Authority of Truth, and characteristically descriptive of the several Qualities that distinguish their present Possessors. To which are added several Samples, neatly etched by an eminent Engraver (London, 1785), i.

14 Isaac Cruikshank, A legal method of thrashing out grain or forestallers & regraters reaping the fruits of their harvest (Samuel Fores, 12th August 1800).

ideal: allowing a burin to cut shallow grooves in the plate, an etching needle to score a wax-coated plate sufficiently for an acid bath to eat away at the plate as required, and a burnisher to spread copper back into incised or etched lines made in error.[15]

Once the artist-engraver was happy with his work – perhaps of a few days or week or more depending on the level of detail included in the design – a printer could run-off impressions. He would start by gently warming the plate before spreading thick ink made from mix of ground black and linseed oil onto its surface. Using various cloths and chalk, the plate would be cleaned everywhere except for the incised lines, and then placed beneath a sheet of high–quality, wetted rag paper and passed through a wool–lined, hand-operated roller press with a combination of meticulous care and brute force. Inking and printing took around ten minutes, after which the printer had a single black-and-white impression. The printing process could then be repeated for perhaps up to five-hundred impressions before the soft copper plate – so useful for an artist's purposes – would have worn at the edges of the incised lines so as to require retouching and recutting to extend its life, perhaps to as much as one-thousand impressions. But no two plates would wear the same. Mezzotint plates and finely etched areas – especially of text – would weaken sooner. An irregular pull through the press could wear a plate unevenly. And both under-heating and over-heating a plate could shorten its usable life.

Preparing copper plates for reproduction and printing from copper plates were, then, craft processes. Alongside this there was a crucial point of exchange between artist-engraver and publisher, at which interaction all the processes by which satirical prints were made converged. At this point the plate moved from the control of the artist-engraver to the publisher: either in fulfilment of a longstanding agreement, a prior ad-hoc arrangement, or a mid- or post- engraving deal. This is not to say, however, that publishers had no control over the plates before they were purchased from artist-engravers. If not direct, the publishers certainly had indirect influence: for having invested in space, tools and materials, the artist-engraver's control over his side of the process – the particulars of the design, the quality of engraving – did not exist in a vacuum, but rather was shaped and constrained by both his exchange with a publisher and his prospective publisher's future sale of impressions from the plate to potential customers. Entrepreneurs such as Samuel Fores, who operated a busi-

15 To work up decorative areas in particular, an etching needle was used to scratch through a wax coating applied to the plate. The plate was then placed in an acid bath to eat away the exposed metal and produce lines deep enough to hold ink during printing. Sweeping lines required the use of an engraving burin, which cut shallow grooves into the plate. Any scratches or shallow lines made in error could be removed by rubbing the area with a burnisher: the use of which spread the copper into unwanted incised lines so that they would not accept ink. For further discussion of print making see Anthony Dyson, Pictures to Print: the nineteenth-century engraving trade (London, 1984), Mary Pedley, The Commerce of Cartography: making and marketing maps in eighteenth-century France and England (Chicago, 2005) and Coolie Verner, 'Copperplate printing' in Five Centuries of Map Printing, ed. David Woodward (Chicago, 1976), pp. 51–76.

ness on Piccadilly from 1783, were discerning businessmen, sensitive above all to the commercial environment their wares entered. Filthy lucre it may be, but money and the market are, then, central to understanding the content of late-Georgian satirical prints, for having purchased a reproducible form of a print from the artist-engraver, a publisher such as Fores would, as one would expect from a businessman, seek to make a profit from their investment. In order to do this, he would need to buy paper and ink, invest in space to house printing equipment and spend time reproducing prints from the plates in his possession (or employing a printer to do so). He then needed to sell this stock at a price which would reimburse his labourers, suppliers and landlord, whilst still also generating enough capital to invest in the next project and to make a profit. This was, as should now be clear, a delicate balancing act. The technologies required to bring satirical prints to a reproducible form shaped and constrained what could be made and in what quantities. Consequently late-Georgian satirical prints were not only challenging but also expensive to bring to market, and hence not cheap objects at point of sale: from 6d–1s for a small uncoloured print to 3s–6s – or more – for a larger coloured impression. Thus the egalitarian print shop window crowd we all know so well was part of the magic of satire, but it was a smaller number of potentially paying customers who fuelled demand.[16] In sum it was they, their money, and the wares for which it was predicated they might be persuaded to part with it – as opposed to creative agency or artistic whim – that drove the content of the satirical prints that men such as Samuel Fores sold.

Understanding the process by which satirical prints came to market makes clear the obvious appeal of royal scandal, especially involving the Wales household, to businessmen such as Fores even during the 1790s: so long as one remained the correct side of taste, the topic possessed huge commercial potential. And yet whilst the narratives of princely misbehaviour we have seen were hardly novel, the innuendo and forthrightness present in prints such as *THE NEW BIRTH* and *MY GRANDMOTHER* – published a full four years after marriage rumours emerged – certainly was. The Prince's earlier affairs had been tolerated as trivial offences of youth. His connection aged seventeen with Mary Robinson became jovially located within Shakespeare's *The Winter's Tale*: with George as the love struck Florizel and Robinson – in reference to her role in Garrick's Drury Lane adaptation – as the commoner Perdita.[17] A mock heraldry from 1785 repeats this light-hearted attitude toward his sexual adventures:

16 The small size of the Georgian print marketplace underpins a narrative of Regency and early-Victorian expansion, innovation and growth in Brian Maidment's excellent Comedy, Caricature and the Social Order 1820–1850 (Manchester, 2013).

17 See Anonymous, *Florizel and Perdita* (10th November 1780) [BM 5767], James Gillray, *MONUMENTS lately discovered on Salisbury Plain* (Hannah Humphrey, 15th June 1782) [BM 6115] and Anon, *THE LADIES CHURCH YARD* (B Pownall, 22nd September 1783) [BM 6263]; Jonathan Bate, Shakespearean Constitutions: Politics, Theatre, Criticism 1730–1830 (Oxford, 1989), p. 75.

The_____ [Prince]
Arms. First, azure, the prince's cap, feathers disordered, second argent, four decanters azure; third, gules, a fringed petticoat between three maiden-heads; fourth, sable, the ace of spades proper; fifth, argent, a horse courant between three rattles, sixth, gules, a quiver, the arrows scattered.
Supporters. The dexter, Cupid, the sinister, a monkey, proper.
Crest. A deer wounded.
Motto. Fionsal'avenir
Better days hereafter[18]

But these 'better days' had not arrived by the mid-1790s and Robinson's pension in exchange for her silence would be the first of many handed out at the public's expense.[19] And so increasingly the Prince's public actions chimed oddly with what Tamara Hunt describes as 'a point when the British public was encouraged to embrace its monarch on the strength of his personal virtue'.[20] With the heir to the throne setting an increasingly destructive domestic example, concerns over royal dalliances were extended to his brothers, to social elites and – in social satires concerning marriage and custom – to the very fabric of the British social compact. Such was the heady mix of outrage and prurient rubbernecking that the famous debate between Lord Rolle and Fox on 30 April 1787 over the supposed marriage between Fitzherbert and Prince George took place, recalled Nathaniel Wraxall, with 'silence pervading the house, which, as well as the gallery, was crowded to the utmost degree'.[21] 'The matter had been discussed in newspapers, all over the kingdom', he continued, 'impressing with deep concern every individual who venerated the British constitution'.[22] These 'newspapers' had brought the Prince's private dispute into a public realm – the locus of scandal – in doing so providing an exemplar of broader compromises to the domiciliary ideal.[23]

This exemplar was most troubling because those who publicly transgressed boundaries of acceptable behaviour remained unpunished. In the wake of George's marriage to Caroline of Brunswick on 8 April 1795, it was Lady Jersey who would emerge as the archetypal unpunished individual: a women who, irrespective of the Prince's complicity, brought the bawdy house into a marital home by combining the roles of senior royal mistress and Lady of the Bedchamber to the Princess of Wales. The King may have suggested to his son that he banish her from Carlton House in June 1796,

18 Anonymous, The Heraldry of Nature, op.cit., ii. see note 12.
19 Wardroper, op.cit., p. 115.
20 Tamara L. Hunt, Defining John Bull: political caricature and national identity in late Georgian England (Ashgate, 2003), p. 242.
21 Nathaniel William Wraxall, Posthumous Memoirs of His Own Time (2nd ed., London, 1845), p. 243.
22 Wraxall, op.cit., p. 243.
23 For a discussion of domiciliary ideals and the use of egregious transgressors to secure the boundaries of acceptable domestic behaviour, see Michael McKeon, The Secret History of Domesticity: public, private, and the division of knowledge (Baltimore, 2005), especially pp. xix–xxi.

and the Queen may have disliked the royal household's public role in the 1790s due to, she suggested on 22 January 1797, 'being privately connected with Ldy Jersey',[24] but they could not and did not force the liaison to cease. It was instead media such as satirical prints which virtually punished Jersey for her social crimes, addressing the perceived paradox that in contrast to the fate of the common whore, Jersey's position as courtesan was neither challenged legally nor by the customs of high society: as moral and legal censure were being focused on those vulnerable souls who prostituted themselves in order to survive, so the exemption of society courtesans was discursively problematic.[25] It is, then, to the appearance of Jersey-as-courtesan in prints sold by Samuel Fores to which we now turn.

The development of this anti-courtesan discourse helps explain the content of prints on the Prince's indiscretions which were printed by Fores during the mid-1790s. Whilst scandal was a tempting subject to exploit, Fores – perhaps cautious not to test the loyalism of his potentially wealthy West End clientèle – chose to bring to the marketplace designs which deflected blame (if only slightly) away from the Prince. In *Thoughts on Matrimony,* for example, it is a youthful reimagining of Jersey upon which the engaged Prince is transfixed.[26] His 'thoughts on matrimony' are not with his future wife, a miniature of whom he holds with disregard, but a married sexualised harlot. This woman, Lady Jersey, is positioned above a lit fireplace, quite literally stoking the Prince's passion, pre-emptively burning the prospective marital compact. It is within this Princely idolatry for Jersey that Cruikshank's imagines for Fores's customers the eventual sexual union between the Prince and Princess. Published on 15 April 1795, seven days after the royal wedding, OH! CHE BOCCONE! – or 'Oh! What a mouthful' – depicts the prince's shock at the soon to be renowned lack of personal hygiene practised by his new bride.[27] Rumours spread that to make bearable the consummation of their marriage George drank himself into a stupor, and thus for Cruikshank he required an aphrodisiac ('Cantharides') to complete their union. Yet – postcoital – he remains shocked at the thought: an image mounted above the bed of Zeus raping Leda in the form of a swan signalling both past and future sexual perversity.[28]

24 Aspinall, op.cit., ii, p. 536. Somewhat ironically it was the Queen who had secured Lady Jersey a position at Carlton House (Wardroper, op.cit., p. 169). For the royal household in public see Barrell, op.cit., pp. 103–44.

25 See for example Richard Newton, *September in London – all our Friends out of Town!!!* (William Holland, 21st September 1791); David Alexander, Richard Newton and English Caricature in the 1790s (Manchester, 1998), figure 1; Wardroper, op.cit., p. 281; James Grantham Turner, 'Understanding Whores', *Eighteenth-Century Life,* 33:1 (Winter 2009), pp. 97–105.

26 Isaak Cruikshank, THOUGHTS on MATRIMONY (26th January 1795, Samuel Fores) [BM 8611].

27 Isaak Cruikshank, OH! CHE BOCCONE! (15th April 1795, Samuel Fores) [BM 8643].

28 The gloom surrounding the prospect of George and Caroline producing an heir contrasts with the eagerness of satirists for the Princess Royal and Prince Frederick of Württemberg to produce legitimate offspring: see James Gillray, *The BRIDAL-NIGHT* (Hannah Humphrey, 18th May 1797) [BM 9014] and Isaac Cruikshank, *The Wedding Night* (Samuel Fores, 20th May 1797) [BM 9015].

Illustration 3: Isaac Cruikshank, *WASHING the BLACKAMOOR* (Samuel Fores, 24th July 1795), BM 8667 © The Trustees of the British Museum

Beyond this scene lurks Jersey: a trumped-up whore, negligent royal attendant and, as Cruikshank-Fores underlined three months later in *WASHING the BLACKAMOOR* (Illustration 3), a woman of irreparable repute.[29] Here we find Jersey, in an echo to *Thoughts on Matrimony,* cast as a mere, dispensable distraction from domestic duty: the Princess, commenting on the failure of the Prince and two attendants to whiten Jersey's stained skin, or, metaphorically, to wash her dirt away, states "It vont do she must put on anoder face". Evidently this anti-Jersey print was a commercial success. Two surviving impressions derive from a copper plate at seemingly vastly differing stages of its life, and yet are printed on paper bearing identical watermarks. We can rule out, therefore, the possibility that the weaker impression was printed at a much later date, and suggest that Fores may have printed a significant number of impressions of the plate – up to the 500 sheets which comprised a ream – in one run. To do so Fores, his apprentices, and his staff would have worked his press in teams to reduce the delay between Fores acquiring the plate from Isaac Cruikshank and a significant quantity of stock reaching the marketplace.[30]

29 Isaac Cruikshank, *WASHING the BLACKAMOOR* (Samuel Fores, 24th July 1795) [BM 8667].

30 See British Museum Registration number 1868,0808,6457 and 1917,1208,4109. The latter uncoloured impression is the considerably weaker of the two.

Rarely however did West End satires show the Princess to be quite so knowing, quite so accepting and stoic in the face of her husband's indiscretions. The following year in *SKETCHES from NATURE!!!* (Illustration 4) the Prince's liaison with Jersey is retrospectively retold over four compartments, creating (for the initiated) an artificial dramatic tension. The print's principal task is to narrate the destruction of two separate domestic compacts: Jersey and Wales. In the first panel, marked 'The Sultan RETIRING', we see Lord Jersey bidding the rakish couple goodnight. Emblem here is of particularly pertinence, showing that they retire to *her* bed – variously decorated with the coronet of the Earl of Jersey – and reinforcing the domestic subversion with the placement of the Prince's chamber-pot underneath. In the second panel, marked 'Fashionable PASTIME', the ridicule of Lord Jersey is complete, as both his wife and the Prince raise the cuckold sign. The Prince mounts Lord Jersey, a reference to his position as Master of the Horse to the future monarch.[31] Lord Jersey is weak, deferential and complicit,[32] but his wife is the chief sinner: indeed it is she who lounges provocatively on the marital bed for someone other than her husband and mocks him, bare-chested, with the question 'Buck-Buck how many Horns do I hold up'.[33]

In these first two panels the prince himself is proactive in undermining Jersey's domesticity, however in the remaining two panels he becomes a reactive character, as Wales's domesticity is shattered. First the Princess discovers the adulterous couple and then attempts to send word to her father, the Duke of Brunswick. The demeanour of the Prince is noticeably changed, his earlier self-confidence and jollity replaced with dismay and suicidal thought: in panel four, 'Confidence Betrayed', he reaches ominously for a gun. Yet Lady Jersey remains the proactive agent of domestic disunity, sleeping peacefully on the chest of her lover whilst the Princess, adopting a romantic posture, weeps. Moreover, she betrays the confidence of her lady, reading aloud to the Prince the contents of an intercepted private letter intended for the Princess's father. Jersey even mocks the predicament of her lover, saying 'here would have been a rare Kettle of Fish to have served up to a German Prince'. She is, as the King privately remarked, the 'shaddow' over marital reconciliation',[34] and through the active destruction of two households, the personification of subverted domesticity over and above her rival Mrs. Fitzherbert.

---

31 Jersey's eldest son was also made Lord of the Bedchamber (Wardroper, op.cit., p. 167).

32 Indeed a print within the second panel compares him to a similar figure of derision, Sir Richard Worsley. For public prints exposing the cuckolding of Worsley see Vic Gatrell, City of Laughter: sex and satire in eighteenth-century London (London, 2006), pp. 1–4.

33 A phrase repeated by Gillray days later in *FASHIONABLE-JOCKEYSHIP* (James Gillray, 1st June 1796) [BM 8811]. The Earl denied encouraging the affair in a sycophantic letter to the King, 13 May 1796: 'Under the state of cruel aspersion which I believe, it is not unknown to your Majesty to have been thrown upon me & my family, do I presume too much upon the most gracious condescension & favor of many years in now laying myself at your Majesty's feet?'; Aspinall, op.cit., ii, p. 474.

34 Aspinall, op.cit., ii, p. 491.

Illustration 4: Isaac Cruikshank, *SKETCHES from NATURE!!!* (Samuel Fores, 28th May 1796), BM 8809 © The Trustees of the British Museum

Illustration 5: Isaac Cruikshank, *FUTURE PROSPECTS* or *Symptoms of Love in HIGH LIFE* (Samuel Fores, 31st May 1796), BM 8810 © The Trustees of the British Museum

Few images summarise this characterisation better than the Cruikshank-Fores 1796 work, *FUTURE PROSPECTS or Symptoms of Love in HIGH LIFE* (Illustration 5). The Princess is once again a romanticised victim, demure and motherly in contrast with her violent and obstinate husband: 'Marriage has no restraints on me!' he proclaims, 'no Legal tie can bind the will – tis free & shall be so'. Set within a staged aesthetic, which extenuates the theatricality of the scene, the front stage action is subverted by that occurring backstage: the only avenue of princely escape from this claustrophobic drama.[35] Lord Jersey – resplendent with cuckold horns – provides an ocular bridge, straddling the two private arenas and drawing the attention of the viewer by stating 'My Wife is waiting for you in the next room'. Here, literally and metaphorically behind the royal domestic failure, is the royal mistress lounging in a lewd posture on a settee. Lady Jersey is the visual antonym of Caroline: their furniture may be similar, but their uses of them vastly differ. Thus freed from earlier direct swipes at her age, Lady Jersey emerges the typographical harlot, mistress and adulterer: an anecdote for domestic upheaval.

Filtered through Carlton House the micro becomes macro. George tramples on a number of papers, one marked 'marriage a la mode', the Hogarthian 'corrective to

35 Chris Roulston, 'Word and Image in the long Eighteenth Century', in Word and Image in the Long Eighteenth Century: An Interdisciplinary Dialogue, eds Christina Ionescu and Renata Schellenberg (Newcastle, 2008), p. 38.

the misuse of the institution of marriage for profit and gain' and a symbol of societal dysfunction.[36] Under this purview of princely domesticity interacting with national morality, he kicks over a tea table, signifying a broader amoral sexual conduct.[37] The scandal of his affairs therefore suggests a more national affliction, a more national disrespect for the inherent goodness of domesticity promoted in loyalist rhetoric.[38] Further, the Prince's marriage is once again compared to his father's. On the wall behind and between the pair hangs *The Constant Couple,* a wistful and affectionate satire on the King's familiar 'soubriquet "Farmer George"',[39] appended to which is a textual reminder that outside of the fashionable 'HIGH LIFE' that his sons moved in, chivalry was far from dead:

> The little Wants, dislikes, preferences, antipathies, fancies, whims, & even impertinence of Women must be officiously attended to, flattered & if possible guesed [sic] at, and anticipated by a well bred Man.

By 1796, then, the Prince takes centre stage and is constructed decisively as a potential threat to national unity, as a man whose immoral actions – and companions – fall outside and thereby threaten the very legitimacy of the customary standards recognised elsewhere in society. As the footnote to *SKETCHES from NATURE!!!* states with some pertinence: 'the very Stones look up to see, Such very Gorgeous Harlotry, Shameing an Honest Nation'.

Notwithstanding this centrality, the Cruikshank-Fores prints which followed were reluctant to fully ostracise the Prince, to make him a lost cause. Instead they were undercut by a notable defence of the Prince and an acceptance of his future role. In short, they can be read as attempts to shape his behaviour for the better. Despite failing to adhere to the principle that 'family affection', as John Barrell describes of the era, was 'if not the first qualification for citizenship, at least the *sine qua non* of good citizenship',[40] the future King was not cast as a lost cause within graphic satire. As we shall see, much of this behavioural reconditioning took the form of comparing him to his father. This is hardly surprising. The symbolic strength of the King's reputation should not be underestimated, given his sheer popularity from the 1780s onwards, a period during which 'God Save the King' became all but institutionalised as the

36 Roulston, op. cit., p. 37.

37 Maxine Berg, Luxury and Pleasure in Eighteenth-Century Britain (Oxford, 2005), p. 231.

38 Barrell, op.cit., pp. 233–34.

39 [James Gillray], *The Constant Couple* (Samuel Fores, 24th February 1786) [BM 6918]; Grayson Ditchfield, George III: An Essay in Monarchy (Basingstoke, 2002), p. 7. See also John Ashton Cannon, 'The survival of the British Monarchy', in: Transactions of the Royal Historical Society, 5th series, no. 36 (1986), pp. 143–64.

40 John Barrell, Imagining the King's Death: Figurative Treason, Fantasies of Regicide, 1793–1796 (Oxford, 2000), p. 51.

national anthem in honour of this moral and spiritual leader of the nation.[41] Reporting from Weymouth in 1789 of events following the King's recovery, Frances Burney wrote:

> The King, Queen, and Princesses, and their suite, walked out in the evening; an immense crowd attended them – sailors, bargemen, mechanics, countrymen; and all united in so vociferous volley of "God Save the King," that the noise was stunning […] Not a child could we meet that had not a bandeau round his head, cap or hat of 'God Save the King".[42]

We might expect superlatives from Burney, one of the Queen's attendants, but as Linda Colley argues, the trials of George III as a man, monarch and father sought only to create an 'increased public protectiveness towards the king himself'.[43] Moreover his 'seniority among European monarchs' would surround him with the folklore of a moral and domestic king indispensable to national stability, so much so, argues Grayson Ditchfield, that by the 1790s 'even the satirists had become hopelessly entangled in the myth of royal ordinariness'.[44] Songs that bemoaned the hypocrisy of the church and state found time to eulogise the King, to set him apart from perceived institutional malaise and malpractice:

> Though I sweep to and fro, old iron to find,
> Brass pins, rusty nails, they are all to my mind,
> Yet I wear a sound heart true to great George our king,
> And though ragged and poor, with clear conscience can sing –
> Though I sweep to and fro, yet I'd have you to know
> There are sweepers in high life as well as in low.[45]

41 An anthem derived from The Holy Bible, 1 Samuel 10:24. For anthems as community builders, see Benedict Anderson, Imagined Communities: Reflections on the Origin and Spread of Nationalism (rev. ed., London, 1991), p. 145.

42 Frances Burney, Diary and Letters of Madame D'Arblay.Author of Evelina, Cecilia, &c. Edited by her niece, 5 vols. (London, 1842), v, p. 33.

43 Linda Colley, Britons: Forging the Nation, 1707–1837 (New Haven, 1992), p. 233; Ditchfield, op. cit., p. 152.

44 Ditchfield, op. cit., p. 45; Colley, Britons, p. 233. This narrative has been questioned in Barrell, op. cit., p. 10, pp. 103–144, however his argument is too couched in radical (or at least reform-inclined) pamphleteering and the acute circumstances of 1795 (when the whole architecture of state, not just the King, was unpopular) to convincingly challenge the prevailing paradigm. Indeed the criticisms levelled at the King during this crisis year – tacit alignments of Father George with forestalling farmers; a demystification of the king through his lack of majesty; an overzealous desire to be seen as ordinary – seem insignificant compared to those aimed at other political figures. Moreover he remained for some a majestic warrior King, see James Ward after WilliamBeechey, *George III with the Prince of Wales and Duke of York reviewing troops* (1st June 1799) [David Bindman, The Shadow of the Guillotine: Britain and the French Revolution (London, 1989), fig. 213].

45 Wardroper, op. cit., p. 278.

After his death even radicals such as John Mitford memorialised this model king, if, with more than a little retrospective idealism, as a device with which to bemoan the comparative failures of his successor:

> He never deserted his house and his wife,
> To lead a debauch'd and dissolute life;
> He never would sanction knaves, bunters, and vice.
> And gamsters [sic], whose only strength centres in dice. [...]
> He did not lie snoring with wantons at noon,
> And when he was call'd, cry '*You'vewak'd me too soon!*'
> With one virtous woman to live he made shift,
> And cherish'd his honour as Heaven's best gift.
> He was not afraid to be met in the street.
> He was not asham'd honest women to greet;
> He never consider'd that oaths were dull nonsense,
> But died as he liv'd – with an unsullied conscience.
> A friend and a father to all the forlorn,
> The pleasure of the vicious he treated with scorn.[46]

Thus for Mitford the late George III was the antithesis of the newly crowned King, a man who, having lived apart from Caroline of Brunswick from shortly after their marriage, *had* 'deserted his house and his wife', who *had* succumbed to 'vice' and 'dice'.[47]

As we have seen, satirists had previously ridiculed this divergence of morality between the royal father and royal son: the motif was hardly novel.[48] Indeed if, as Ditchfield comments, George III 'appeared to his subjects as a family man, and his family circle touchingly brought regality and domesticity together in a way that endeared him to a public which was increasingly exhorted to the pursuit of morality', the Prince must have seemed intent on destroying this union of state and domesticity.[49] And yet as we move through the 1790s, the dangers of couching royal legitimacy in terms of private virtue – emphasized by the centrality of domestic dysfunction to anti-Paineite pamphleteering – did not, as might be expected, manifest itself into some kind of pre-regicidal intent.[50] Indeed in Cruikshank-Fores productions such as

46 John Mitford, A Peep into W----- Castle, after the lost mutton (London, 1820), pp. 12–13.

47 Ditchfield, op. cit., p. 15; Aspinall, op. cit., ii, p. 491 and iii, p. 6. Colley, op. cit., pp. 195–236.

48 'The contrary character of his [the King's] Successor' with respect to 'private virtues' is expressed by Coleridge in a letter to John Fellows, 31 May 1796; cited in Leslie Griggs (ed.), Collected Letters of Samuel Taylor Coleridge, 6 vols. (Oxford, 1956–71), i, p. 219.

49 Ditchfield, op. cit., p. 143. See also Corinna Wagner, Loyalist Propaganda and the Scandalous Life of Tom Paine: 'Hypocritical Monster!', in: *British Journal for Eighteenth-Century Studies* 28:1 (2005), p. 98, and Marilyn Morris, The Royal Family and Family Values in Late Eighteenth-Century England, in: *Journal of Family History* 21 (1996), pp. 519–32.

50 Accusations of perverted domesticity were used to cast Paine as the antithesis of civic and patriotic humanitarianism; Wagner, op. cit., pp. 108–11.

THE ROYAL JER[A]SEY!! (Illustration 6) something very different is in evidence. Here lightly caricatured and shown in profile, the Prince holds a scroll marked 'Thoughts on a Restricted Regency'. George's natural wig, known colloquially as a 'jazy' or 'jasey', hides a lice-ridden head observable through a parting on the back of his neck. The suggestion is that the damage to the Prince's reputation as a result of his post-marital dalliances with Lady Jersey (see the deliberately altered title) can only be concealed and not washed away; leaving open in the public mind the idea of restrictions to George's power should a Regent be required. The print therefore skilfully negotiates the fraught discursive territory between critique and radicalism that so few pamphlets and tracts were able to do: it advocates a reform of princely behaviour, towards which his wearing of a jasey (which did not require the hair powder popularly believed to diminish food stocks) goes some way to repair, whilst at the same time avoiding questioning directly the notion of Hanoverian primogeniture: this in spite of George's betraying, both in itself and in what it fails to cover, his ungenteel nature.[51] It *warns* the Prince only of the displeasure he has caused his subjects, rather than of any revolutionary activity they may undertake, should he not improve his ways when king.[52]

In the late 1790s this fear of destruction was played out in public warnings regarding the Prince's lavish lifestyle and diet. A slew of prints in May 1799, for example, imagined the Prince receiving a visitation from the ghost of his great-uncle, William Augustus Duke of Cumberland (1721–65).[53] In the first of these, a Gillray-Humphrey print published 7 May 1799 (Illustration 7), the Prince's private torment is revealed to us by the actions of his great-uncle. The Duke draws back a once obscuring curtain, is obese and naked (illustrating that prince and pauper alike are equal in the grave) and holds aloft an hourglass running out not for him but for the Prince. The print was successful, and in response a Cruikshank-Fores print appeared a week later entitled *The GHOST or the CLOSET SCENE in HAMLET,* a design whose reliance on text and lack of background detail betrays a somewhat hasty preparation. On this occasion the Prince, supported in his moment of horror by one Honor Gubbins, is aware of the apparition predicting in literal speech his imminent death:

> Dont be frightened George, dont be frightened but next Monday fortnight must come & take a Glass of Burgundy along with us dont be frightened I just slip'd of to tell you I heard the Governor tell some of his runners to fetch you!! glad to see you dont be frightened.

Two days later a Cruikshank design appeared entitled *THE GHOST OR SECOND WARNING* (Illustration 8). Evidently in preparation when the previous design was

---

51 For the contemporary debates surrounding Pitt's Hair Powder tax of 1795, and the belief that powder limited bread supplies, see Barrell, op. cit., pp. 145–209.

52 For further discussion of this print see James Baker, Satirising a Prince, or Making Light of a Culture of Errors, in: *The Comics Grid* 3(1): 3 (March 2013).

53 William Arthur Speck, William Augustus, Prince, Duke of Cumberland (1721–1765), ODNB online edition.

Illustration 6: Isaac Cruikshank, *THE ROYAL JER[A]SEY!!* [E and R struck through and replaced with A] (Samuel Fores, 22nd February 1797), BM 8988 © The Trustees of the British Museum

Illustration 7: James Gillray, *DUKE WILLIAM'S GHOST* (Hannah Humphrey, 7th May 1799), BM 9381 © The Trustees of the British Museum

published, this more complex print brazenly imitates various elements of Gillray's *GHOST* – the Ducal unveiling, the discarded bottles and the unkempt bed are all compositional quotations to Gillray – and in doing so attempts to exploit the commercial opportunity afforded by the limited life of the original plate. Text, however, retains a more central role than in the Gillray-Humphrey design. Minded towards pleasing his favoured publisher, some text is used by Isaac Cruikshank for overtly commercial purposes: 'Oh Dear Dear what can the matter be, these Amusements of High Life dont suit me' states Honor Gubbins, a inter-textual play on the Fores-published *FUTURE PROSPECTS,* specifically the subtitle *Symptoms of Love in HIGH LIFE.*[54] But *in toto* this text is more than a puff, for it is used by Isaac to differentiate his message from Gillray's, to present to Fores' customers a much less malevolent scene than Gillray's. Rather than imagining the future death of the heir apparent, Cruikshank suggests how what was to Gillray inevitable could be prevented. To quote the ghost of the Duke:

54 See also Richard Newton, *A Sketch from Highlife* (1791) [Alexander 3]. For Gubbins's association with high living in resorts such as Bath see Isaac Cruikshank, *The LILLIPUTAN SATIRISTS* (Samuel Fores, 22nd June 1797) [BM 9088] and Isaac Cruikshank, *SYMPTOMS of LOVE!!* (Samuel Fores, 1st January 1796) [Bmund].

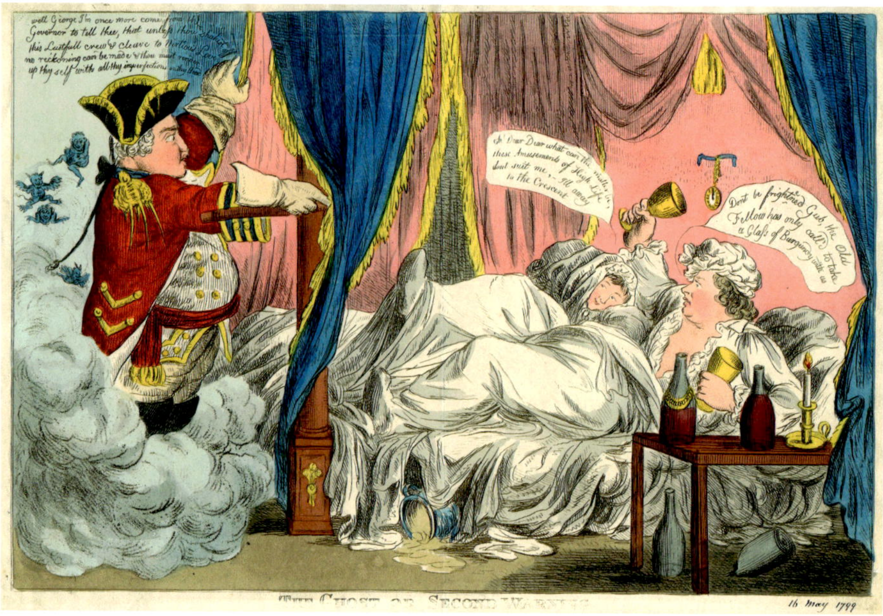

Illustration 8: Isaac Cruikshank, *THE GHOST OR SECOND WARNING* (Samuel Fores, May 1799), BM 9384 © The Trustees of the British Museum

> Well George! I'm once more come from the Governor to tell thee, that unless thou shakest off this Lustfull crew & cleave to Virtious [sic] Love no reckoning can be made & thou must render up thy self with all thy imperfections on thy Head.

Another Fores print, Charles Williams's *THE GHOST* (Illustration 9), confirms Fores's commercial intentions. Not only is the print – published two days before Cruikshank's – clearly derived from the same original design, suggesting Fores charged both of his preferred artist-engravers with collaborating in his response to Gillray-Humphrey, but it also goes further in offering instruction as opposed to hopeless critique. As Williams's Duke states:

> Most noble youth, I am thy Uncles Ghost, Doom'd for a certain time to walk at night, and win the Fates; shake off the Traitorous Crew that lurk around thy Table; expose their treacherous schemes, inform the ruling powers what plots and treasons deep they meditae [sic] against the State; and thus by one bold patriotic deed restore Britannia's darling Son; then shall the sentence be revers'd and------shall live again.

George did indeed 'live again'. As Regent the Prince would remain separated from his wife and once King this decision would explode into a scandal which threatened the very existence of the British establishment. Unsurprisingly the passing years saw little change in his desire to drink, gamble and cavort with women. Indeed in 1799

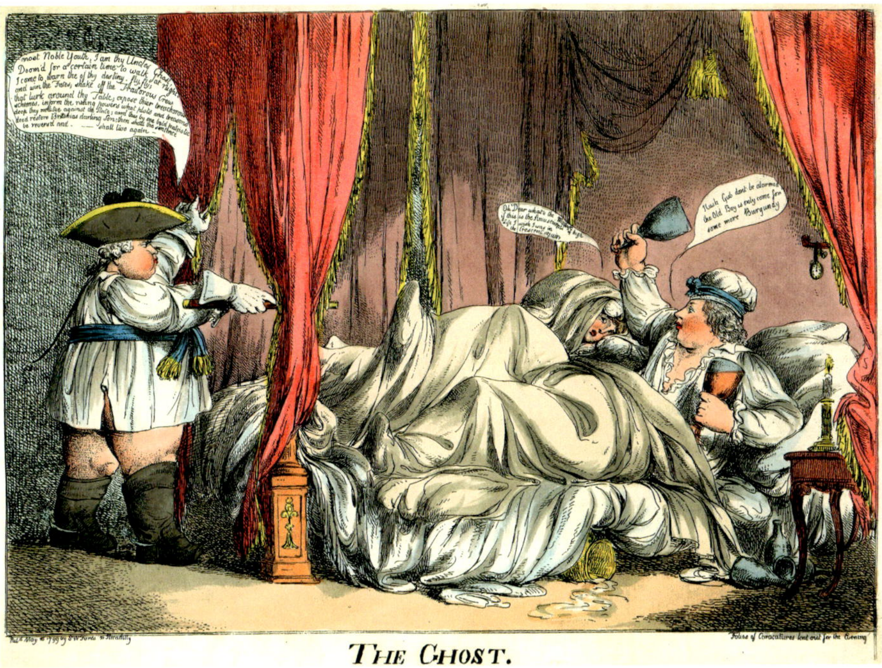

Illustration 9: Charles Williams, *THE GHOST* (Samuel Fores, 15th May 1799), BM 9385

he had returned to Fitzherbert. Lord Wallingford recorded in a private letter dated 13 December 1806, 'I never saw more apparent cordiality than between [the Prince] and Mrs.Fitzherbert', an association we are alerted to once more in 1816 when the industrialist Robert Heywood mentioned the Prince having by this date – though one presumes only recently, for why else mention it – 'quite discarded Mrs. Fitzherbert'.[55] For critical conservative commentators there would however be an unforeseen benefit to George's persistent extra-marital transgressions. Fitzherbert and Lady Hertford, with the latter of whom he had an attachment from 1807, would persuade the newly installed Regent to reject his former Whig friends and affiliate himself politically with his father's Tory allies. Thus the prophecy of Solomon did not come true. Governance of customary liberty, although mocked by the Prince for so long, was not to be handed over to a party seen by many loyalists as anarchists and republicans: rather, a critical, conservative iteration of John Bull, so long ignored, now had positioned himself through public pressure at the Regent's ear.[56]

55 Hampshire Record Office, 1M44/122/11; Bolton Archive and Local Studies Service, ZHE/12/43.
56 As early as 1794, Cruikshank had alluded to the power of middling discourse over the Prince's affairs, see Isaac Cruikshank, *John Bulls Hint for a PROFITABLE ALLIANCE* (Samuel Fores, 26th September 1794) [BM 8487].

Between the late-1780s and late-1790s Samuel Fores published a number of satirical prints which made fun of the Prince of Wales. As we have seen, those designed by Isaac Cruikshank show how Fores – and his marketplace – gradually warmed to direct critiques of the Prince. At the beginning of this period Maria Fitzherbert and Lady Jersey were used to deflect blame from the Prince. By 1799 the Prince stood alone. But by charging Cruikshank and Williams with aping Gillray's DUKE WILLIAM'S GHOST, whilst simultaneously toning down its hopeless message, Fores was hedging his bets: commercial success would come from both those who had failed to pick up a copy of Gillray's successful design before stocks ran out and from Londoners unimpressed by Gillray's dispiriting vision. Fores, then, was a responsive, flexible and opportunistic publisher. But he was also cautious, keen both to protect and to develop the respectability of his business and, in turn, the custom of his clientèle. In part this caution was a response to the complex, time-consuming and expensive process of bringing a satirical design to market. With so much invested in terms of time, and such a small window of opportunity to exploit a plate for profit, the designs he chose delicately possessed a message of sufficient breadth to capture the attention of a broad range of London's consumers. Allied with this, Fores's caution came from his surroundings. Located at the heart of the fashionable West End, Fores occupied a different metropolitan milieu to City publishers such as James Aitken, an eastward geographical influence which would grow through names such as Thomas Tegg and John Johnston as the Golden Age of graphic satire wore on.[57] But location alone does not explain Fores's caution. His closest competitor throughout the 1790s and his nearest equal in terms of volume of output was located from 1797 just doors away at 27 St James's Street: from Hannah Humphrey's shop James Gillray would publish – irrespective of his secret government pension – some of the age's most vicious assaults on the Prince. How then, did Fores's business differ?

Unlike Humphrey, Fores traded in a range of wares. An early glimpse of Fores' shop, or at least how he wished his shop to be imagined, is evident in the 1786 print, *THE COCK of the WALK, DISTRIBUTING HIS FAVOURS.*[58] Here at the back of the scene, Fores presents to the public the latest satirical and portrait prints. Three years later a newspaper advertisement for 'FORES's Grand Caricature Exhibition' shows his business also traded in illustrations after comic songs, fashion prints and various items of stationery.[59] In 1795 Fores moved his business from No. 3 to No. 50 Piccadilly, a large property on the corner of Sackville Street, and diversified his business portfolio further still. A Cruikshanks-Fores print from 1810, which uses this second property as its stage, locates the door to these premises at a 45° angle to both streets

57 For further discussion see Timothy Clayton, Transfer of Caricatures. The London Printing Trade and the Export of English Graphic Prints in this volume.

58 *THE COCK of the WALK, DISTRIBUTING HIS FAVOURS* (Samuel Fores, 31 May 1786) [BM 6961].

59 *Nouveau Guide des Étrangers* (London, 1789), back page.

Illustration 10: Isaac and George Cruikshank, *Folkstone Strawberries, or more Carraway Comfits for Mary Ann* (Samuel Fores, 20nd June 1810), BM 11565 © The Trustees of the British Museum

(Illustration 10).[60] Inside is a high and well-stocked bookcase accessible by ladder, two adjacent bookcases above a few small pictures and a counter at which Fores sits, well-dressed, attending to an open book – probably a ledger. Next to the door on the Sackville Street side are five small window panes forming a single column. Within these, from top to bottom, is a print in profile, a caricature, four books spines facing outward, four books face outward and one open book. On the Piccadilly side is a thirty-three pane window (11 by 3) within which are books large and small, some open, others closed, two containing illustrations. This is a picture of a diverse business, for which satirical prints formed, or are presented as forming, a modest role. And although by 1810 the volume of satirical work Fores was publishing had reduced from its 1790s peak, then, too, there was more at stake than just consumers of satirical prints, when Fores was considering which designs to publish under his name. One false move and he could alienate a range of both existing and potential customers. Making fun of George Augustus Frederick was a delicate business.

60 Isaac and George Cruikshank, *Folkstone Strawberries or more carraway comfits for Mary Ann* (Samuel Fores, 20nd June 1810) [BM 11565].

Karl Janke

Counter-Image, Anathema, Vision of Terror: Republic and Popular Rule in English Caricature of the Eighteenth Century

Revolution und Hannoveraner Königtum gehören aufs engste zusammen. Das Bild der Republik in der englischen Karikatur des langen 18. Jahrhunderts wird von vier, die jeweilige Staatsform begründenden Revolutionen beeinflusst – drei davon begründeten Republiken, die Englische von 1649–60, die Amerikanische und die Französische. Nur die vierte, die ‚Glorreiche' von 1688, begründete mittelbar die eigene, monarchische Herrschaft. Grund genug also, nach dem Republikanischen im Royalen zu fahnden, in der Bildwelt des sich in diesem Zeitraum herausbildenden neuen Mediums der politischen Karikatur. Das Versagen der Bildpolitik der puritanischen englischen Republik zeigt sich im Unvermögen der Whig-Opposition im letzten Drittel des 18. Jahrhunderts, der loyalistischen Dämonisierung der eigenen politischen Position im Schreckbild der (Französischen) Republik eine eigene Bildargumentation entgegenzusetzen. Das Bild des Republikanischen wird weitgehend im Zerrbild seiner loyalistischen Gegner überliefert – und ironisch als Beitrag zu ‚einer neuen Geschichte des Republikanismus' angekündigt. In der Auseinandersetzung um das richtige oder falsche Bild des Gemeinwesens rekurriert die loyalistische Karikatur auf Grundlagen politischer Perzeption oder auf das Narrativ zeitgenössischer Medien- und Kleinkunstformen, um republikanische Anschauungen zu korrigieren. Zugleich bietet diese zusätzliche Brechungsebene eine Basis, um das Spannungsfeld zwischen loyalistischer Botschaft und einem möglichen satirischen Selbstbehalt, wenn nicht republikanischen Selbstbewusstsein, zu artikulieren.

Revolution and Hanoverian monarchy are very closely interlinked. No less than four revolutions shape the context for their rule. Three of these established republics, the English one of 1649–60, the American and the French one. Only the fourth, the Glorious Revolution of 1688, established indirectly their own monarchic rule. This is reason enough to search for the republican in the monarchic idea, in the imagery of the new medium of political caricature emerging during this period.

I would like to start with the 'Heraldry of the constitution', to use the words of Edmund Burke, with an overview of emblematic and symbolical representations of the community, which was not oriented towards an individual; depictions that come closest to a representative image of the republic in caricature. In the second part, I will look more closely at the preconditions and the perception of the republic, as they are broached in the caricatures themselves.

The only English republic that was actually set up, which due to its short duration its critics disparagingly called an interregnum, left behind little, if any, visual heritage. One exception is its Great Seal of 1651, which shows the parliament in session: 'In the third Year of Freedom by God's Blessing Restored' (Illustration 1a). Its claim is obvious: to replace the traditional image, on coins, of the monarch, the sovereign ruler, with an image of the egalitarian collective organ representing the people, whilst at the same time laying claim to continuity and patriotism.[1] Here, the republic is justifying its claim to the legal principle whereby the ruler is equivalent to the community in image and name (princeps rei publicae imaginem et nomen gerit), with the difference that here the citizens themselves are the sovereign (civitas sibi princeps),[2] after the army had declared England to be a free Commonwealth in 1649, 'ruled by the representatives of the people in parliament, without king or upper house'. However, apart from this seal, there is hardly any serious self-image of the English Republic in the 17th century. Incapable of disseminating its new sovereignty in political imagery that would have been capable of displacing the culturally dominant image of the king, it died largely without images.[3] Its tradition is literary; its enemies are generally the ones who draw its image.[4]

Thus in 1683, before the start of the period under consideration, there is a horrifying image of the Restoration period that is parodying the English Republic as a dragon that has devoured the monarchy: *The Common wealth ruleing with a standing Army* (1683), (Illustration 1b). The unknown satirist has now placed the parliament in the belly of the beast, which is swallowing up the Commonwealth's resources, while the people are lying in chains and are being covered in dragon excrements in the form of taxes and duties. This demonic formulation of the periodically recurring royalist trauma warns against returning to republicanism.

However, under such conditions it is clear that pictures of the republic and the republican idea can only be found sporadically, in particular if the specific demands of the caricature genre are taken into account, which to some extent only formulates political matters in a negative way; in such exceptional cases as, for example, James Barry's image of republican mourning, *The Phoenix, or the Resurrection of Freedom* (1776/1790), (Illustration 2), which, along with the death of freedom, also postulates

1 Kevin Sharpe, Image Wars. Promoting Kings and Commonwealths in England, 1603–1660 (New Haven et al., 2010), pp. 437–438.

2 Wolfgang Mager, 'Republik', in: Historisches Wörterbuch der Philosophie, vol. 8 (Basle, 1992), pp. 858–878.

3 On the dominance of the royalist tradition, the image of which seeped into all parts of one's life and immunised people against everything else and which the English Republic in the 17th century had not been able to overcome. Cf. Kevin Sharpe, An Image Doting Rabble. The Failure of Republican Culture in Seventeenth-Century England, in: ibid. and Steven N. Zwicker (eds), Refiguring Revolutions. Aesthetics and Politics from the English Revolution to the Romantic Revolution (Berkeley et al., 1998), pp. 25–56.

4 Sharpe, Image Wars, op. cit., pp. 439 f. Rachel Hammersley, French Revolutionaries and English Republicans: the Cordeliers Club 1790–1794, (Woodbridge, 2005), p. 1.

Illustration 1a: Anonymous, The Great Seal of the Common Wealth of England (London, c. 1750–1800), etching, BM 1880,0911.1240 © Trustees of the British Museum

the end of the republican tradition of 17th-century England and projects hopes for its resurrection onto the Elysian Fields of the New World. This is a singular image of avowal in two respects, since, firstly, it incorporates the artist's own person (at the top far right of the picture) alongside the great English republicans Algernon Sidney, John Milton, Andrew Marvell and John Locke, who are gathered on the rubble of the ancient republics around the grave of freedom in Europe. Secondly, because Barry reprinted the sheet in 1790, when radical publicists and political activists did not tire, in their fight against clerical intolerance, loyalist reaction and state repres-

Illustration 1b: Anonymous, The Common wealth ruleing with a standing Army (London, 1683), etching and engraving, BM 1127 © Trustees of the British Museum

Illustration 2: James Barry, The Phoenix, or the Resurrection of Freedom (London, 1776), etching and aquatint in brown ink, BM 1848,1221.109 © Trustees of the British Museum

sion, of appealing to the republican classics as witness.[5] The figure in the foreground with the leg irons and the tattered copy of the Habeas Corpus Act peeking out from his coat is an early version of the satirical figure of the Free-Born Englishman, who is later silenced by a padlock in his lips.

Republican ideas, however, put in an unexpected appearance elsewhere. A small, anonymous etching with the title *The Constitution of England* (ca. 1770), (Illustration 3a) – clearly a book illustration, perhaps for a work on constitutional theory in the context of William Blackstone's *Commentaries on the Laws of England* (1765–1769) – formulates the republican idea in the monarchic most clearly. In the geometric figure of the trīpus, the political powers that support the constitution are symbolised by three strong tree trunks, each recognisable by the various crowns at their tops: monarchy, Lords Spiritual and Temporal with two crowns on top of each other and the Commons. These too are represented by a crown, similar to that of the speaker's mace in the lower house. At their intersection, the constituent parts of parliament are held together by the common bond of the *res publica,* as the inscription states, by public matters, which according to Cicero are the res populi, the concerns of the people. The common good not only connects the different powers with diverging interests, but it also binds them to each other. 'And herein indeed consists the true excellence of the English government, that all the parts of it form a mutual check upon each other,' Blackstone states, and very similarly the young George III, who under direction of his mentor, Lord Bute, had written a hymn of praise to the (unwritten) English constitution.[6]

With a 'mixed and compounded constitution' (Blackstone), the post-revolution monarchy showed itself to be a monarchical republic – not an unusual set up for classic constitutional theory. Contemporary republics in existence at the time such as Venice or the Netherlands were certainly compatible with the power systems of their time. In the picture it makes little difference whether in the upper section of the picture it was a sovereign ruler or a collective body that defined the hierarchy. Thus the image of the king graces the title page of Thomas Smith's description of the Commonwealth of England of 1633 just as naturally as the allegory of the republic graces Le Petit's

5 David Bindman, The Shadow of the Guillotine. Britain and the French Revolution (London, 1989), Cat. 6, p. 84.

6 William Blackstone, Commentaries on the Laws of England. In Four Books. Ed. George Sharswood (Philadelphia, 1893), p. 154. 'Thus have we created the noblest constitution the human mind is capable of framing, where the executive power is in the prince, the legislative in the nobility and the representatives of the people, and the judicial in the people and in some cases the nobility, to whom there lies a final appeal from all other courts of judicature, where every man's life, liberty and possessions are secure, where one part of the legislative body checks the other by the privilege of rejecting, both checked by the executive, as that is again by the legislative; all parts moving, and however they may follow the particular interest of their body, yet all uniting at the last for the public good.' George III, quoted from John Brooke, King George III (London, 1972), pp. 56–57.

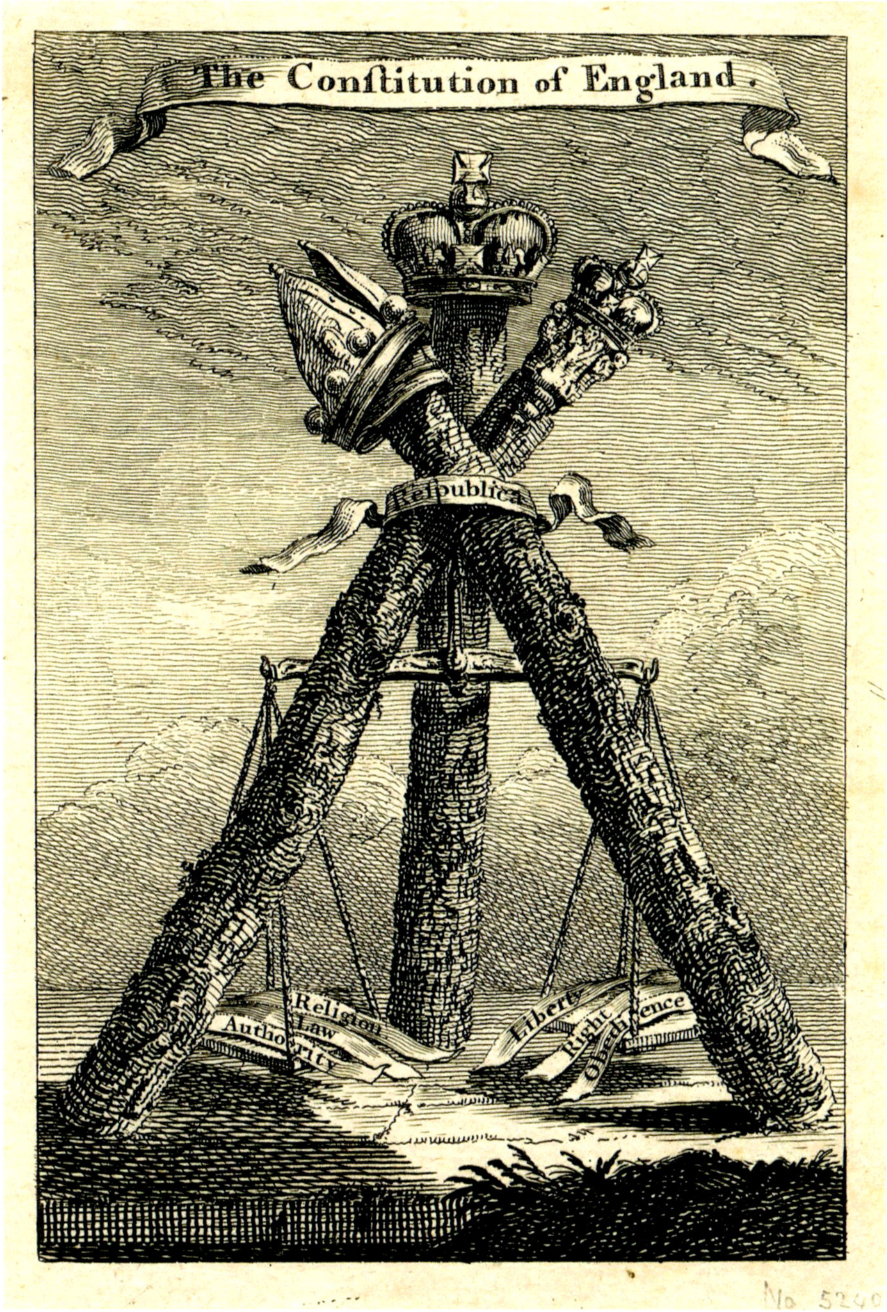

Illustration 3a: Anonymous, *The Constitution of England* (London, 1770?), etching, BM 5240

description of the Low-Country Commonwealth in the English translation of 1609.[7] Even arch-republican Thomas Paine hesitated in his Common Sense of 1776 as to what name he should attribute to the English state system, that of a republic or that of a monarchy, before deciding on the latter and accepting only the Commons as the republican part of the constitution. Rousseau, too, and even Robespierre recognised a crowned republic.[8] 'The Constitution of England is in truth a republic, and has been ever so considered by foreigners, and by the most learned and enlightened Englishmen,' as the later US president John Adams summarised in 1787.[9] In other words, the broad 18th-century concept of republicanism is heavily dependent on a subjective understanding of the state. Or, as Frank Prochaska expresses it: 'Republicanism is in the eye of the beholder.'[10] Later this concept will make it much easier for loyalist caricature to make out the supporters of parliamentary reform to be radical republican.

This triad of constitutional powers, which is actually composed of four, namely alongside the King in Parliament, the three estates of the Lords Spiritual and Temporal and the Commons, also forms a relevant element of counter-revolutionary iconography. It appears in caricature again and again in different manifestations: in the three pillars of the temple of the constitution, in the image of the tree of monarchy with its three roots or in the pyramid-shaped triangle of the constitutional framework. Almost equally important: hanging from this solid tripod, symbolising the system's stability and soundness, there are scales, in the pans of which Religion, Law and Authority on the one hand and Liberty, Right and Obedience are exactly balanced. Together these stand for the classic law of motion in British politics: the Balance of Power, a movement, however, that exhausts itself in seeking compromise and serves to maintain the status quo.

The moralising print after Robert Dighton's *Keep within Compass* (1784–86) appears not only as the triad's structural equivalent, but also as a forceful affirmation on an individual level, which implicitly raises doubt about the claimed stability: 'keep within compass and you shall be sure to avoid many troubles which others endure.'[11] Like the central constitutional components on a large scale, the young

7 William F. Marshall, Title-page to Thomas Smith, *The Commonwealth of England* (1633), BM Hind III.182.235 and F. Le Petit, *The Low Country Commonwealth* (1609), BM 1866,1208.1010.

8 'Die Unsicherheit, ob die Republik ein königsfreundliches oder ein königsfeindliches Wesen sei, entsprach durchaus einer begriffsgeschichtlichen Konstellation, in der Republik einmal jeden übergeordneten Staat, dann aber auch den Oppositionsbegriff zur Monarchie bezeichnen konnte.' cf. Martin Warnke, Die Demokratie zwischen Vorbildern und Zerrbildern, in: Exh. cat., Zeichen der Freiheit. Das Bild der Republik in der Kunst des 16. bis 20. Jahrhunderts (Bern, 1991), p. 86.

9 John Adams, A Defence of the Institutions of Government of the United States of America (1787), in: Works, ed. Charles Francis Adams, vol. 4 (Boston, 1851), pp. 284–5. quoted from Wolfgang Mager, 'Republik', in: Geschichtliche Grundbegriffe. Historisches Lexikon zur politisch-sozialen Sprache in Deutschland, vol. 5 (Stuttgart, 1984), p. 592.

10 Frank Prochaska, The Republic of Britain, 1760–2000 (London, 2001), p. xv.

11 Robert Dighton, Keep within Compass and you shall be sure, to avoid many troubles which others endure (1784–86), BM 6903.

gentleman (and the gentlewoman in a companion piece) is, on a small scale, being admonished to stay within the compass or his sphere and to take the checks and balances to heart in order to avoid evil and produce prosperity. The community just as the individual will rush headlong into disaster, should they try to promote their own part at the expense of the whole and to disregard the corporative rules, as the side scenes illustrate, which show morally reprehensible behaviour and the resulting disasters of shipwreck and prison.

It is precisely this act of leaving one's sphere and interfering egoistically in the mechanism of government, leading to breach of the constitution, that Lord Bute, the Scottish mentor of George III and prime minister for a brief period, is being accused of in the anonymous caricature, *The Constitution* (1770), (Illustration 3b). Bute makes use of the monarch's 'invisible hand' to his own advantage and to eliminate the republican elements (Bill of Rights, Magna Charta, Freedom of Election, Liberty of the Press). He thereby causes the building of the republic (in the right background) to collapse, as did Charles I's favourite, Lord Strafford, who was executed in 1641, to whom the subtitle refers. For his selfish interference in the sensitive mechanism of government, Bute used his secret influence on King George III. Long after withdrawing from office, Bute was still being pursued by criticism in the shape of the symbol of the Scottish thistle. His misuse of power with the help of the royal little finger appears to scoff at William Blackstone's definition of the "true line of liberty and happiness of the community,' which he said resulted from the diverging individual powers.[12] (Paine sees in monarchy the master fraud, which covers up all others; arbitrary rule in the interests of the individual, not of the res publica.)[13] But it is not the mechanism of government, the principle of the tria junta in una, as it appears in nimbus-like form on three legs, that is fundamentally being questioned here, only its misuse.

However, the constitutional reality of such a monarchic republic was also contested in principle. The anonymous etching, *An Emblematical Pile* (1774) (Illustration 3c), sees in it just an old pile of wood, grown rotten under Scottish influence and eaten away by political worms, its survival a mere question of the passing of time: the ragged flag of liberty is now only being upheld with much effort by the rights of liberty wrested from the monarchy, such as the Magna Charta, Common Hall and the Bill of Rights, and by patriotism and the whole is being held together by ropes. Religion has already broken off and the right to elections is lying on the ground, destroyed by the axe of corruption. As a warning, the scales of divine justice, citing the Bible, shine down from the clouds onto the destroyed earthly justice. 'Monarchy hath pois-

---

12 'Like three distinct powers in mechanics, they jointly impel the machine of government in a direction different from what either, acting by itself, would have done; but at the same time in a direction partaking of each, and formed out of all; a direction which constitutes the true line of liberty and happiness of the community.' See William Blackstone, Commentaries on the Laws of England, In Four Books, ed. George Sharswood, Vol. 1 (Philadelphia, 1893), p. 154.

13 Thomas Paine, Rights of Man, 1791–92, ed. with an introduction by Henry Collins (Harmondsworth 1971), pp. 226 and 200.

Illustration 3b: Anonymous, *The Constitution,* (London, 1770), etching and engraving, BM 4430

Illustration 3c: Anonymous, *An Emblematical Pile* (London, 7th November 1774), etching, BM 5239 © Trustees of the British Museum

ened the republic, the crown hath engrossed the commons', were the words written by Thomas Paine two years later.[14]

The precarious constitutional construction saw itself submitted to further stress tests. In 1784, in *The Unfortunate Ass* (1784),[15] the ass of the English people is standing obstinately between two signposts: while the king is tugging it in the direction of absolute monarchy using his sword of prerogative rights, Charles James Fox, leader of the Whig opposition, is pulling it in the opposite direction, towards republicanism. An impasse, which leaves the people, burdened by heavy taxes, refusing to move – as in a mixture of *Hercules at the Cross-roads* and *Buridan's Ass* – having already left the path of aristocracy, as a third signpost in the background indicates.

The triad-like constellation of powers, described both in Blackstone's *Commentaries* and Thomas Paine's *Common Sense,* proved itself, historically, to be flexible enough to even withstand the momentous effect of the French Revolution. But under the influence of the American and above all of the French Revolution, the positive image of the monarchic republic very quickly changed to a terrifying image of the republic, as did the term 'revolution', which before 1789 had almost exclusively positive connotations and, as *The Revolution,* had referred to the peaceful revolution of 1688.[16] This change is illustrated by *The Grand British Balloon* (1784), (Illustration 4b), which appeared in two versions, fourteen years apart. The first version shows the techno-fantasy project of an armed airship, which was created following the balloon euphoria triggered off by the Montgolfier brothers in 1783 and only three months after Lunardi's first balloon ascent in London. A large balloon is carrying a war ship, hanging from shrouds and ropes, with open gun ports, and flying through the air by means of 'inflammable air'. The different parts are introduced using the encyclopaedic technical illustration's vocabulary with its detailed, descriptive legend (in the British Museum's copy the legend has been cut off, but can be partially reconstructed using the later version): there is A Tent for the Inspector of the Cordage, Tents for the Aerial Navigators and Pumpers, a Gallery for mounting Guard, Aerial Officers on the look out, The General's House, Apartments for Officers, The Lodge of the Helm-Keeper, The Hospital, a huge telescope etc., not forgetting the 'small wings for Ornament'. Three factors make of this technical utopia, as it is often understood, a political one: 1. The attribute of the British Lion holding an admiral's flag on the balloon's crest and the attribute of the king's crown with the initials GR for Georgius Rex and the dedication *Pro Bono Publico* (for the Common Good or Commonwealth) on the balloon's surface. The number *2440* above the crown is an allusion to Louis-Sébastien Mercier's utopian novel of the same name, which was published in Amsterdam in 1770 and criticised contemporary

14 'Why is the constitution of England sickly but because monarchy hath poisoned the republic, the crown hath engrossed the commons?' See Thomas Paine, Common Sense, 1776, ed. Jim Manis (Hazleton, PA, 1998), p. 25.

15 William Humphrey (publ.), *The unfortunate ass* (1784), BM 6446.

16 The peaceful nature is disputed by some modern historians such as Steven Pincus, 1688. The First Modern Revolution (New Haven and London, 2009).

Illustration 4a: Anonymous, Frontispiece to Thomas More, Libellus vere aureus nec minus salutaris quam festiuus de optimo reip. statu, de noua Insula Vtopia … cura M. Petri Aegidii Antuerpiēsis … nunc primum accuratissime editus (Leuven, 1516), woodcut

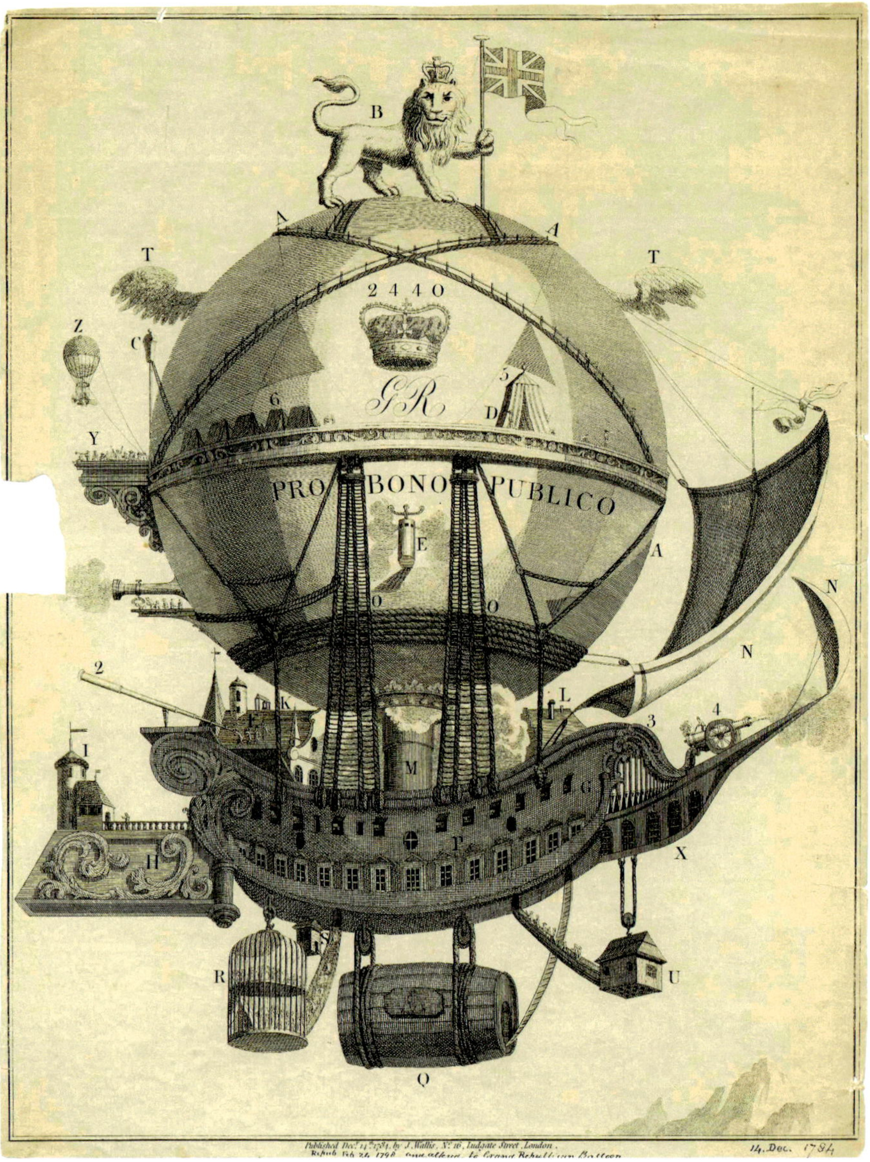

Illustration 4b: John Wallis, *The grand British balloon* (London, 14th December 1784), BM 6710 © Trustees of the British Museum

Illustration 4c: John Wallis, *The Grand Republican Balloon* (London, 24th February 1798), etching, hand-coloured, BM 9176 © Trustees of the British Museum

Parisian society by using a projection into the future.[17] With its clear formal references to the frontispiece of the first edition of Thomas More's *Utopia,* Leuven 1516, the print reverts to the past, positioning itself in the tradition of English utopian societal models (1516) (Illustration 4a).

So seen as a whole, we have before us an allegory of the state ship, thus extending an old tradition that reaches back to Plato's *Politeia* (which is generally translated as 'Republic' in English) into the future. The ship's symbolism, which signals functionality and effectiveness, lets the airship appear as an embodiment of the republic with a king, as a thoroughly militarised society on a journey to nowhere with coffee houses, an attached brothel and water closet, which presents itself ironically 'as the rule of laws for the good of the people – pro bono publico'.[18] In the later, minimally altered version of *The Grand Republican Balloon* (1798) (Illustration 4c), this mild parody of the monarchic republic is transformed into a lampooning image of the republic and the export of revolution. Here, too, the political iconography is more interesting than the perspective of military technology: the state ship has mutated into an aggressive, goal-directed military machine, which, under the Gallic cockerel, is setting off for the invasion and enslavement of England. The satirical, utopian dimension of the monarchical republic's airship, which has its real foundations in the early, dangerous attempts at flying, conducted under the threat of explosion and crashes, has become, by intensifying the connection with the present, a definite dystopia. A largely unaltered state ship becomes a hostile threat, by adding the guillotine as the pivotal point (the machine which had killed the king and has replaced his symbol) and by alienating the 'false' republic, which now only champions the promise of liberty as a mock show and propaganda.[19] The universal human rights appear as a threat to the hierarchical order of society in England. The pilloried republican ideas threaten to bring the ruinous storm of revolution to 'Old England' as well and rouse loyalist caricature to produce an intensified, legitimising response. In the second part of my essay I will now address the new interest, thus becoming evident, in the tactical dimensions of political perception.

The French Revolution of 1789 was initially received in England along the lines of the Glorious Revolution and of the constitutional monarchy that this had established. It

17 Louis-Sébastien Mercier, L'an deux mille quatre cent quarante, rève s'il en sût jamait [sic]. (London, 1771).

18 Mark Philp, Republicanism, in: Iain McCalman et al. (eds), The Romantic Age. An Oxford Companion to British Culture 1776–1832 (Oxford 2001), p. 673; Eckhart Schäfer, Das Staatsschiff. Zur Präzision eines Topos, in: Peter Jehn (ed.), Toposforschung. Eine Dokumentation (Frankfurt a. M., 1972), pp. 259–292.

19 Viewed closely, the difference in subject matter is not between a royal and a republican variant, as the BM catalogue claims, it is between the British concept of the Republic and the French concept. The British balloon is also a *Grand Republican Balloon.* Burke preferred the firm ground of the British constitution to the *desperate flights* of the *aëronauts of France.* Cf. Edmund Burke, Reflections on the Revolution in France and on the Proceedings in Certain Societies in London Relative to that Event, 1790, ed. Conor Cruise O'Brien (Harmondsworth, 1973), p. 376.

was expressly welcomed by Gillray, amongst others, or even put forward as an example for Britain that stood in stark contrast to William Pitt's repressive regime.[20] However, it lost its position in the familiar political system of coordinates and its importance as a central point of reference in political life, as soon as it became clear that the revolutionary process in France had not stopped in its constitutional phase.[21] The image of the Republic 'explodes' right at the moment when ideas of the sovereignty of the people unite with those of the Republic. Instead, personified nightmare visions of the Republic now dominate: I. Cruikshank's reminiscences of the Parisian fishwomen, his terrifying woman with fish between her sagging breasts, dagger, snake-head and a corona of violent crimes on barrels of Dutch alcohol; Gillray's smoke monster, likewise with legs apart, with a guillotine at his neck; or George Cruikshank's monster of *Universal Suffrage* from a later period, which envisages the scum coming to power on the inverted social pyramid (1819), may suffice as examples.[22]

In 1790, with his *Reflections on the Revolution in France* (his 'Manifesto of a Counter Revolution' as James Mackintosh expressed it in 1791)[23] Edmund Burke had triggered off the revolution alarm and the revolution debate of the 1790s. He not only provoked political counter-statements, such as Thomas Paine's *Rights of Man,* but also a series of caricatures, which attacked the new, hostile Republic, but at the same time making political perception and its manipulation the subject of discussion. Whilst the republican and radical side can hardly muster up any visual and argumentative resistance,[24] loyalist caricaturists follow Burke's programme of dramatisation. The author of the *Philosophical Enquiry into the Origin of our Ideas of the Sublime and Beautiful* (1757), an experienced politician and conscious propagandist, describes the Revolution in categories of the lowly hybrid of the Grotesque. He carefully avoids all forms that could lead to an ennobling of the opposing side by using modes of the sublime or the beautiful.[25] By defining the Revolution as a Grand Spectacle and a monstrous,

20 James Gillray, 1789, BM 7548, esp. BM 7546.

21 On the English reception of the French Revolution cf. Ronald Paulson, Representations of Revolution, 1789–1820 (New Haven and London, 1983), esp. Ch. 2, The View from England: Stereotypes; John Brewer: This monstrous tragi-comic scene, British reactions to the French Revolution, in: David Bindman (ed.), Exh.cat., The Shadow of the Guillotine. Britain and the French Revolution (London, 1989), pp. 11–25.

22 Isaac Cruikshank, A peace offering to the genius of liberty and equality (1794), BM 8426; James Gillray, The genius of France triumphant, -or- Britannia petitioning for peace. –Vide, The Proposals of Opposition (1795), BM 8614; George Cruikshank, Universal suffrage, or- The scum uppermost-!!!!! (1819), BM 13248.

23 'It is the manifesto of a Counter Revolution and its obvious object is to inflame every passion and interest.' James Mackintosh, Vindiciae Gallicae (London, 1791/Indianapolis, 2006), p. 9.

24 Diana Donald, The Age of Caricature. Satirical Prints in the Reign of George III (New Haven and London, 1996), p. 168.

25 Joseph Crawford, Raising Milton's Ghost. John Milton and the Sublime of Terror in the Early Romantic Period (London, 2011), pp. 60–61.

tragi-comic scene he more or less outlines the storyboard for English caricature of the French Republic.[26]

It is therefore no coincidence that caricaturists belong to the main beneficiaries of the aggravated ideological confrontation and the concentration on questions of political perception. In the conflict over notions, language and political imagination,[27] caricature constitutes an essential component of the conservative counter-offensive against the flood of republican writings and activities due to its specific means of visualising the concept of the enemy. Arguing ad oculos, the dimension of the visual, and the staging of political opinions play a special role here: in analogy and based on the model of Burke‘s dramaturgy – refracted time and again by the double lenses of British history and politics, the English Revolutions of 1688 and 1649, to use John Brewer's expression.[28]

The clash of republican and loyalist views forms the point of departure, if a change of opinion is to be brought about through visual argumentation. The existence of opposing political views leads to a type of 'optical metadiscourse' on the republican image. On the basis of the contrast formula (John Barrell), caricaturists develop an iconography of political perception and illusion, of deception and unmasking, which reflects the medialisation of politics in the 18th century also in a self-referential manner. The whole spectrum of the visual – from the naked eye to the armed eye, from spectacles, through binoculars to techniques of illusion – as well as artists and caricaturists as those who make things visible, and naturally theatre of every description are drawn upon to belittle the republic and the republicans.

As the revolution progressed, the battle for state symbols, conducted between monarchist and republican iconography, is portrayed as a full-blown, potentially violent, cold civil war of images across national boundaries, preceding the 'hot' war, as in James Sayers's *Loyalty against Levelling* (1792) (Illustration 5a). The civil Association for Preserving Liberty and Property against Republicans and Levellers, founded in 1792 to support the government, opposes the iconoclastic onslaught of French and local sans-culottes such as Thomas Paine and seeks to organise the closing of ranks among the patriots in alliance with sailors and soldiers. Sayers's chiastic visual formula, which interlocks the interaction of both sides, falls back on a royalist propaganda print from the time of the English Civil War. William Marshall's title page to Francis Quarles's *The Shepherd's Oracles* (London, 1646) is cited as the supposedly comparable plight of a monarchy battling against infiltration and hostile ideology (Illustration 5b).

The contrasting perception of the political situation is staged by William Dent's *A View of modern France, or the end of a country without a constitution* (1793) (Illustra-

26 Brewer, op. cit., p. 16.

27 John Barrell, Imagining the King's Death. Figurative Treason, Fantasies of Regicide 1793–1796 (Oxford, 2000), pp. 1–46.

28 Brewer, op. cit., p. 17.

tion 6), as a model – a cross between an oversized open-air theatre, peep-show scenery and a hall of mirrors. He confronts a distorting mirror with a mirror, progressing in the direction of reading from the wrong to the right view. To the very left, Citizen Reynard, alias Charles James Fox, is on a platform, looking through a peephole in the False Mirror; on the right, John Bull, the Plain and Honest, is looking through a similar hole in the True Mirror at the Jacobin Republic with the tree of liberty and its fruits of turmoil and rebellion – didactically secured through the clear classification of secondary figures: to the left, the devil has Fox in his power, to the right, Britannia is supporting Bull as a representative of the simple people in drawing the right conclusions from what he is seeing.

Sayers proceeds in a similarly didactic way in an early representation of Burke's *Reflections: Mr Burke's pair of spectacles for short sighted politicians* (1791) (Illustration 7a). As its title claims, the image, half a ghostly necromancy, half an emblematic allegory of the constitution, wants to offer a political, optical remedy for short-sighted politicians with the help of spectacles held into the picture by a hand at the left edge of the picture. Sayers thus presents four different ways of viewing things: 1. Edmund Burke's view represented by the spectacles, as he had formulated it half a year earlier. 2. The views of the 'Republicans' surrounding Fox and Sheridan, codified in a demonic counter-image of the Republic. 3. The observer's view; he is, of course, first and foremost invited to put on Burke's spectacles. 4. The aloof view of the cartoonist, who knows all three ways of looking at things, who knows how to reduce it to one common denominator and who literally 'manipulates' with his seeing-aid in the hand. Here, too, Sayers calls on the help of the royalist pictorial tradition in the battle against the republicans: *The Royal Oake of Brittayne,* the frontispiece to Clement Walker's *Anarchie Anglicana* (1649) (Illustration 7b). Later engravings concentrate solely on the spectacles or spectacle-like constellations of round images and contrast the politically controversial views apodictically. Take for example probably the most widespread image of political agitation of the whole anti-radical campaign, *The Contrast* (1792),[29] drawn for the Association by Lord George Murray and engraved by Rowlandson; or Richard Newton's *Spectacles for Republicans* (1795) (Illustration 8): in both cases the alternative – cosy British freedom and prosperity here, French bondage and murderous despotic rule there – is intended to make the observer's decision in favour of the monarchist British side inescapable.

Sayers selects another tactic in 1794 with his series of eight satirical portraits under the title of *Illustrious Heads designed for a new History of Republicanism in French and English dedicated to the Opposition* (1794) (Illustration 9). The portraits of leading English Whig politicians are each given the name of a French revolutionary. Charles James Fox becomes Robespierre, the Duke of Grafton becomes Louis Philippe, Duc

29 Thomas Rowlandson, The Contrast (1792), BM 8149; Bindman op. cit., Cat. 71; John Barrell, The Spirit of Despotism. Invasions of Privacy in the 1790s (Oxford, 2006), pp. 235 ff.; Donald, op. cit., pp. 152–153.

Illustration 5a: James Sayers, *Loyalty against Levelling* (London, 15th December 1792), etching, BM 8138 © Trustees of the British Museum

Illustration 5b: William Marshall, *The Tree of Religion protected by Charles I* (1645). Title-page to Francis Quarles, The Shepherds Oracles (London, 1646), etching and engraving, BM 426
© Trustees of the British Museum

Illustration 6: William Dent, *View of modern France, or the end of a country without a constitution* (London, 1793), etching, hand-coloured, BM 1988,1001.3 © Trustees of the British Museum

Illustration 7b: Anonymous, *The Royal Oake of Brittayne,* frontispiece to Clement Walker, Anarchie Anglicana, or, The History of Independency, the Second Part (London, 1649), etching and engraving, BM 737 © Trustees of the British Museum

Illustration 7a: James Sayers, *Mr Burke's pair of spectacles for short sighted politicians* (London, 1791), etching, aquatint, BM 7858 © Trustees of the British Museum

Illustration 8: Richard Newton, *Spectacles for Republicans* (London, 24th November 1795), etching, hand-coloured, BM 8695 © Trustees of the British Museum

d'Orléans, Sheridan appears as Barère, the Earl of Stanhope as Anacharsis Cloots, etc. One component of the series is a red Phrygian cap printed on paper, which can be put on the portraits, as the satyr on the front page announces: *'If the Cap fit put it on.'* An ironic game, which had been stimulated by official-looking French engravings of the French king, which had been furnished with a cap of liberty retrospectively as a *'gift of the French people dated 20th June 1792'*, as stated in the title.[30] A *nota bene* remarks: 'The work will not be compleat/till all the heads are taken off.' Sayers formulates an ideological riposte, which wishes to pay back potential British Jacobins for the monarch's humiliation by anathematising the members of the English Whig opposition: the loyalist satire casts them out of the community of patriots as 'republicans' and expatriates them symbolically to the French Republic. It is stated bluntly in Richard Newton's *Spectacles:* 'The land *we* live in and may those that don't like it leave it' [my emphasis]. In this negative way something rather like a pictorial record of the English reform movement and of republicanism emerges in loyalist caricature, in a distorted manner and dressed up in French clothes.

By revealing at the same time the caricaturist dispositif in a comparatively naïve manner – like representing different political views all at once, deconstruction,

30 On 20th June the people had invaded the Tuileries and forced the red cap on Louis XVI.

demasking, exaggeration, understatement and the self-referential exploration of how political life is staged – the question does present itself of whether there is possibly an alternative way of reading anti-republican caricatures. Gillray's frequently noted ambivalence, which cannot be tied down to one way of reading, might serve as an example:[31] In *A connoisseur examining a Cooper* (1792), Gillray has the art connoisseur, Georg III, examine a miniature portrait of Oliver Cromwell done by Samuel Cooper (1609–1672).[32] The king's authoritative appearance as well as the relative sizes leaves no room for doubt that George has got a 'good grip' on everything. But there is something disturbing about the shining candle stump, mounted in the solid candlestick's economising fixture. On the one hand it can be read as an aspect of the king's thrifty, economical character. However, on the other hand, the fact that the candle will soon go out points to a possible end of his rule (radical taunts about *'George the Last'* were to go the rounds later).[33] The monarch is indeed acutely conscious of the danger of republicanism, which also wishes to put an end to the de-charismatised Hanoverian monarchy, yet the miniature portrait also appears like a mirror. The king can see himself in it as Cromwell with an open mouth, just like Ch. J. Fox previously in James Sayers's *The Mirror of Patriotism* (1784, BM 6380). Gillray seems to be insinuating something like a self-portrait in the enemy's image: parallels to Cromwell's repressive power politics can be discovered in the king – for example only a few weeks previously, in May 1792, the king had issued the proclamation against 'wicked and seditious writings,' including Tom Paine's *The Rights of Man.*

Gillray brings it all to a head, literally, in 1797 with his proposal to execute the leading republicans immediately in order to save the country: *The Tree of Liberty must be planted immediately!* (1797, BM 8986). Here one sees Fox's head dripping with blood on a pike under a red Phrygian cap as a tree of liberty in the middle of the cut-off, bloody heads of Thelwall, Lord Derby, Erskine, Sheridan and Horne Tooke. All this on the crest of a grassy hill with an executioners' hatchet and a paper entitled *Lectures on the Fall of the Republic by J. Thelwall.* With his portrayal of extreme violence, Gillray seems to be following Burke's tactic of *'being mobbish',* by using a highly emotive language, as the politician had urged in the trial against Warren Hastings in 1791.[34] Its aim is to increase the psychological pressure on the opponent and to incapacitate him[35] and to bring about something that one could call monarchist catharsis, cleansing oneself of, or liberating oneself from, republican, democratic passions. This tactic

31 Paulson, op. cit., pp. 183–214.

32 James Gillray, A Connoisseur examining a Cooper (1792), BM 107.

33 Hubertus Fischer, Wer löscht das Licht? Europäische Karikatur und Alltagswelt 1790–1990. (Stuttgart, 1994), p. 112; Barrell, op cit., p. 124.

34 Yet even in the *Reflections* this tactic is already outlined, when Burke remarks that our natural feelings, our passions teach reason and when kings are thrown off the throne, we would be shocked into thought. – cf. Burke, op. cit., p. 175.

35 Conor Cruise O'Brien, 'The Manifesto of a Counter-Revolution'. Introduction to Burke, op. cit., pp. 11–81.

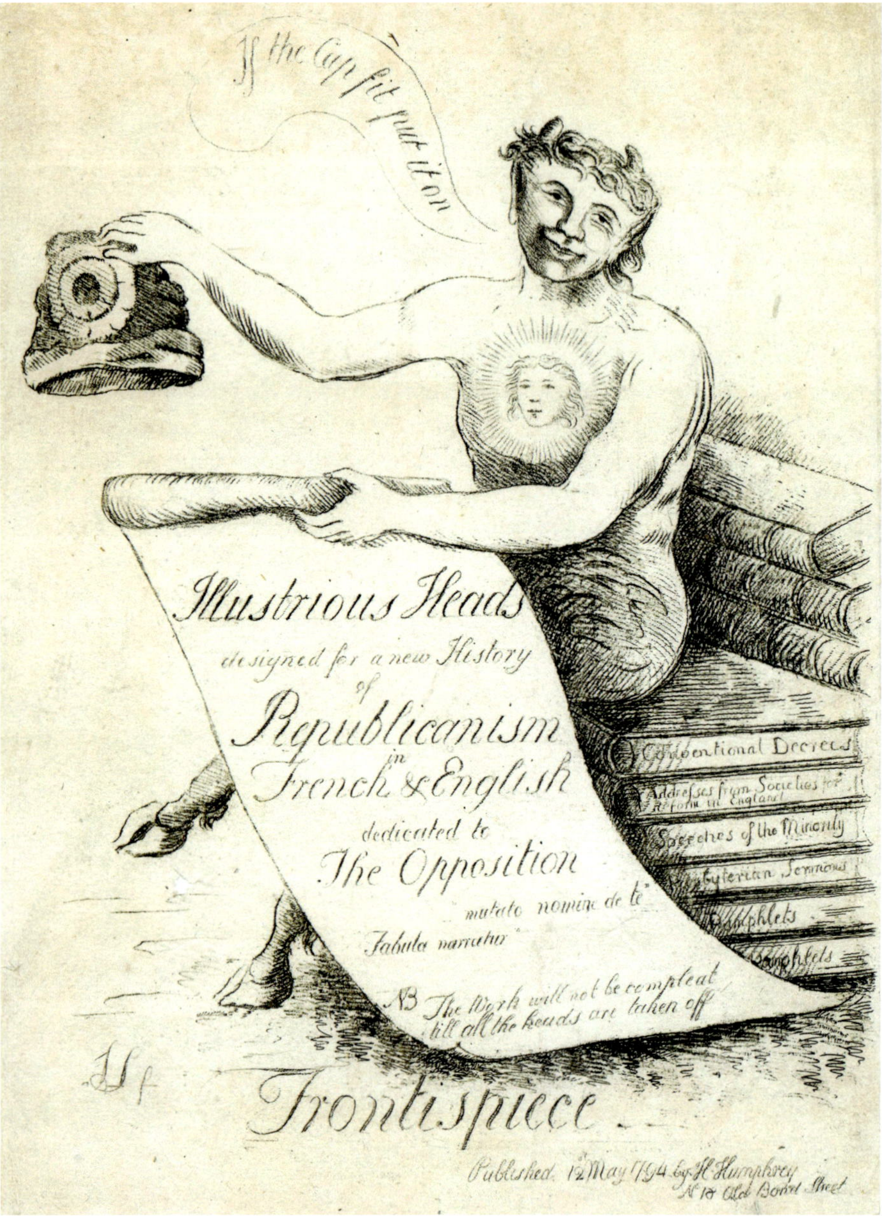

Illustration 9a: James Sayers, Illustrious Heads designed for a new History of Republicanism in French and English dedicated to the Opposition/Frontispiece (London, 1794), etching, BM 8449 © Trustees of the British Museum

Illustration 9b: Anonymous: Louis Seize Roi des Français | Né la Versailles le 23 Août 1756. Marié le 16 May 1770. et sacré à Reims le 11 Juin 1775. | Bonnet de la Liberté, Présenté au Roi par le peuple Français, le 20 Juin 1792, engraving, hand-coloured (Paris, 1791), BnF, Inv.Nr. Qb 1 1791 – M 101 224
Illustration 9c: James Sayers, Illustrious Heads … Charles James Fox as Robespierre, BM 8450 © Trustees of the British Museum
Illustration 9d: James Sayers, Illustrious Heads … George Henry Fitzroy, 4th Duke of Grafton as Louis Philippe, duc d'Orléans, BM 8457 © Trustees of the British Museum

has a great affinity to caricature and satire, in particular to the characteristic use of hyperbole specific to the genre, thus also making caricature particularly suitable for constructing an image of the enemy.[36] With its will to exaggerate, the tactic of verbal or visual violence is confronted with the problem of the appropriate dosage and tends to run the risk of aesthetic 'overkill'. In analogy to the legally defined offence of excessive force, it can be understood as an excessive use of visual force. It goes further than necessary to reach its goal (as distinct from the question of the moral or political boundaries of caricature and satire).[37] But along with obtaining this goal, it implies the possibility of a collateral damage, i. e. of an alternative reception. The excessive caricaturing of the original facts itself becomes the occasion for political and aesthetic reflection and under certain circumstances becomes decipherable as a criticism of criticism and is connected with concrete political processes.[38] Used intentionally, loyal subversion or an undermining loyal to the government, so-to-speak, in the crown's indirect service, as one can understand a large part of Georgian caricature before the emergence of the mass press, turns, on the quiet, into its opposite, into subversive loyalty.[39] Contrasting images can become reversible figures, ones that can also be read against the grain, these being the collateral damage of satirical overkill. Gillray's proposal of massacring the republicans would accordingly be the opposite of what it claims to be, an ironic disapproval of the hunt for radicals (which he then retracts again in his *Democratic Transparency,* 1799, BM 9369).

For caricaturists this gives rise to the possibility of keeping a back door open for phrasing something that I would like to call the satirical self-retention, a recognisable divergence from the image's official task. Even minimal deviations from the propaganda task, for example by inserting small disruptive motives such as Newton's small grinning imp or his slightly lascivious housewife can, up to a point, reverse the *Spectacles for Republicans* (Illustration 8) and make of them a true Spectacle for *Republicans,* which can be enjoyed with 'secret pleasure' in times of repression – admittedly these are minimal signals of political and social deviance, yet important for a minority's self-confidence. Similarly, the caricaturist's ability to adapt to the imagery of the minor art forms, the 'stepsister arts', ostracised from the high arts, is also a smart move in an 18th-century sense.[40] For example, when the little respected caricaturist

36 Elke Anna Werner, 'Feindbild', in: Uwe Fleckner et. al. (eds), Handbuch der politischen Ikonographie, vol. 1 (Munich, 2011), pp. 301–305.

37 The question whether satire and caricature go too far because they violate social norms is a different one from the question of whether caricature and satire obtain their goals and whether, by using their means excessively, they might not produce unintended or even counter-productive effects.

38 Barrell, op. cit., p. 629.

39 Robert Poole, The March to Peterloo. Politics and Festivity In Late Georgian England, in: *Past and Present* 192 (2006), pp. 143 and 152.

40 Karl Janke, 'Stepsister Arts'. Zum streitbaren Verhältnis von Karikatur und Malerei in London Ende des 18. Jahrhunderts, in: Peinture et caricature. Actes du colloque de Brest, 13–15 mai 2004, (Brest, 2004), pp. 27–42.

Illustration 10a: Richard Newton, Self-portrait with a caricature of Mr. Follet as the Clown (1797/1798), ink, pen, pencil and water-colour, © Hanover, Wilhelm Busch – Deutsches Museum für Karikatur und Zeichenkunst

compares himself with the harlequin or court jester, as Richard Newton does in his *Self-portrait with the caricature of Mr. Follet as a Clown* (1797) (Illustration 10a and b); with a figure who, under the cover of apparent social and semantic harmlessness, was granted traditional liberties, which were useful even under the conditions of relative freedom of the press.[41] The harlequin is the caricaturist's *alter ego.* In him, Newton

41 Harlequin's cheeky, anti-authoritarian attitude perhaps received an impulse from a radical leaflet, *Harlequin Impeacher or John Bull will have his own* with its figures of Harlequin-accuser and Citizen Stand-Up, that appeared in 1795. Under the pretext of making a theatre announcement and

Illustration 10b: Richard Newton, *Mr. Follet as the Clown in the Pantomime of 'Harlequin and Oberon'* (3rd April 1797), etching, hand-coloured, BM 9003, © Hanover, Wilhelm Busch – Deutsches Museum für Karikatur und Zeichenkunst

emancipates himself from the comical without relinquishing the comical. He overcomes Lairesse's formula of the clownesque for representing the common people[42] and frees himself from the humble genre of caricature by making this the permit of the sovereign individual, who knows himself to be not only at eye level with his sovereign, but with his image also has him at his command.

There is a remarkably similar self-portrait of James Gillray, of uncertain date and obviously created just a short time later, which suggests a connection to Newton's self-portrait: *James Gillray. The Caricaturist* (ca. 1800, BM 9569). Both Newton and Gillray define themselves by way of an image of themselves and of the attribute of their own work, caricatures. Understood as the political public displayed objectively, these drawings reveal the caricaturist himself to be 'the ensemble of the social relations', 'the subjective existence of imagined and experienced society […]'. So both of them in fact demonstrate republican self-confidence: they show themselves as an individual community[43] and visibly dispute the royal monopoly on representing society. The modern journalistic media

with the subtitle *Pro bono publico* it announces the performance, soon to be made, of a large ballet pantomime in the huge theatre of the world, i. e. a revolutionary action, that will lead to fraternity, love and peace and at the close ironically cheers the king and queen. John Barrell, Exhibition Extraordinary!! Radical Broadsides of the mid 1790s. (Nottingham, 2001), pp. 61–63.

42 Gérard de Lairesse, The art of painting, in all its branches, Methodically demonstrated by Discourses and Plates, … (London, 1778), p. 33; John Brewer, The Common People and Politics 1750–1790s (Cambridge, 1986), p. 21.

43 Karl Marx, 6. Feuerbachthese (1845), MEW 3, p. 534 and the same: 1844, EB 1, pp. 539 and 538.

are thus harlequin's heirs:[44] In 1821, George Cruikshank's *My Eye* (BM 14168) combines the individual organ of (artistic) perception with the universal machine of the Enlightenment, the printing press, which banishes the powers of darkness.[45] With this new technical means of mass production, he lets caricature act as the *Universal safety lamp* (1821, BM 14224) and the guarantor of freedom in the face of monarchic 'black lights' (bottom centre: George IV's pear-shaped head). So in this new sense, too, republicanism is also in the eye of the beholder.

Finally, a comforting postscript – maybe not just for continental minds – which may prove how lively the tradition of British caricature is, just as is British republicanism. When furious demonstrators bombarded the royal limousine with projectiles on its journey through London a good three years ago, in December 2010, the Guardian's caricaturist, Martin Rowson, commented on the *Royal Car Attack* with a paraphrase of Gillray's *The Republican Attack* (1795, BM 8681) from a similar occurrence, the militancy of which the caricaturist had visibly enjoyed two hundred and seventeen years earlier. Zooming in on the passengers, Rowson puts words into the shocked Prince Charles's mouth: 'For God's Sake, Driver! Get us back to Versailles'[46] – or, if I may say so, punk's not dead!

---

44 Dirk Schümer, Hofnarren. Illustrationen von Martial Leiter, in: Vontobel-Stiftung (ed.), Schriftenreihe 2060 (Zurich, 2012).

45 This does not prevent him in turn being caricatured by his brother, who accuses him and the radical press of having special interests in the shape of a likeness of Queen Caroline (BM 1977,U.312).

46 Martin Rowson, On the Royal Car Attack, in: The Guardian (11th December 2010).

Temitope Odumosu

In Bad Taste? Slavery and the African Presence in the Subversive Mockery of Royalty[1]

Nichts beunruhigte das Gewissen der Öffentlichkeit am Ende des achtzehnten Jahrhunderts in England stärker als das Thema der Sklaverei. Gegen Ende der 1780er Jahre und im darauffolgenden Jahrzehnt leiteten Mitglieder der Anti-Sklaverei-Kampagne aus den Reihen der Quäker und Evangelikalen eine populärpolitische Offensive ein, indem sie den Briten die Gewalt des Handelssystems und ihre moralischen Folgen für die Nation vor Augen führten. Die Propaganda war effektiv, wirkte jedoch polarisierend, denn sie zwang die Menschen, sich angesichts der unleugbaren Unmenschlichkeit für eine Position des ‚für' oder ‚wider' zu entscheiden. Die satirischen Künstler bezogen selten Stellung zu moralischen Fragen. Sie untergruben jedoch die Ideen und Ikonographie der Anti-Sklaverei-Bewegung, indem sie darauf hinwiesen, wie diese neue Philanthropie ausgenutzt werden konnte, und indem sie zur Veranschaulichung der negativen Auswirkungen des florierenden Handels gesellschaftlich abgedrängte Afrikaner in ihren Arbeiten erscheinen ließen. Der folgende Beitrag untersucht eine kleine Auswahl von Drucken, die in einzigartiger Weise zeigen, wie das Thema der Sklaverei und die Darstellung afrikanischer Figuren benutzt wurden, das königliche Privileg während der jahrelangen Kampagne zur Abschaffung der Sklaverei anzugreifen. Es wird auch besprochen, warum das Verhältnis zwischen den königlichen Untertanen und den schwarzen Koloniebewohnern mit ihren tabuisierten Leibern – in öffentlich verbreiteten Druckgraphiken erdacht und dargestellt – möglicherweise den ultimativen Akt loyaler Subversion darstellte.

On the 27th March 1792, at the height of public campaigns to abolish the slave trade, James Gillray produced a memorable print showing the royal family boycotting sugar. In *Anti-Saccharrites, or John Bull and his Family leaving off the use of Sugar,* (Illustration 1) King George III, Queen Charlotte and their six daughters are seated around a

1 I would like to extend my sincere thanks and gratitude to the Volkswagen Foundation, the Wilhelm Busch Museum of Caricature, and the organisers of the Herrenhausen symposium for inviting me to participate in the discussion that informed this essay. In particular many thanks to Anorthe Kremers, Karl Janke and Elisabeth Reich for their kindness and generosity. I would also like to acknowledge the unending support of my family, friends and esteemed colleagues whilst conducting this research for my doctoral thesis on African characters in Georgian caricature. Further thanks go to my research supervisor, Professor Jean Michel Massing, and additionally to Elizabeth McGrath, Sheila O'Connell, Brian Maidment and Vic Gatrell.

Illustration 1: James Gillray, *Anti-saccharites, or John Bull and his family leaving off the use of sugar,* hand-coloured etching. Published in London by H. Humphrey, 27 March 1792 © Trustees of the British Museum

small table to share plain bitter tea. The king is sipping from his cup saying the tea is 'delicious', whilst the sour-faced princesses are reluctant to drink their tea. Encouraging sacrifice, the queen reminds them all to: 'consider how much Work you'll save the poor Blackeemoors by leaving off the use of it! – and above all, remember how much expence it will save your poor Papa!'.

Abstinence from sugar was an antislavery intervention that followed soon after the failure of an abolition bill presented to parliament by William Wilberforce MP in April 1791. Rather than focusing on political debate, the idea encouraged a more direct social response that highlighted consumer responsibility. It had been promoted by the radical bookseller William Fox, who argued that all Britons were implicated in the crimes of slavery when consuming West Indian sugar and rum, and that 'in every pound of sugar used (the produce of slaves imported from Africa) we may be considered as consuming two ounces of human flesh.'[2] These words were strong, but certainly had an impact. Fox's pamphlet went on to be published in many editions,

2 William Fox, An Address to the People of Great Britain: On the Propriety of Abstaining from West India Sugar and Rum (11th ed., London, 1791), sold by M. Gurney and C. Forster (unpaginated).

and by 1792 the boycotting of sugar was being practised by thousands of ordinary people. Gillray's print on royal abstinence is, however, also critical. Playing on the king's notorious miserliness, he describes the family as a 'Noble example of oeconomy', suggesting that the king and queen are enthusiastic only because the idea will save them money.

Nothing troubled the public conscience more intensely in Britain at the end of the 18th century than the subject of slavery. During the late 1780s and the 1790s, Quaker and evangelical antislavery campaigners invaded popular politics by opening the eyes of ordinary Britons to the violence of the trading system and its moral implications for nation. Josiah Wedgewood's antislavery motif of a supplicating African asking 'Am I not a man and a brother?' (Illustration 2) invoked an image of the punished slave not as an individual but as a sympathetic emblem embodying devotion and the capacity for redemption.[3] The propaganda was effective but polarising, forcing people to take a 'for' or 'against' position in the face of undeniable inhumanity.

Aside from the financial implications, abstinence from sugar highlighted several moral issues underpinning the slave trade. Firstly, African people were being maltreated and endangered for the sake of sugar production. This onerous work took place under the strict control of planters, who often abused their power by punishing the Africans they did not like or who disobeyed their orders. This meant that an extreme culture of violence was fuelling the sugar economy, which was made prosperous by the growing demand for sweetened goods and sugar-derived spirits in Britain. So the great irony was that British material luxuries and social pleasures were being enjoyed at the expense of uncountable African lives.

When they entered the debate, satirical artists rarely took a particular stand on the moral issues, but they did subvert antislavery ideas and iconography: pinpointing the ways this new philanthropy could be exploited, and including peripheral African characters whose presence signified the consequences of a life made prosperous by the trade. The following essay will analyse a small selection of prints that uniquely demonstrate how the subject of slavery and the presence of African characters challenged royal privilege during the abolition years. By exploring the potential meanings of these images in the context of the times, the discussion will also consider why the relationship between royal subjects and taboo colonial bodies, imagined and depicted in publicly circulated reproductions, potentially represented the ultimate act of loyal subversion.

Six days after the publication of Gillray's *Anti-Saccharrites* print, on 2nd April 1792, William Wilberforce gave an important speech to parliament, closing another debate

3 For a more detailed discussion on abolitionist iconography see Sarah W. Parsons, The arts of abolition. Race, representation, and British colonialism, 1768–1807, in: Interpreting Colonialism, eds Byron R. Wells and Philip Stewart (Oxford, 2004), pp. 345–68.

Illustration 2: Josiah Wedgwood, *Antislavery medallion*, Jasperware, metal and gold. Produced in Etruria, UK, c.1790 © Trustees of the British Museum

on the abolition bill. Characteristically, his words were emotionally charged and full of moralistic polemic. The political historian William Belsham was later to write of these speeches in his memoirs that:

> The crimes and villanies to which this horrid traffic had given rise were detailed with a minuteness which placed not merely the persons actually concerned, but human nature itself, in a light the most degrading and detestable…[4]

In this particular speech, Wilberforce reported that an English slave ship captain named John Kimber had tortured an African girl to death on a recent voyage from Calabar to Grenada. The girl, aged fifteen, was unwell with gynaecological complaints and kept herself in a crouched position, unable to eat or 'dance' on deck – a common practice used to exercise Africans. The captain interpreted her withdrawal as stubbornness and had her humiliated in front of the crew whilst bound by her wrists. She was then flogged and suspended upside down by her ankles for three days, during which time she suffered convulsions and eventually died.

Newspaper reports of Wilberforce's speech inflamed the public's attention, bringing Britons face to face with the worst of aspects of the trade. A week later Isaac Cruikshank went a step further by illustrating Kimber's crime in a disturbing satire titled *The Abolition of the Slave Trade* (1792) (Illustration 3). Staged on the ship's top deck, it shows Kimber grinning and holding a whip whilst the distressed naked girl is hoisted upside down. The scene is watched by a seated group of three enslaved women in the background with the remaining crew turning their backs in dismay.

---

4 William Belsham, Memoirs of the Reign of George III from His Accession, to the Peace of Amiens Vol. 4, 8 vols. (6th ed., London, 1813), p. 391.

Although the print appears to speak for itself, Cruikshank's message here is uncertain. The print's subtitle takes on a moral tone, explaining the image as 'the Inhumanity of Dealers in human flesh exemplified in Captn Kimber's treatment of a Young Negro Girl of 15 for her Virjen [sic] Modesty.' The sailor who is hoisting the girl by one leg even admits: 'Dam me if I like it. I have a good mind to let go.' And yet here dealing in 'human flesh' has a double meaning, for the later site of murder is also sexually charged. Kimber's phallic sword is pointed directly at the girl's flailing body, which is presented less for the crew than for the viewer's inspection. The group of naked women also suggests that more is going on here, and their detached manner in the print implies availability, anonymity and selection – qualities that liken them (as well as the tortured girl) to the London prostitutes from Wapping mentioned by one of the sailors. Open to several interpretations, one could ask if the other women, too, will suffer the whip held by the smiling Kimber? And if so, for whose pleasure?

The ambiguity of Cruikshank's position on John Kimber's crime could be read either as disapproving or indifferent – potentially reflecting awareness of the uncomfortable truth that having command of a slave ship containing African captives incited sexually expressed abuses of power. This is certainly the underlying attitude conveyed in an ironic poem from 1738, which warned the English wife of a slave ship's captain to expect disloyalty, once he was exposed to the naked bodies of enslaved African women:

> That constant truth, and faithful vows,
> Made by a sailor to his spouse,
> Were all a jest and folly.
> Some young black slave they bid him view,
> Who, though she is of different hue,
> May have a pow'r to charm him;
> They shew her limbs, her pouting breast,
> Panting and courting to be press'd,
> With soft desire to warm him.[5]

The Kimber incident contained aspects of the trade that were both troubling and distasteful, with absolutely nothing about which one could laugh. But Cruikshank cited the case again days later, this time continuing the joke about royal abstinence. In *Gradual Abolition off [sic] the Slave Trade, or Leaving of [sic] Sugar by Degrees* (1792) (Illustration 4) the king and queen are seated at the breakfast table, piled high with two generous stacks of dripping muffins. They are joined by two of their daughters and Mrs Schwellenberg, the keeper of the queen's robes. The conversation reveals

5 From 'To Mrs**** Wife to a Capt. of a Merchant-man', in: *Gentleman's Magazine* 8 (June 1738), p. 320. The poem is an imitation of an ode by Horace.

Illustration 3: Isaac Cruikshank, *The abolition of the slave trade,* hand-coloured etching. Published in London by S. W. Fores, 10 April 1792 © Trustees of the British Museum

mixed responses to abstinence, ludicrously contradicting the obvious signs that they are well catered for. At the centre of the scene the king is pouring the contents of his tea cup onto the table, telling Princess Elizabeth to 'leave off at once, you know I have never drank any since I was married'. Raising her cup she tells him: 'Indeed papa, I can't leave of a good thing so soon, I am sure of late I have been very moderate, but I must have a bit now & then.' But her sister rejects the talk of moderation and turns away from the scene saying: 'for my part I'd rather want altogether than have a small piece.'

Next to the king, Queen Charlotte is speaking to Mrs Schwellenberg and is about to weigh a small lump of sugar on balanced scales, which resemble those of justice. In a Creole-type dialect (mimicking the one thought to be used by Africans) she says: 'Now my dear's only an ickle bit, do but tink on de Negro Girl dat Captain Kimber treated so cruelly ha, Madam Swelly & Rum too.' A sketchily drawn child's face, possibly another princess, is grimacing in the background. Mrs Schwellenberg, however, admits her weakness and copies the Queen in Creole speech saying: 'Oh to be sure I was taken but an ickle at a time, an ickle and often you know & as for de rum I don't care about it. Good cognac will make shift aha!!'

The gathering of the royal women as depicted by Cruikshank (and also by Gillray) certainly reflects the growing politicisation of women within the antislavery move-

Illustration 4: Isaac Cruikshank, *The gradual abolition off the slave trade, or, leaving of sugar by degrees,* hand-coloured etching. Published in London by S. W. Fores, 15 April 1792 © Trustees of the British Museum

ment.[6] Seeing the royal women as effective and potentially influential role models, the abolitionists publicly petitioned them for support. In fact during early abolitionist campaigning, Queen Charlotte was petitioned directly by the African writer Olaudah Equiano (Illustration 5), who published the letter in his popular autobiography *The Interesting Narrative* of 1789. He wrote:

> I presume, therefore, gracious Queen, to implore your interposition with your royal consort, in favour of the wretched Africans; that, by your Majesty's benevolent influence, a period may now be put to their misery; and that they may be raised from the condition of brutes, to which they are at present degraded, to the rights and situation of free men, and admitted to partake of the blessings of your Majesty's happy government.[7]

Cruikshank's print, however, makes a mockery of this 'influence', which has been reduced to domestic teatime chatter with women who have no political weight. And

6 For a discussion on contemporary references to women's participation in the sugar boycott see Clare Midgley, Women against Slavery: The British Campaigns, 1780–1870 (New York and London, 1992), pp. 35–42.

7 Olaudah Equiano, The Interesting Narrative of the Life of Olaudah Equiano: Or Gustavus Vassa, the African. Written by Himself. (4th enlarged ed., Dublin: printed for, and sold by, the author. Sold also at the *Dublin Chronicle Office,* by W. Sleater, and the other booksellers in Dublin, 1791), p. 352.

Illustration 5: Daniel Orme after William Denton. Olaudah Equiano, or, Gustavus Vassa, the African. The frontispiece for The Interesting Narrative of the Life of Olaudah Equiano: Or Gustavus Vassa, the African. Written by Himself. London, First published in 1789

all of their words describe sugar like a romantic companion that is both seductive and hard to let go of, making their responses about abstinence not only fickle but also crude. For a subject of such a contentious nature Cruikshank does little more than highlight the privileged distance between royalty and reality, which is perhaps the ultimate aim. Added to this, he also hints at both a tedium and discomfort with the subject, as emphasised by the word play in the print's title: 'abolition *off* the slave trade' and 'leaving *of* sugar'.

Wilberforce's spotlight made a public example of John Kimber, which resulted in his arrest and trial. The case was eventually heard on 7th June 1792, but lasted only five hours without a single testimony from Kimber. It consisted of evidence presented by the ship's surgeon and a member of the crew, who subsequently had their credibility undermined by claims of a conspiracy. Kimber also had several high-profile supporters, and so he was quickly acquitted. One of Kimber's 'friends' was the King's third son, Prince William Henry (Duke of Clarence), who attended the trial. In the final words of the published proceedings it was noted that the Duke:

> … appeared from his looks and gestures, to be particularly interested, in favour of the man who was accused of having murdered a slave.[8]

8 Anonymous, The Trial of Captain John Kimber, for the Murder of Two Female Negro Slaves, on Board the Recovery, African Slave Ship, Tried at the Admiralty Sessions, Held at the Old Baily, the 7th of June, 1792 (London, 1792), p. 36.

Another pamphlet on the trial, possibly published by Kimber's associates, writes:

> We were pleased to see his Royal Highness the DUKE OF CLARENCE present, as he is looked up to as the support of the British seamen; his anxiety on this occasion therefore, did him honour…[9]

Prince William was a naval man with wealthy friends in the West Indies and, unlike his parents, he publicly defended slavery on the basis of its economic advantages.[10] Like so many proslavery voices, he disregarded abolitionist arguments about the maltreatment of Africans, and the brutalities of plantation conditions, as the ramblings of 'fanatics and hypocrites.'[11] It was certainly an unpopular standpoint in Britain during the 1790s, even though it gained the prince support among the influential elite. But these associations also had cultural implications for his image in the popular sphere, linking the 'royal sailor', as they did, with corruptive colonial influences and the taboo theme of miscegenation.

Seen though words and images published in London, life in the sugar colonies was regarded as a hazardous combination of disease, heat, violence and sexual exploitation. Away from the prying eyes and constraints of metropolitan social protocols, male Britons conducted virulent and uncontested sexual relations with enslaved African women. In his seminal thesis *Sex and Race* (1972), Joel A. Rogers, exploring the history of these dynamics, details how British male residents in the West Indies, with diminished marriage prospects, depended on an extreme habit of African concubinage.[12] He maintains that the British West Indies, and particularly the islands of Jamaica and Barbados, 'present the most unrelieved scene of immorality.'[13] This view is clearly revealed in the writings of the period that documented life in harsh tropical conditions. The surgeon and physician John Williamson, for example, writing about the prevalence of venereal disease in Kingston, Jamaica, notes:

> … The truth requires that it shall not be concealed, the whites on estates follow the same habits, on many occasions, to a greater extent. Black or brown mistresses, are considered necessary appendages to every establishment: even a young bookkeeper coming from Europe,

9 Taken from the pamphlet 'Address' in: The Trial of Captain John Kimber: For the Supposed Murder of an African Girl, at the Admiralty Sessions, before the Hon. Sir James Marriott, Knt. (Judge Advocate) and Sir William Ashurst, Knt. &c. On Thursday, June 7, 1792 (London, 1792) (unpaginated).

10 See William IV, King of Great Britain [not king at the time], Substance of the Speech of the Duke of Clarence on the Motion for the Recommitment of the Slave Trade Limitation Bill (4th ed., London, 1799).

11 Thomas Clarkson, The History of the Rise, Progress, and Accomplishment of the Abolition of the African Slave-Trade by the British Parliament, 2 vols. (London, 1808), p. 464.

12 Joel Augustus Rogers, Sex and Race. A History of White, Negro, and Indian Miscegenation in the Two Americas 3 vols. (6th ed., New York, 1972), pp. 122–137.

13 Rogers, op. cit., p. 122.

> is generally instructed to provide himself; and however repugnant may seem the idea at first, his scruples are overcome, and he conforms to general custom.[14]

'Nearly everyone', wrote James Mursell Phillippo, 'down to the lowest white servant had his native female companion.'[15] Janet Schaw would also complain in her West Indies journal that 'the young black wenches lay themselves out for white lovers, in which they are but too successful.'[16] Visitors to the islands also indulged in this 'custom' and Prince William was no exception. His escapades were politely summarised by Admiral Nelson, under whom he served at sea, in a letter to a friend as follows:

> 'He has his foibles as well as private men, but they are far over-balanced by his virtues. In his Professional line, he is superior to near two-thirds, I am sure, of the List; and in attention to orders, and respect to his Superior Officers, I know hardly his equal: this is what I have found him. Some others, I have heard, will tell another story. The Islanders have made vast entertainments for him. But all this you will see in the English papers.'[17]

Although scandal was rife in the papers, giving the prince a public reputation as a royal Lothario, it was a print by James Gillray, produced a few years before the Kimber trial, that had already given his manly image a risqué colonial twist.

In *Wouski* (1788) (Illustration 6) we find Prince William lying in a hammock, lovingly embracing an Afro-Jamaican woman. The couple are in the hold of a ship, with a stack of rope, a barrel of Jamaican rum, and a chest with the prince's name beneath them. The royal sailor is wearing red, striped naval breeches, as his costume was normally shown in prints, and his beloved a yellow spotted dress with a revealing décolletage. Gillray represents 'Wouski' as a Creole: dark-skinned but with a full-cheek blush. He also engraves these lovers with intimacy and without physical caricature, suggesting a real rather than imagined encounter.

According to published gossip at the time 'Wowski' was a young girl that Prince William brought home to England in January 1788, following a naval tour with Admiral Nelson to Canada and the West Indies. It is claimed that upon arrival she was hidden on board ship like a mole, whilst the prince disembarked at Portsmouth, awaiting the King's permission to return to London. The society newspaper, *The World,*

---

14 John Williamson, Medical and Miscellaneous Observations Relative to the West India Islands 2 vols. (Edinburgh, 1817), p. 49.

15 James Mursell Phillippo, Jamaica. Its Past and Present State (Second thousand edition, London, 1843), p. 124.

16 Janet Schaw, Journal of a Lady of Quality: Being the Narrative of a Journey from Scotland to the West Indies, North Carolina, and Portugal, in the Years 1774 to 1776, eds Evangeline Walker Andrews and Charles McLean Andrews (New Haven, CT, and London, 1923), p. 112.

17 'Letter to William Locker Esq. sent on December 29th 1786' in: Horatio Nelson and Sir Nicholas Harris Nicolas (eds), The Dispatches and Letters of Vice Admiral Lord Viscount Nelson 7 vols. (London, 1845), p. 205.

Illustration 6: James Gillray, *Wouski,* hand-coloured etching. Published in London by H. Humphrey, 23 January 1788 © Trustees of the British Museum

was the first to report that the prince had with him: 'a small Negro girl. He saw her dancing in the West Indies, and made purchase of her. 'Wowski' is said to have been grateful ever since.'[18]

With a large dose of irony, the newspaper had named the mysterious girl after a comic black servant in George Colman's adaptation of *Inkle and Yarico.* The popular play had recently made its debut on the London stage and retold an old, 17th-century colonial story of an English trader (Inkle), who first falls in love with an Indian maiden who had saved his life, then sells her into slavery for profit. In Colman's comic version, a touch of abolitionist sentiment sees Inkle eventually recognising the error of his ways. In addition, Inkle and Yarico are joined by their aspirant servants – the mimicking comic duo of Trudge and Wowski.

In *Wouski,* Gillray has borrowed, but slightly adapted, the newspaper's epithet for the prince's mistress, replacing the 'w' with a 'u' to mock the original name phonetically. By implication, Prince William is shown in the guise of the doting colonial servant, but is simultaneously acknowledged as a member of royalty through an inscription from another 17th century play at the bottom of the print, which states:

18 *The World,* No. 319: Monday 7th January 1788, p. 2.

------Far be the noise
Of Kings & Crowns from us, whose gentle souls
Our kinder fates have steerd another way.
Free as the forest birds we'll pair together
Without rememb'ring who our fathers were.
And in soft murmurs interchange our souls.

Representing the prince with a 'black' woman was certainly a daring intervention at this moment. For the meanings ascribed to African women's bodies were a potent mix of exoticism and hyper-sexuality, coupled with notions of blackness as being unattractive, alien and corruptive. Georgian men therefore imagined African women through a distorted lens of fascination and revulsion, encapsulated here uniquely in a joke once related to the actor David Garrick:

> Mr. Blake, a gentleman of great possessions in the West Indies, upon his return from paying his first visit to that climate, was expressing to Mr. Garrick, his great aversion to the charcoal ladies; 'however, says he, I was made very drunk one night, and an ebony beauty was put to bed to me. When I waked in the morning, I was greatly astonished, and cried with much surprise, who is this? 'Tis I, massa,' replied the black beauty; 'What did you do then?' says Mr. Garrick. 'Why' answered Mr. Blake, 'I lamented the loss of *rosey cheeks,* and went *into mourning.*'[19]

This seemingly unconscious attraction to African women – who were either enslaved or disenfranchised and therefore technically 'off-limits' – fetishized their inclusion in British sexual life as a transgression or disloyalty. Graphic satirists therefore often conveyed encounters with African women (like Garrick's joke) as a mistake or mishap in the bedroom. This can be seen for example in the dramatic encounter illustrated by Isaac Cruikshank in *The Morning Surprise* (1807) (Illustration 7). To emphasize their connection with the London underworld, artists also included black prostitutes on the edges of caricatures or, literally, on the periphery of the city, waiting at the docks for sailors.

Taking the royal 'couple' in Gillray's *Wouski* seriously, then, at a moment when interracial mixing was so taboo, seems to be the simple, but political, sting of this visual joke. Almost as an inversion of the bedroom surprise, Gillray uses the sincerity of a 'portrait', coupled with layers of literary subtexts, to deliver a jibe at the prince that was direct and memorable. But what were the implications for the representation of the ultimate taboo? To what extent was Gillray's print indicative of the medium's growing disobedience when it came to safeguarding the royal image? Certainly *Wouski* demonstrates satirical audacity in connecting the royal household to the sexual life of the colonies – depicting private indiscretions that were supposed to be out of sight, even if they were

---

19 Anonymous, The English Roscius. Garrick's Jests: Or, Genius in High Glee. Containing All the Jokes of the Wits of the Present Age (London, [c.1785]), p. 29.

Illustration 7: Isaac Cruikshank (after George Woodward), *A morning surprise. Why who the devil have we got here!! It is only me Massa,* hand-coloured etching. Published in London, c.1807 © Trustees of the British Museum

not out of mind. Critically the print also signaled physical accessibility to royalty for colonial and working class subjects, through a libertine and undiscerning manly culture.

African people experienced numerous social perils in London during the abolition years that ranged from precarious liberty to the denial of authentic citizenship. On the one hand abolitionist propaganda urged Britons to see African people as equally human, and they showcased the work of writers such as Phyllis Wheatley, Equiano and Ignatius Sancho, to demonstrate how social and intellectual advancement could be attained through humanitarian patronage. But these African icons were the exception. In general, Africans were disregarded as belonging to a social underclass, thereby suffering the discriminations involved with being poor, misrepresented and foreign. They very rarely enjoyed the benefits of British privilege, even if ironically they were part of its public display.

Various eighteenth century portraits attest to the way African domestic servants in particular, participated as attendants at aristocratic social rituals. This can be seen for example in a hunting portrait of the politician Charles Lennox (3rd Duke of Richmond) from the 1760s, which represents an intimate scene of master-servant harmony in the country landscape. A well-dressed boy is smiling affectionately as he brings the duke his shooting prize. Direct gazes and a pose that suggests physical closeness connect their two bodies. However even in this moment of intimacy, the use of props (a hat and dead bird) maintains the literal distance between the two figures, and therefore upholds hierarchical distinctions. Such paintings idealised enslaved African boys as doting recipients of paternal protection and captured their devotion in lasting expressions of British privilege and power.

As signs of wealth and worldliness, African pages were naturally members of Britain's notable aristocratic households, and evidence reveals both their prevalence and unfortunate disposability. Georgiana, the Duchess of Devonshire, is quoted as having been sent 'a Black boy, eleven years old and very honest',[20] but as being unable to keep him since the Duke did not approve. Instead she offers to send the child to her mother, writing: 'he will be a cheap servant and you will make a Christian of him and a good boy; if you don't like him they say Lady Rockingham wants one.'[21] Looking back on the history of these African servants in Britain, an article from 1866 was to note:

> The fashion of employing black servants in the households of 'the quality', survived to quite recent times; but the negro footmen have now disappeared almost altogether, and the fancy of attiring them in Eastern garb expired long previously. The turban gradually yielded to the gold-bound European hat, and Turkish trousers were replaced in due course by plush small-clothes and silk stockings.[22]

Satirical prints were peppered with similar figures, but here they were enlivened with performative qualities that made them active elements of humour. Instead of the voiceless petted page portrayed in fancy attire, they became animated figures like the irritable and grimacing youth, resentfully carrying a skewer of dripping meat in wind-swept streets behind a feline woman in Thomas Rowlandson's *Cat in Pattens* (1812) (Illustration 8). Including such peripheral but exotic characters on the urban stage proved useful for expressing the strange excessiveness implied by the relationships between British masters and African servants – relationships that symbolised the troubled connection between metropolis and colony.

In a royal context, these meanings and dynamics are utilised in a discomforting manner by Richard Newton in his scurrilous print *The First Interview, or an Envoy from Yarmony to Improve the Breed* (1797) (Illustration 9). Here, an African footboy is shown carrying Prince Frederick of Württemberg's fat projecting stomach on his back, towards the King's oldest daughter Princess Charlotte. The couple were soon to be married, in a dynastic arrangement that was intended to enhance Anglo-Ger-

20 Victoria Sackville-West, Knole and the Sackvilles (London, 1922), p. 191. No citation is given for the reference to the letter.

21 Ibid.

22 From 'Othello's Costume', *Once a Week: An illustrated miscellany of literature, popular science, and art,* New series 2 (1866), p. 273. The article was originally published on 8th September 1866.

man relations. But Newton is more concerned with representing the German prince's excesses. Clearly a glutton and adorned in showy regalia, he proclaims: 'I was come from Yarmony to love you dearly, and was take you to Yarmony to love me'. Stunned and blushing, a similarly stout Princess Charlotte says: 'Lord what a Porpoise Pho!!!'.

Between them the African footboy is yelling with visible pain: 'Oh Lord oh lord my neck will break, I can't carry it any farther.' The pain expressed conveys obvious allusions to enslavement and labour, but here it is literally doubly loaded, for the prince's groin is pressed graphically against his bottom. This vulgar connection between the prince and his footboy is further commented on by a carpenter in the background, modifying a table to accommodate the royal gut. He murmurs knowingly:

> Egad they did well to order a piece to be cut out of the Table, or he never could have reached his Dinner, and how he will reach her, God only knows. I suppose he has some German Method a rare Ram this to mend the Breed.

The burlesque of Newton's graphic style gives the print an intensity that emphasises its violence, making it difficult for a contemporary viewer to see (or even want to see) beyond its racial and sexual biases. When historian Marcus Wood described this print in *Blind Memory* (2000) as representing abuse between 'white royalty' and a 'black child',[23] he asked some critical questions concerning the challenges of deconstructing the artist's meaning and intent:

> Is the black to be pitied, does he represent racially disadvantaged and abused childish innocence, the powerless fall-out from the slave trade, or is it just all good fun, and as a black is he ridiculous anyway?[24]

Certainly the African body here becomes a mirror for projected sexual deviances, in ways that reference the unmitigated promiscuity of the plantation. But is there anything else to be seen that makes this image function other than as the reason for a cheap bawdy laugh? It is clear that Newton would have heard rumours that the prince was bisexual, and almost certainly would have known about the difficulties of his former marriage to the king's niece, Duchess Augusta of Brunswick-Wolfenbüttel. Purportedly the prince had been abusive towards her, and she eventually died in labor with an illegitimate, but stillborn child. The tragedies of his previous marriage, coupled with the obvious issue of the prince's physical excess, also turn Newton's print into a nuanced mockery of royal inbreeding. And in spite of the graphic abuse meted out on the African child's body, his role as a mediator for this marriage of cousins shows again a daring satirical impetus to conjure up taboos and have them enacted

23 Marcus Wood, Blind Memory: Visual Representations of Slavery in England and America, 1780–1865 (New York, 2000), p. 159.

24 Ibid., p. 160.

Illustration 8: Thomas Rowlandson, *Cat in Pattens,* hand-coloured etching. Published in London, 1812 © Trustees of the British Museum

Illustration 9: Richard Newton, *The first interview, or an envoy from Yarmony to improve the breed (1797),* hand-coloured etching. Published in London by S. W. Fores, 19 April 1797 © Trustees of the British Museum

for political effect – in this instance using sexualized physical contact to toy with latent national anxieties about lineage, and the mixing of 'race' and foreign influence in the royal bloodline.[25]

When the king's second son, the Duke of York, married Princess Frederica Charlotte of Prussia at Buckingham Palace in November of 1791, the sugar abstinence campaign was in full swing. In good favour with the public, the duchess was viewed as a virtuous royal role model and within months she was petitioned to support the sugar campaign by abstaining and helping to influence the royal circle. Strongly worded, the petition pamphlet pleaded:

> Be persuaded then to discontinue the use of a drug, which is the produce of cruelty and barbarity! Let sugar never be brought into your presence! Let it be proscribed your household, till its connection with fraud, robbery, and murder, be entirely broken![26]

25 For a detailed exploration of the complex matrices of royal inbreeding see Karina Urbach, ed., Royal Kinship: Anglo-German Family Networks, 1815–1918 (Munich, 2008).

26 Anonymous, An Address to Her Royal Highness the Duchess of York against the Use of Sugar (London, 1792), p. 16.

Was it in bad taste to capture the new bride's attention with the language of violence? How much sugar would have been consumed at the royal wedding banquet? Metropolitan debate about the sordid details of slavery invoked strong emotions of disgust, guilt and condemnation, forcing Britons to face a difficult aspect of their modern lives. These emotions were effective in soliciting public support for abolition, but they also framed perceptions of African people detrimentally, by psychologically linking their bodies to shameful acts, and making their maltreatment for racist reasons the focus of collective discomfort and anxiety. The public discourse also infiltrated class and gender boundaries, thus widening the social scope of politics and critically challenging royalty to demonstrate empathy and share opinions with their loyal subjects.

In this tense atmosphere satirical artists played the devil's advocate and crossed hallowed cultural boundaries, which perhaps revealed their disquiet with the ways antislavery had invaded public consciousness in a similar way. The socially contentious body of the African was made further grotesque in prints by physiognomic caricature, but by their very inclusion in the genre the Caribbean plantation was mirrored by the British living room. And thus this linkage of slavery to the private world meant that no one, not even the king, was exempt from its influence. For modern eyes, reproductions of the queen discussing slavery at her breakfast table or of Prince William and his black lover on a British naval ship, provide lasting impressions of a moment when humourists could use race to sell jokes about royals. The very existence of these images is therefore an indicator of a graphic culture that was being innovative in a complex way and disregarded symbolic proprieties in order to introduce contentious topics into royal personal space – space that in real life was revered by British citizens.

Timothy Clayton

The London Printsellers and the Export of English Graphic Prints

Als die Hannoveraner den englischen Königsthron Thron bestiegen war die Produktion von Drucken in Großbritannien international unbedeutend. Eine wachsende Nachfrage nach gedruckten Bildern gab es erst, nachdem die Mezzotinter John Smith und William Hogarth internationalen Ruhm erwarben. Karikatur war schon immer ein spezialisierter Bereich des Druckhandels. Dieser war zunächst eng mit dem Handel von politischen und aktuellen Broschüren verbunden. Karikaturen wurden begehrter und die Drucker eröffneten Läden in den teuersten Wohngegenden der Bond Street, der St. James Street und in Piccadilly; die Bilder wurden größer, ehrgeiziger, bunter und immer teurer. Oft erforderte die Karikatur eine große Vertrautheit mit den politischen und sozialen Beziehungen in London, die ausländische Betrachter hätte abstoßen können. Doch es scheint tatsächlich beträchtliches ausländische Interesse an britischen Karikaturen gegeben zu haben. Dieser Bereich ist bisher nur marginal erforscht, weswegen im letzten Teil dieses Beitrags einige Beispiele für einen internationalen Handel mit Karikaturen näher erläutert werden.

In 1714, when George I became King of Great Britain, print production in England was small-scale and internationally insignificant. However, the economy was expanding fast and with the end of the War of Spanish Succession and the resumption of international trade an ever-increasing demand for printed images was satisfied first of all by large scale importation from France and Italy of both the latest contemporary design and the finest modern interpretations of the great art of antiquity and the renaissance. Numerous picture shops sold such items in London, while auctioneers and booksellers began to sell them in the provinces. At the same time the London publishing trade began to expand.

The only field in which artists working in England had shown any marked distinction was mezzotint, a tonal process in which the plate was first roughened (gathering ink and printing black) and then scraped smoother (printing white when perfectly smooth). The first English printmaker to gain an international reputation was the finest early mezzotinter, John Smith, who engraved Godfrey Kneller's coronation portrait of George I. Smith's work, the engraver and art historian George Vertue wrote, 'was universally known to all ingenious persons of his time in England' and 'of no less esteem abroad in foreign countries in France, Holland, Flanders, Germany

& Italy, all concurring in a settled opinion, for…the honour…of this nation, that he excelled all others in that art'.[1]

Mezzotint was easy enough to learn and quick to undertake, so no great investment was required, but a plate would not yield many hundred good impressions and required frequent refreshing by the engraver. A host of lesser exponents satisfied less demanding customers for portraits. Portraits often carried political messages and their display signalled allegiance, but specifically political prints were published and sold in shops that also handled political pamphlets. Such topical prints were usually etched but in the early years of the eighteenth century some publishers made woodcuts which were conveniently combined with letterpress (because they could be printed using the same press) in pamphlets or broadsheets.

At the opposite end of the qualitative spectrum, significant foreign artists were tempted to come to London to undertake major projects, of which the most significant was the publication by Nicolas Dorigny, a Frenchman who had been working in Rome, of the Raphael Cartoons at Hampton Court. Claude Dubosc came with him as an assistant and in 1714 took the opportunity to engrave a flattering allegorical piece to celebrate the coronation:

> Just publish'd a new print of the Coronation of King George, curiously engrav'd on a Sheet of Paper; wherein is contain'd his Majesty sitting on a Throne, and crown'd by Fame, and the Genius of the People; on one side is Minerva, talking to the Prince and Princess who shews 'em the King as a Pattern of Wisdom and Prudence; and Justice, who offers him England, and puts a Scepter in his Hand; with many other Hieroglyphick Figures. Presented to his Majesty by Charles Dubosc, Engraver. Pr. 2s. 6d. Sold by T. Bowles Print and Map-seller, next to the Chapter House in St Pauls Churchyard; and by James Regnier, in Newport street near Long-Acre; at the former of which Places is sold, a new Print in which is contained divers views and Plans of Blenheim-House; a new Print of Powis-House; a new Print of the Queen's Statue at the West-end of St. Paul's; and all the different views of the said Cathedral. Price 1s. each.[2]

Dubosc worked with the printseller Thomas Bowles on *Marlborough's Battles,* an English series modelled on Louis XIV's prints celebrating his victorious campaigns. Whereas Louis's prints were published for the king at the king's expense, the British prints were a commercial enterprise published by subscription (Illustration 1).

Paris dominated the print market. About 1720, Vertue noted that 'that City being the great Mart for prints. They from thence do disperse to all part of Europe.' The government taxed prints imported from abroad at 30 % of their value until 1729 and subsequently at a more easily calculated 6d per print. By adding 50 or 100 % to

1 George Vertue, Notebooks, III, pp. 113–14 (*Walpole Society,* XXII, 1934). On Smith see 'Early Mezzotint Publishing in England – I John Smith, 1652–1743', *Print Quarterly,* VI (1989), pp. 242–57.

2 Post Boy, 10–12 February 1715. The English pound sterling (£) contained 20 shillings (s.) of 12 pennies (d.) each. A guinea (g.) was one pound and one shilling, or 21 shillings.

Illustration 1: *Thomas Bowles's shop, one of the oldest in London, Spectators at a shop in Saint Paul's Churchyard,* published by Carington Bowles (London, 1774). BM 1880,1113.3311 © Trustees of the British Museum

their price this duty must have greatly discouraged the importation of cheap foreign prints, which became prohibitively expensive in comparison with cheap prints produced in London, whose production was thus stimulated: typically, William and Cluer Dicey advertised in 1754 that they were continually publishing copies 'from the various Inventions of the best French, Dutch, and Italian Prints.' But the duty had a relatively slighter effect on more expensive prints, where 6d. was a small proportion of the price.[3]

The scale of the import trade can be deduced from surviving customs registers that cover the period from 1725 to 1774 and list total numbers of prints upon which duty was paid under their country of origin. The biggest supplier throughout the period was France, followed by Italy, then Holland, and by much smaller totals from Flanders and Germany. The Italian figure fluctuated dramatically, suggesting that collections imported by individuals, rather than regular supplies to dealers, made up a substantial part of it. The total number of imports per annum rose to a high of 19,000 in 1729, then dropped during the 1730s to about 7,000 per annum and dropped further during the War of the Austrian Succession to about 5,000 per annum, especially between 1744 and 1748 when French imports ceased entirely, although a corresponding rise in imports from Holland suggests that shipments from France were rerouted. The figure then rose to about 8,000 before the Seven Years War, increased slightly during the War when shipments from France appear to have been sent through Flanders, rose to an average of about 15,000 during the 1760s, before dropping to about 10,000 during the 1770s. Since prints were easily smuggled it is possible that the figures under-represent the scale of trade and it is also remarkable that a number of the most eager print collectors were Commissioners of Excise.[4]

Nevertheless, by the mid-century there was widespread desire to compete with France in this field and in 1751 Malachy Postlethwayt's *Universal Dictionary of Trade and Commerce* was determined that soon 'instead of importing immense quantities of foreign prints, we may not only supply ourselves, but become exporters of a commodity that is universally vendible'.[5] London production of prints in the middle price range expanded enormously during the first half of the century, supplying growing provincial and colonial markets, but for British publishers to export fine prints they needed to create a demand abroad for British designs.

The initial breakthrough came when William Hogarth launched *A Harlot's Progress* in 1731, a project that transformed Hogarth into a celebrity with international acclaim. He envisaged a set of six prints that would tell a story of his own invention: 'I have endeavoured,' he wrote, 'to treat my subject as a dramatic writer; my picture is my stage, and men and women my players, who by means of

---

3 Vertue, op. cit., VI, 1948–50, p. 189; Timothy Clayton, The English Print 1688–1802 (London, 1997), p. 33, p. 125.
4 Clayton, op. cit., p. 25, p. 123.
5 Malachy Postlethwayt, Universal Dictionary of Trade and Commerce, I (London, 1751–55) p. 725.

certain actions and gestures are to exhibit a dumb show.' George Vertue was startled by the originality of this, 'the most remarkable Subject of painting that captivated the Minds of most People persons [sic] of all ranks and conditions from the greatest quality to the meanest'.[6] It was the financial success of the project that most impressed Vertue. Hogarth endeavoured to cut out the printsellers who had backed his previous ventures and keep all the profit to himself. The increasingly wide circulation of newspapers offered new opportunities to entrepreneurs, for by advertising in the newspapers read by potential customers, artists could now make direct contact with their public and they used the newspapers to make subscription a viable method of publishing prints. Hogarth announced a subscription for a set of prints that was to be completed in the future, inviting potential subscribers to come and see the paintings at Hogarth's house, and if they liked the paintings, they gave Hogarth their name and address, paid half the price of the prints in advance and Hogarth gave them an etched subscription ticket as a receipt. Newspaper advertisements kept subscribers informed of the progress of the project and eventually they collected their sets.

George Vertue had observed the progress of every project of this kind, but none succeeded like Hogarth's: 'these prints at a guinea a Sett had the greatest subscription – & public esteem that any prints ever had.' Hogarth's printer told Vertue that 1,240 sets had been printed, and Hogarth was equipped with the names and addresses of so many enthusiasts for his prints who might buy his future publications.[7] To Hogarth's frustration, however, the prints were copied by a number of printsellers in various cheaper formats.

In 1733 he published *A Midnight Modern Conversation,* selling it for 5 shillings. Smaller engraved copies priced at 6d. (one tenth of Hogarth's price) were published by a number of printsellers, including John Clark, Bispham Dickinson and Robert Sayer. This was the price commonly charged for topical prints, political satires and pamphlets until about 1770 and it placed them within reach of artisans and traders. In Henry Overton's 1754 catalogue Hogarth's design appeared as

> 'a 3 foot x 2 foot engraving at 1s., on a royal sheet by George Bickham at 6d., and as a truly popular print: a copper 'royal sheet' probably at 3d. and as a woodcut, probably at 1d. or 1½d.

The copies spread his fame even wider but he did not benefit financially from these piracies of his ideas, nor could he control their quality.

In 1735, Hogarth and a small group of fellow petitioners obtained an Act of Parliament to secure copyright for those who designed and engraved prints, or who employed others to engrave prints after their design. Unauthorised copies of their publications became illegal, but exactly which prints were covered by the Act was

6 Vertue, op. cit., III, xxii 1933–34, p. 58.
7 Vertue, op. cit., VI, p. 191.

slightly obscure and in 1767 a second, better worded Act vested protection for the owner of the plate for a term of twenty-eight years from the date of publication, which was engraved on the plate. This radical extension of copyright provision to all prints encouraged a rapid increase in speculative publications. Unlike most European copyright systems, where a *privilège* had to be purchased, copyright in England was free and with rates of duty leaning heavily in favour of English exports, there was some justice to the complaints of French publishers that they received far less help from their government than the English.[8]

Hogarth found that foreign collectors wanted to buy his prints. Despite or because of the innovative nature of his 'modern moral subjects', his work was widely collected in Europe. In order to explain his designs to Europeans Hogarth commissioned Jean Rouquet to write explanations in French and included a copy of these with sets that he sent abroad.[9] In 1747 one writer claimed that Hogarth's 'celebrated pieces are esteemed all over Europe', and six years later Matthew Maty noted in his *Journal Britannique,* a periodical published in the Hague to promote British culture, that Hogarth's prints had claimed a place in all the best collections in Europe with the result that few fashionable continentals were not familiar with his principal designs.

Interest in Hogarth survived his death, remaining at a high level throughout the eighteenth century. Both John Nichols' 'Biographical Anecdotes of William Hogarth' and a German translation of it were announced in the *Magazin des Buch- und Kunsthandels* in 1781. Georg Christoph Lichtenberg's twelve-volume ‚Ausführliche Erklärung der Hogarthischen Kupferstiche, mit verkleinerten aber vollständigen Copien derselben von E. Riepenhausen' commenced in 1794.[10] Hogarth's immediate followers were also reviewed and collected. He had several imitators, most notably John Collett, whose designs, like Hogarth's, were published in a series of large engravings. Collett and others – Hannah Humphrey's brother William was one – also published 'droll mezzotints', which were comic with some mild social satire in a smaller, 10 by 14 inch, format.

The art exhibitions held in London after 1760 fuelled interest in contemporary artists – as a commodity to be collected or displayed. Artists such as Joshua Reynolds, Benjamin West, Richard Wilson, Thomas Gainsborough, George Stubbs, Johann Zoffany and Joseph Wright of Derby showed their work through the Society of Artists to several thousand people each year in April and May. Engravers exhibited their prints in the same show as the painting it reproduced and subscriptions were launched and prints were often published during the period of the exhibitions when the art-loving

8 On copyright for prints in Britain and abroad see Clayton, op. cit., pp. 81–88, p. 198, pp. 274–76.

9 John Nichols, George Steevens and Thomas Phillips, The Genuine Works of William Hogarth, 3 vols. (1808–17), I, p. 428: 'the Pamphlet was designed and continues to be employed, as a constant companion to all such sets of his Prints as go abroad'.

10 Georg Christoph Lichtenberg's Ausführliche Erklärung der Hogarthischen Kupferstiche, mit verkleinerten aber vollständigen Copien derselben von Ernst Ludwig Riepenhausen, 12 vols. (Göttingen, 1794–1816).

public was gathered in the metropolis. High quality prints – usually mezzotints – of contemporary paintings suddenly became fashionable and collectable. The print trade in London expanded accordingly, with the main areas of growth in the finest prints, for which a substantial export trade to Europe developed.

In 1759 the influential, new aesthetic magazine *Bibliothek der Schönen Wissenschaften und der freyen Künste* (founded in 1757), commenced a regular series of reviews of English prints written by Georg Friedrich Brandes, the Hanoverian official responsible for the University of Göttingen, who enthusiastically recommended the products of the new English school to German-speaking collectors. Prints fuelled a wave of admiration for English culture (Shakespeare, Sterne, Wedgwood, Chippendale, steam engines, telescopes as well as art) that enjoyed a lasting vogue throughout Europe. By 1772 the fashion for English design and manufactures had reached St Petersburg where Nikolay Novikov reported that 'the English have replaced the French: nowadays women and men are falling over themselves to imitate anything English; everything English now seems to us good and admirable and fills us full of enthusiasm.'[11]

All of this led to a boom in exports of English prints. The *Morning Chronicle* estimated in 1785 'that a balance of Thirty Thousand Pounds annually, in favour of this Kingdom, hath for many years arisen from the exportation of our Prints in general'. By the end of the century much larger figures were quoted for the annual profit to Britain – £200,000 in 1803, £300,000 in 1805.[12] At that date the economist David Macpherson argued in *Annals of Commerce* that:

> 'With respect to trade with foreign nations in the article of prints, the imports, which used to be considerable, are now so small, and the exports so great, that the value of the latter is estimated to that of the former as five hundred to one.'[13]

The *European Magazine* claimed in 1792 that 'these exports are not confined to one, or two, or three countries – they extend from one end of Europe to the other'.[14] This market was severely disrupted during the 1790s by the French conquest of the Austrian Netherlands, Holland and the Rhineland, where the principal dealers operated and many collectors were concentrated. During the Peace of Amiens the most successful of the London printsellers, John Boydell, commented on the effect that this had had on his business: 'I certainly calculated upon some defalcation of these receipts by a French or Spanish War, or both,' he wrote in 1803, but with France or Spain I carried

11 Anthony Cross, The British in Catherine's Russia: A Preliminary Survey, in The Eighteenth Century in Russia, ed. John Gordon Garrard (Oxford, 1973), p. 233.

12 *Morning Chronicle,* 31 May 1785; Hansard, Parliamentary Debates, i, 1803–04, p. 849; John Pye, Extraordinary Characters of the Nineteenth Century (London 1805), p. 244n.

13 David Macpherson, Annals of Commerce, Manufactures, Fisheries and Navigation, 4 vols. (London, 1805), IV, pp. 183–84.

14 *European Magazine,* xxi (London, 1792), p. 244.

on but little commerce – Flanders, Holland, and Germany, who, no doubt, supplied the rest of Europe, were the great marts: but alas! they are now no more!'[15] This suggests that Boydell dealt with middlemen such as Santo Tessari, whose business was based in Augsburg but had a branch in Liège in the Austrian Netherlands, or with Carl Artaria, based in Vienna with a branch in Mannheim. Surviving documents demonstrate that these men supplied English prints wholesale to other dealers further east in Prussia and Poland.[16]

Meanwhile, reviews continued to keep Germans informed of what was being published in other countries. This is Brandes's review of an engraving published in 1780 by William Ellis:

> 'An idea from Goldsmith's novel *The Vicar of Wakefield;* namely where Mr Burchell rescues Sophia, the good vicar's young daughter, from the water. The painter, Thomas Hearne, has set the scene by a mill, where Sophia has been overcome by the strength of the current and thrown from her horse. Now however her companion Burchell has sprung to her, picked her up, and is carrying her unconscious from the torrent. Meanwhile the old father, who is on the bank with the rest of his family, kneels and prays for her preservation. The figures are by W. Woollet, and the landscape is very finely engraved by W. Ellis. If there are no more plates from this story, we await at least a companion piece that has already been announced. It costs 6 shillings and measures 12 inches high by 16 inches wide.'

This relatively detailed review of Ellis's plate appeared with a number of shorter notices of prints published from Autumn 1779 to early summer 1780. Another concurrent periodical, the *Magazin des Buch- und Kunsthandels,* contained appendices listing the stock of the Braunschweig printseller Bremer & Sohn. All of the prints that Brandes reviewed could be bought from Bremer at the time that the reviews appeared. The working exchange rate was three shillings to the Thaler of 24 Groschen and the prices charged in Braunschweig were the same as those charged in London. This standardisation of prices was normal with English prints sold abroad. In 1787 Giacinto Micali e Figlio of Livorno, supplied (to judge from their stock) chiefly by Boydell, also promised 'il vantaggio de prezzi originali di Londra'. This was made possible by the habit of English printsellers of taking the risk of supplying for-

15 'Alderman Boydell's Letter to Sir J.W. Anderson, Bart, M.P., read to the House of Commons, on his applying for Leave to Dispose of his Property by Lottery, cited in Pye, op. cit., p. 245n. as Annual Register, xlvi, p. 366.

16 On Artaria see Christoph Frank, Zu den Anfängen des etablierten europäischen Graphikhandels: Das Wiener Unternehmen Artaria & Comp (gegr. 1768/70) in Interkulturelle Kommunikation in der europäischen Druckgraphik im 18. und 19. Jahrhundert, eds Philippe Kaenel and Rolf Reichardt (Hildesheim, 2007), pp. 609–45. On Santo Tessari see Timothy Clayton, The export of English Prints to Germany 1760–1802, in Commercio delle stampe e diffusione delle immagini nei secoli XVIII e XIX, ed. Alberto Milano (Rovereto, 2008), pp. 156–58 and ditto, From Fireworks to Old Masters: Colnaghi and Printselling c.1760–c.1880, in Colnaghi, established 1760: The History, ed. Jeremy Howard (London, 2010).

eign dealers with prints on commission. The *Magazin des Buch- und Kunsthandels* informed readers that Bremer's prints can be ordered in Leipzig from Herr Geyser who is in correspondence with them on commission. The goods would have been sent by ship from London to Bremen and then up the Weser and Aller, or via Hamburg and the Elbe.

The review journals were supplemented by a series of art dictionaries and guides for print collectors. Several of these, including a catalogue of Brandes's own collection, were written by Michael Huber, long resident in Paris and subsequently Professor of French at the University of Leipzig. His 'Notices générales des graveurs divisés par nations et des peintres rangés par écoles' (1787), like several other similar works of the period, arranged artists according to national schools and then listed their published work – that is, whatever had been engraved and published. Modern English prints figured along with those of earlier continental masters, and the lists provided collectors with an idea of the major works of the more important masters. The most complete account of this kind would have been Carl Heinrich von Heinecken's 'Dictionnaire des artistes, dont nous avons des estampes' (1778–) had it ever got past the letter D.

However, English prints were not aimed solely at the collector. They were also, or alternatively, designed for display on the wall. For this reason, they were usually printed in shades of red or brown, rather than the normal black. These colours looked more sympathetic on the wall, especially with a gold frame. For a higher price they could also be had printed in colours (and usually finished by hand). Some were gauged to blend in with neo-classical interior furnishing. Others were visual collectable accessories to popular modern novels. English literature was in wide vogue in Europe, especially in Germany.[17] The extraordinary popularity of Laurence Sterne's 'A Sentimental Journey through France and Italy' (1768) was reflected in the very large number of prints representing incidents in the novel, and fashionable foreign authors were treated in the same manner. One of the massive international bestsellers of the late 1770s and early 1780s was Goethe's short novel 'Die Leiden des jungen Werther' published in 1774. It was widely translated and adapted for the stage, and was one of the novels that inspired the most prints for the wall. One of the artists who produced designs for prints of Werther was James Northcote, who described how poverty drove him to it:

> 'Being in the awkward state before described and deprived of all resource in the line of portrait painting, I betook myself from necessity to painting small historical and fancy subjects from the most popular authors of the day, as such subjects are sure of sale amongst the minor print-sellers, being done in a short time, and for a small sum. From those which I executed there are prints taken such as Sterne's 'Sentimental Journey', the 'Sorrows of Werter', Gay's

17 See Bernhard Fabian, English books and their eighteenth-century German readers, in The widening circle, ed. Paul J. Korshin (Philadelphia, 1976) and The English book in eighteenth-century Germany (London 1992).

> pastorals, &c. I did also small pictures, or rather sketches, of the events of the moment, such as at the time were the topics of general conversation. But all this was against my will, work of necessity, & to me who panted for higher employment but bitter work.'[18]

Northcote's *The Last Interview of Werter and Charlotte* was engraved by Charles Knight and published by John Harris in 1784. It was announced in the *Neue Bibliothek* in that year as available for 7s. 6d. and was reviewed again with a group of three other prints from 'Werther' and one from Sterne's 'Sentimental Journey' in Johann Georg Meusel's Museum für Künstler und für Kunstliebhaber in 1787. The reviewer, 'K.' from Ansbach, quotes from the book: '"He did not resist, released her from his arms and threw himself before her". He holds her left hand with both hands and wets it with his tears…'. The quote used on the print, 'It is the last time Werther, you will never see me more', occurs two lines later, so the reviewer evidently knew his text. Northcote's print was quickly copied. One version was published at Augsburg by J.J. Haid and Son. Gaetano Canali, who worked for the Remondini of Bassano, produced a smaller, cruder engraving and the Remondini changed the name of the painter from Northcote to 'Angelica Kauffman'. She was a much more famous artist than Northcote, a woman, and a Swiss, all of which would help the Remondini's salesmen to place the print in their particular markets.[19] A false painter's name was one danger, a false engraver's name another. Giuseppe Wagner warned customers against copies 'col falso nome del Bartolozzi', a danger that need not concern them with prints bought from him. There were a great number of these. Wolfgang Cillessen has discovered a contract between Domenicus Zimmermann, a printseller from Hanover, and an engraver named Salietto from Rotterdam to copy Hamlet and his mother, the Sorrows of Werter by Bartolozzi, a pair of prints of Werther by Thomas Ryder and two of cupids by Knight. There was evidently a thriving market for cheaper versions of these decorative but very expensive English prints, as well as for the real thing.

Political satire was always a specialised sector of the print trade. In the 1740s it was still sold primarily along with topical prints from little shops and booths around Temple Bar and Westminster. These prints were usually made by and for the politically active and sold together with small portraits and other newsworthy prints like views of battles or theatrical novelties. Anonymous political insiders and hired professional authors both wrote pamphlets and there is no reason to suppose that the pattern with prints differed from the pamphlets sold alongside them. William Holland initially shared premises in Drury Lane with a pamphlet seller and was eventually

18 Stephen Gwynn, Memorials of an Eighteenth-Century Painter: James Northcote (London 1898), pp. 199–200.

19 A representative selection of Remondini copies of English prints can be seen in Antonio Suntach, Un incisore del settecento tra Bassano, Roma e l'Europa (Bassano del Grappa, 2012).

arrested for selling a pamphlet by Thomas Paine.[20] Until about 1780 political prints were usually relatively small, usually priced at 6d, hawked about the streets of London and sold in specialised shops. Where they were collected, it was as an alternative commentary on historical events.[21] They were quite distinct in size, kind and ambition from Hogarth's 'modern moral subjects', which were much larger and priced typically at about 3s. 6d., belonging by price and presentation to the genre of 'fine art' prints.

Caricature proper arrived in England from Italy in the mid-eighteenth century through the designs of Pier Leone Ghezzi published by Arthur Pond (1742). Thomas Patch resided in Florence and made Italian-style caricatures of British grand tourists (1769). In London caricature drawing – the exaggeration of physical features – caught on as a fashionable pastime for amateur artists, and Mary Darly became the outstanding publisher of caricatures, while her husband Matthew had always etched political prints. Both often executed and published designs supplied to them by amateurs and in 1779 they advertised that 'Ladies or Gentlemen furnishing hints or sketches will have them duly honoured, and published (if required) with the utmost secrecy and Dispatch' (Illustration 2).

The Darly shop was the cradle of 'golden age' satire: they published the earliest work of both Bunbury and Gillray. Amateurs continued to supply ideas and drawings to caricaturists and to get their own caricatures published, for in the next decade Samuel William Fores advertised 'Gentlemens designs [sic] executed gratis', and the manuscript correspondence in the British Library demonstrates amply the degree to which amateurs supplied Gillray with commissions.[22] It was not long before caricature was applied to the political print – a development usually attributed to the amateur artist George Townshend, but his caricatures remained small and cheap. The big change in the appearance of caricatures came with a great increase in size and the application of colour and that development should probably be associated with the comic drawings of Henry Bunbury, which became very fashionable in the 1770s and 1780s (Illustration 3). His principal publishers, James Bretherton, who was also a drawing master, and William Dickinson, established shops in Bond Street, in the fashionable residential area of the West End and the caricature printsellers also moved in this direction during the 1780s. Elizabeth d'Archery had a shop in St James's Street by 1782, Samuel William Fores set up in Piccadilly in 1782, Hannah Humphrey was in Bond Street probably by 1783, and William Holland moved to Oxford Street about 1787. William Humphrey and Rudolph Ackermann remained on the principal shopping street, the Strand, rather further East. Their choice of location implies that Bretherton, Dickinson, Humphrey and Fores all expected the same fashionable, wealthy

20 See David Alexander, Richard Newton and English caricature in the 1790s (Manchester, 1998).

21 Naval Miscellany IV, Naval Records Society XCII, p. 250: Boscawen to wife 13 Sep 1756 on Byng affair: 'I have made a collection of all the Gazettes, prints, songs etc., sent me about this affair and intend to bind them together'.

22 Public Advertiser, 1 January 1779, London; see BM Satires 7125, by anonymous, published by Samuel William Fores "The Scotch Arms" (1787); Gillray papers BL Add. Mss 27337.

Illustration 2: *Mary Darly's shop at 39 Strand, The Macaroni Print Shop,* after Edward Topham, published by Darly (London, 1772). BM J,5.46 © Trustees of the British Museum

people to buy their products, and the move of the printsellers to the aristocratic West End was followed by an increase in the size, price and colourfulness of their product.

All print shops displayed the latest publications in their windows but caricature shops drew larger crowds than most, generating numerous complaints about the inconvenience of getting past and the danger of pickpockets. To some extent this may have increased the social range of the audience.

Several caricature printsellers had exhibition rooms where, for a 1s. entrance fee, or by buying one of the products, visitors could admire an array of prints. Holland's opened in 1788 and Richard Newton drew a view of it soon after the French Revolution (Illustration 4). Among the fashionable clientele depicted, several of the ladies wore tricoleur ribbons to indicate their pro-revolutionary sympathies. Holland's prices are known from a surviving broadsheet and a number of advertisements giving long lists of priced stock.[23] These show that prices had risen substantially from the mid-cen-

23 William Holland, Catalogue of humorous Prints, &c. reproduced in Simon Turner, William Holland's Satirical Print Catalogues, 1788–1794, in: *Print Quarterly,* XVI (1999), pp. 127–36. The catalogue was found in the collection formed by Lars von Engeström (1751–1826) in a volume called 'A Collection of various papers that serve to give an idea of the manners and habits of the English People collected in the years 1794 and 1795'. A number of advertisements are discussed in David Alexander, Richard Newton and English Caricature in the 1790s, Manchester 1998. A further series appeared in the society newspaper, *The World* (London 1787–94).

Illustration 3: *The Caricaturer's Stock in Trade,* published by William Holland (London, 1786). BM 1868,0808.5587 © Trustees of the British Museum

tury sixpence. Holland's ranged from one shilling for a very small Rowlandson to a guinea for long ones printed from several plates. His standard price for his smaller prints was 2s. plain, but larger prints cost considerably more. Rudolph Ackermann's prices ranged from 1s. to 7s., with 2s. also as standard.[24]

During the 1800s a number of other caricature publishers set up in the City and their businesses had a slightly different orientation, often but by no means always giving more space to social than political satire, and generally selling for a cheaper price. The biggest of them, Thomas Tegg sold his cruder prints for a standard price of

24 Rudolph Ackermann, A Catalogue of Various Prints (London 1805) and SLUB Dresden h. 37, 4°, no. 6.

Illustration 4: Richard Newton, *Holland's Exhibition of drawings,* drawing (London, 1794). BM 1876,0510.764 © Trustees of the British Museum

1s., advertising that 'Noblemen, Gentlemen, &c. wishing to ornament their Billiard or other Rooms, with Caricatures may be supplied 100 per cent. cheaper at Tegg's Caricature Warehouse.' It is interesting, though not necessarily accurate, that even Tegg's advertisement was addressed to 'Noblemen, Gentlemen, &c.'[25] In 1811 John Fairburn started publishing caricatures from shops in Blackfriars and Ludgate Hill, having previously published very cheap prints from the Tower Minories. In the same year John Johnston opened a 'cheap caricature warehouse' in Cheapside and the satirical journal the Scourge was launched with caricature plates. Their output, which included savage attacks on the Prince Regent, was aimed at a much broader audience in London and the provinces and sold for lower prices. By this stage caricature had established itself as an important mainstream branch of the print trade.

About 1790 caricaturists began to be sold as artistic personalities. The comic artist William Henry Bunbury paved the way in this respect, but William Holland cultivated the separate identities of his various artists, promoting new prints as the work of an artist whose last production had been well received. By 1794 he offered the oeuvres of particular artists for libraries: 'Compleat Collections of the Works of Hogarth, Rowlandson, Bunbury, Byron, Woodward, Newton and Nixon, made up into Volumes,

25 'New publications by Thomas Tegg' in *Chesterfield Travestie; or a school for modern manners* (London 1808); ('only at 1s. each, equal to any, and superior to most, published at double the price.').

in a few Days after the Order is given.'[26] It is interesting that he could not supply Gillray – presumably only Hannah Humphrey could do that (Illustration 5). Holland also offered to make up more general compilations, and had done so for the Prince of Wales and the Duke of York. The Swedish envoy, Lars von Engeström, was another of Holland's customers, as was the Austrian envoy Count Starhemberg, who formed a large collection of caricatures. In 1814 the *Morning Post* carried an advertisement for:

> An extensive Collection of rare and valuable CARICATURE PRINTS, in twenty folio volumes, and the original works of Hogarth, bound uniformly, with the Works of Austen, R. West, Boyne, Bartolozzi, Bretherton, Collins, Sayers, T. Hook, Lord Townsend, Byron, O'Keefe, Woodward, Williams, Rowlandson, Gillray, Bunbury, and all the celebrated Satirists of the last century, forming a complete Political and Historical Elucidation of that period.[27]

High prices set limits on the circulation of caricatures and so also, probably, did the print run. Evidence is scarce, but a plausible guess is that in most instances print-sellers aimed at a similar total to pamphlet sellers – about 500 for a first edition. Where demand continued plates were reworked or in extreme cases new plates were engraved. On a number of occasions Samuel William Fores published copies of prints by James Gillray that had been published by Hannah Humphrey (Illustration 6). This infringed copyright law, yet he went unpunished, perhaps because no customer of Hannah Humphrey would stoop to buy a Gillray idea that had not been etched by Gillray. Johann Christian Hüttner, who had probably spoken to Gillray, wrote that 'because a caricature is not the kind of thing one would care to go to law about, Gillray puts up with this piracy, without attempting to protect his property'.[28]

In urban contexts the market for cheaper caricatures was wide, but while it might normally include middling tradesmen, it excluded the labouring classes. Only in exceptional circumstances were caricatures aimed at wide, 'popular' consumption. In 1792 the Crown and Anchor club sold *The Contrast,* a loyalist caricature, for 3d. plain or 6d. coloured, or 100 for a guinea plain. With such a cheap prices they sought to extend the normal market. The offer of 100 for a guinea was probably designed to encourage the affluent to give them away.[29]

Caricatures, then, were a peculiar product. Very much a part of elite culture but often violently offensive, they were, to outsiders, quintessentially expressive of British liberty and freedom of speech. Foreigners were fascinated and by the time of the French revolution there is some evidence that caricatures were being exported in significant numbers like other English prints. The most frequently quoted evidence

---

26 Alexander, op. cit., p. 44, Turner, op. cit., p. 128.

27 *Morning Post,* 8th March 1814, London, sale by Harry Phillips.

28 *London und Paris* 18 (Weimar 1806), pp. 7–10; Diana Donald and Christiane Banerji, Gillray Observed: The Earliest Account of his Caricatures in *London und Paris* (Cambridge, 1999), p. 246.

29 On this vexed issue see Eirwen Nicholson, Consumers and Spectators: The Public of the Political Print in Eighteenth-Century England, in: *History* 81 (January 1996), pp. 5–21.

Illustration 5: James Gillray after John Sneyd, *Hannah Humphrey's shop at 27 St James's Street, Very Slippy Weather,* published by Humphrey (London, 1808). BM 1851,0901.1248
© Trustees of the British Museum.

Illustration 6: Samuel William Fores, Samuel William Fores's shop at 50 Piccadilly, Folkestone Strawberries, published by Fores (London, 1810). BM 1868,0808.7949 © Trustees of the British Museum

is that of Pastor Wendeborn of the Lutheran Church in Ludgate, whose comments were published in 1791. He insisted that, like other English prints, caricatures went 'in great quantities over to Germany, and from thence to the adjacent countries.' He remarked on the oddness of it: 'This is the more singular and ridiculous, as very few of those who pay dearly for them, know anything of the characters and transactions which occasioned such caricatures.'[30]

It was not only the characters and transactions that posed problems for foreigners. Few of them spoke much English – although in some areas, such as Germany, knowledge of English was increasing fast. Few caricatures bore bilingual inscriptions. Moreover, a substantial proportion of caricatures relied to some considerable extent on verbal humour for their comic impact. Some prints no doubt seemed more suitable for export than others, but the language barrier does not seem to have been thought insuperable.

Like other printsellers, the caricature publishers sought to interest those making up cargoes for ships or taking out a little private venture. William Holland advertised that 'Merchants, Captains of Ships, and others who buy to export, will be allowed a

30 Gebhard Friedrich August Wendeborn, A View of England towards the close of the Eighteenth Century (London, 1791), I, pp. 190–92 and II, pp. 213–14.

considerable Discount'. Thomas Tegg also tried to attract international traders to his Cheapside warehouse with 'Merchants and Captains of Ship's supplied Wholesale for Exportation.'[31] Rudolph Ackermann also offered the normal discount to overseas traders: 'Merchants and Ship Captains supplied on reasonable terms'. Inevitably, prints left England by sea. The typical routes into Germany were along the Rhein, or through Bremen and the Weser, or Hamburg and the Elbe. British goods generally entered Italy through Livorno, while Russian goods went by ship to St Petersburg. However, merchants took English caricatures to much more unlikely locations, and caricatures bought as a venture might be bound for colonial rather than European markets. In 1793, the gentlemen travelling with Ambassador Staunton to China were surprised to find English caricatures on sale in Rio de Janiero.[32] One of these gentlemen was Johann Christian Hüttner, tutor to Staunton's son, who, when he returned, would become the close friend of Rudolph Ackermann and the principal channel for promoting Gillray in Germany through his articles for the journal *London und Paris*.

If one method of export was to sell groups of prints to those sending cargoes abroad as a venture, another was the establishment of a regular correspondence with foreign printsellers. This was the normal pattern in the upper reaches of the print trade, where prints were sold to collectors. The journal and letters of the engraver and art-dealer Johann Georg Wille demonstrate that in Paris he was at the centre of an extensive network of printsellers, artists and collectors, with correspondents all over the German- and French-speaking world. Some elements of the networks of London printsellers can be reconstructed, but little is known at present about those of the caricature printsellers.

Foreigners residing in London often acted as agents for their friends at home. By 1800, 30,000 Germans were living in the metropolis and the Hanoverian community was particularly large. A few Germans set up as printsellers in London, but only Rudolph Ackermann sold caricatures (Illustration 7). A considerable number of artists, chiefly from Germany, Russia and Italy, were sent to train in London to learn British methods of printmaking and printselling. Johann Heinrich Ramberg of Hanover was a talented caricaturist who did some work for Fores, and prints produced by these artists had a natural market in their home countries. For their English employers the connection often provided the channel through which to do business there.

Newspapers and periodicals helped to let people know what was available. The editor of the *World*, a newspaper in which William Holland advertised repeatedly, claimed that his paper was sold in Versailles, Paris, Brussels and Flanders. It is possible that to some degree advertisements placed in English newspapers were seen by foreign eyes, especially the eyes of the courtiers and government officials who collected prints. Advertisements and reviews of English caricatures in European publications seem to have been unusual but there were exceptions. In 1787 Johann Wilhelm

31 Advertisement in Thomas Tegg, *Chesterfield Travestie*, London 1808.
32 David Macpherson, op. cit., (1805), p. 184 citing Embassy to China, v, i (1792), p. 177.

Illustration 7: Augustus Pugin and Thomas Rowlandson, *Interior of Rudolph Ackermann's Repository of Arts,* 101 Strand, published by Ackermann (London, 1809). BM Heal,100.7 © Trustees of the British Museum

von Archenholz, a Prussian soldier who passed the 1770s in England, established a remarkable periodical in Hamburg. His English-language *British Mercury* ran for four years, discussing cultural affairs and carried some advertisements for prints including caricatures. In 1787, for instance, it noticed five caricatures published by 'Fores, satirist, No. 3 Piccadilly' including Gillray's *Ancient Music* and *Dido Forsaken,* both published in May of that year. The following year von Archenholz was scathingly critical of *Bunbury's Long Minuet at Bath,* 'where in the space of six feet there is about as much wit and satire as Hogarth would have put into six inches'.[33] That year William Remnant set up an English bookshop at the Gänsemarkt, Hamburg, as an importer of English books as well as maps, globes and copperplate prints. He advertised in the *British Mercury* that orders for such items would be 'punctually and expeditiously executed; and sent to any Distance, on previous Security being given for the Payment on Delivery at the Post'.[34]

In 1792 Johann Georg Meusel's 'Museum für Künstler und für Kunstliebhaber', published in Mannheim, also listed New English Caricatures from 1791 published the previous autumn.[35] These were a mixed group, published by Humphrey, by Fores

33 Johann Wilhelm von Archenholz (ed.), *British Mercury,* I (Hamburg 1787), pp. 378–79 and IV (1788), p. 186.

34 *British Mercury,* IV (Hamburg 1788), p. 31.

35 Johann Georg Meusel (ed.), *Museum für Künstler und für Kunstliebhaber* XVII (Mannheim 1792), p. 364.

and anonymously, mostly relating to the marriage of the Duke of York with Princess Frederica, daughter of the King of Prussia, including *The Introduction* and *Fashionable Contrasts*. Most importantly, from 1798 the Weimar-based journal *London und Paris* published a long series of copies of caricatures and commentaries on them from originals sent from London by Johann Christian Hüttner. The first issue of the journal carried an article on 'Gillray and Mrs Humphrey', and one of the last to be published before Napoleon's continental blockade and censorship closed down the journal was a eulogy of Gillray written by Hüttner.

Gillray's publisher, Hannah Humphrey, was well equipped for international trade but little is known at present of her activities. Her elder brother William abandoned a career as an engraver and publisher in favour of dealing in prints. Another specialist in this field, James Caulfield, reported that Humphrey 'carried on this trade for many years with great success, and imported more curious English Portraits than any other individual, and was of the greatest service to the collections of the late Earl of Orford, Sir William Musgrave, Messrs Bull, Storer, Cracherode, Bindley, Tighe, Sykes, &c &c &c'.[36] In 1802 he was in Holland, where he did business with Charles Howard Hodges, an English mezzotint engraver residing in Amsterdam. He wrote to Gillray to ask for a supply of damaged prints and pairs of ovals to sell there, and it is plausible that when Hannah Humphrey sent prints abroad she used her brother's network of contacts. She might also have used those of her brother-in-law, the mineralogist Adolarius Jacob Forster (1739–1806), a leading dealer in minerals with shops in London and Paris and major interests in Spain and St Petersburg. His wife and his nephew and successor Henry Heuland (born Johannes Heinrich Heuland in Bayreuth) witnessed Gillray's will in 1807. Hannah's other brother, George, was an expert international dealer in shells and other natural curiosities.

Like many liberal Englishmen, James Gillray welcomed the French Revolution. At any rate such an attitude is strongly implied by his large 'fine art' engraving of *Le Triomphe de la Liberté en l'élargissement de la Bastille* (1790), dedicated 'à la Nation Françoise – par leurs respectuex [sic] admirateurs James Gillray & Robert Wilkinson'. The French-language inscription implies that Gillray and Wilkinson hoped for foreign sales. William Holland had already expressed similar views and a similar intention to export in *La Chute du Despotisme; The Downfall of Despotism* (1789). The following year he advertised that in his 'Caricature Exhibition Rooms' could be seen 'those Published in Paris on the French Revolution', showing that he could import French prints. Two years later, in Paris, Aaron Martinet opened a shop specialising in caricatures. He displayed them in his window in the English manner and it would be surprising if he did not stock English prints.

For some years after war broke out English goods seem to have been widely available in Paris despite official prohibition. In 1798 *London und Paris* remarked on the existence near the Théatre des Italiens of a shop prominently labelled 'Magasin des

36 *Calcographiana*, 1814, p. 6.

marchandises anglaises' and later in the year announced that a newly-opened print-shop in Paris stocked a large collection of English caricatures.[37] This may possibly have been the same enterprise that issued a catalogue in 1798/9 (an VII) of 'estampes et caricatures Anglaises exposés en vente à la grande galerie d'estampes etc au ci-devant couvent des Capucines, Place Vendôme'. The catalogue listed 313 imported English prints but no caricatures except a few prints after Bunbury that might have been given the name.[38] Certainly some did reach the frontier. Abraham Raimbach, returning from Paris to London in 1802 found himself obliged to wait in an anti-chamber of the French passport office at Calais that was decorated with caricatures by James Gillray of members of the Addington administration.[39]

Gillray was certainly familiar to continental artists and was regarded as the prince of satirists. The Swiss David Hess acknowledged his debt by calling himself 'Gillray junior', while the Berliner Johann Gottfried Schadow signed his anti-Napoleonic etchings ironically 'Gilrai a Paris'. Schadow was a friend of Böttiger so it is likely that he was familiar with *London und Paris* and he may well have been familiar with Gillray's own work for the same reason.[40]

Napoleon's Continental System ended all but clandestine trade with France, but it did not close all of continental Europe. Ackermann showed a sympathetic interest in Spanish affairs as early as February 1805 with *SPANISH COMFORT*, and when large parts of Spain joined the anti-Napoleonic struggle in 1808 Ackermann produced a number of caricatures on Spanish themes. After 1816 Spain and Latin America became extremely important markets for Ackermann (in 1826 his son George was a member of the Mexico City Cricket Club), but the foundations were probably laid around 1808. Some of Gillray's prints were sufficiently well known in Spain for Spanish copies to be published. These might have been British propaganda for Spanish consumption, although the ignorance of Swift demonstrated in the title of *El Rey de Brobdingnag y Gulliver Examinando largamente al Señor Napoleon* (in 'Gulliver's Travels' Gulliver is the Napoleon figure so he cannot be watching) suggests that it was a Spanish print.

Trade with Russia resumed after Napoleon fell out with Alexander if indeed it ever stopped. Newspaper advertisements and surviving examples provide clear evidence that English caricatures were imported and the many anti-Napoleonic caricatures produced by Russian artists between 1812 and 1814 show clear stylistic debts to British examples.[41] The Russian caricatures that were issued with government backing were

---

37 *London und Paris* II (Weimar 1798), pp. 161 and 387.

38 The catalogue, discovered by Peter Fuhring, was described by Antony Griffiths, English Prints in Eighteenth-century Paris, in: *Print Quarterly*, XXII (2005), p. 388.

39 Thomson Scott Raimbach (ed.), Memoirs and Recollections of the late Abraham Raimbach Esq., Engraver (London, 1843), pp. 104–05.

40 Antony Griffiths and Frances Carey, German Printmaking in the Age of Goethe (London, 1994), p. 170.

41 For Russian caricatures against Napoleon, the government's role in them and their relationship with English examples, see Marina Peltzer, From Propaganda to Trade: Russian and European Political

clearly directed at rallying the population and motivating them to resist Napoleon's invasion. A set of adaptations of Russian prints by Terebenev was etched by George Cruikshank for Hannah Humphrey in 1813. They were lettered in English and Russian, one also in German and French, indicating an intention to distribute them in Russia and Germany. Perhaps it was thought that British distribution networks were more extensive and efficient than Russian ones or that Cruikshank's prints were more sophisticated and effective than the originals. Whatever the reason, the English versions celebrating the Russian effort appear to have been intended for distribution in French- and German-speaking Europe. The lesson was presumably that if the Russians could resist and drive out Napoleon, so could others.

When Ackermann resumed trade with Germany after the Battle of Leipzig he imported German prints as well as exporting his own. With some pride he issued copies of Johann Michael Voltz's 'Corpse Head' called *A Hieroglyphic portrait of the Destroyer* and other German prints that were published in almost every country in Europe (Illustration 8). In his 'List of Caricatures Suitable to the Present Times; Just Published by R. Ackermann' these were presented along with twenty other caricatures of his Corsican bête noire, such as *The Two Kings of Terror; or Death and Bonaparte.* Also listed was a portrait of Ackermann's personal hero, 'a most striking Likeness and highly-finished engraving of Marshall Blucher, The Terror of Bonaparte'.

As Napoleon's grasp on power loosened, some English prints began to circulate in Holland with explanatory letterpress in Dutch. In December 1813 Ackermann celebrated the liberation of Holland with *The Sea is Open. Trade Revives* with lettering in English and Dutch. Copies of English prints even began to circulate in France with lettering in French. George Cruikshank's *The Corsican Shuttlecock* was copied as *Le Volant Corse* and the British Museum's impression is inscribed in a contemporary hand 'Cette Caricature et les Cinq Suivantes ont été faites en Angleterre.'[42]

---

prints in Napoleonic Time, in: Alberto Milano ed., Trade and Circulation of Popular Prints during the XVIII and XIX centuries, Rovereto, 2008, pp. 411–34. See also Marina Peltzer, Imagerie Populaire et Caricature: La Graphique Politique Antinapoléonienne en Russie et Ses Antécédents Pétrovien, in: *Journal of the Warburg and Courtauld Institutes* 48 (1985), pp. 189–221.

42 British Museum 1868,0808.12762.

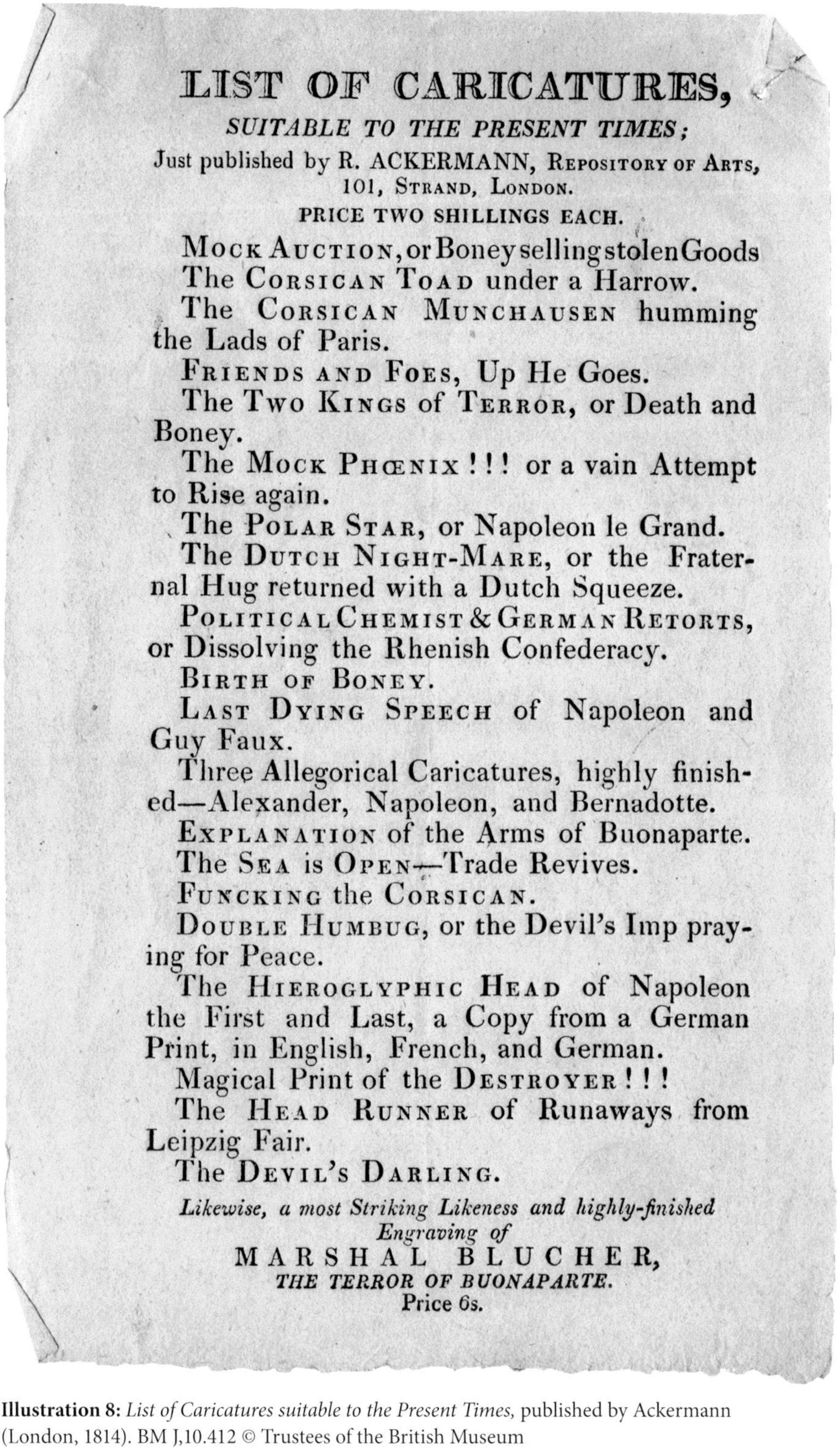

LIST OF CARICATURES,

SUITABLE TO THE PRESENT TIMES;

Just published by R. ACKERMANN, Repository of Arts,
101, Strand, London.

PRICE TWO SHILLINGS EACH.

Mock Auction, or Boney selling stolen Goods

The Corsican Toad under a Harrow.

The Corsican Munchausen humming the Lads of Paris.

Friends and Foes, Up He Goes.

The Two Kings of Terror, or Death and Boney.

The Mock Phœnix !!! or a vain Attempt to Rise again.

The Polar Star, or Napoleon le Grand.

The Dutch Night-Mare, or the Fraternal Hug returned with a Dutch Squeeze.

Political Chemist & German Retorts, or Dissolving the Rhenish Confederacy.

Birth of Boney.

Last Dying Speech of Napoleon and Guy Faux.

Three Allegorical Caricatures, highly finished—Alexander, Napoleon, and Bernadotte.

Explanation of the Arms of Buonaparte.

The Sea is Open—Trade Revives.

Funcking the Corsican.

Double Humbug, or the Devil's Imp praying for Peace.

The Hieroglyphic Head of Napoleon the First and Last, a Copy from a German Print, in English, French, and German.

Magical Print of the Destroyer!!!

The Head Runner of Runaways from Leipzig Fair.

The Devil's Darling.

Likewise, a most Striking Likeness and highly-finished Engraving of

MARSHAL BLUCHER,

THE TERROR OF BUONAPARTE.

Price 6s.

Illustration 8: *List of Caricatures suitable to the Present Times,* published by Ackermann (London, 1814). BM J,10.412 © Trustees of the British Museum

Brian Maidment

The Satirical Image. Politics and Periodicals 1820–1837

Das Hauptziel dieses Beitrags ist, anhand innovativer Beispiele den scheinbar einfachen Nachweis zu führen, wie zwanzig Jahre vor der Thronbesteigung von Queen Victoria begonnen wurde, das satirische Bild oder die Karikatur zu verwenden, um Zeitschriften und andere serielle Medien zu illustrieren und auch zu strukturieren.

The main aim of this paper is the apparently simple one of tracing, through consideration of some key innovative examples, the ways in which the satirical or comic image began to be used to illustrate – or indeed structure – periodicals and other forms of serial publication in the twenty years before the accession of Queen Victoria.

The caricature as it was understood and developed as a commodity in the late eighteenth century seems at first sight to stand at odds with the periodical idea. If the periodical form can be crudely characterised by its regularity of appearance, ease of production, cheapness, popularity, accessibility and brand identity, the caricature, in its single-plate identity at least, was generally expensive, occasional, opportunistic, relatively difficult to produce, sometimes even more difficult to de-code and interpret and, crucially, of a size and complexity that made it difficult to accommodate within the available periodical formats. So a putatively simple narrative of the genesis of the caricature magazine, which occurs precisely at that historical moment when comic image-making in Britain is negotiating its passage from the caricature to the cartoon, and from an essentially political vision to a broad scanning of the socio-cultural structure of the nation, requires more complex explorations of change, adaptation, and the forces at work within an energised but essentially volatile market-place for print culture.

Such forces derive from a wide variety of sources – changing theories of humour taking place in the 1820s and 1830s, where wit, allusiveness and complex iconographical and cultural references were beginning to be replaced by ideas of 'fun', 'humour', miscellaneity and the diversionary; a sense of the beginnings of a mass market for print culture, including visual culture, and a determination to freight traditional print genres like the song-book, the play-text and the almanack with a weighty cargo of graphic embellishment; the new availability of the lithograph as a reprographic medium, a medium that allows for greater immediacy and speed between the draughtsman making marks and the emergence of the image; and, crucially, the beginnings of the rise of the wood engraving into widespread acceptance as a form of reprographic practice in making images that to some extent cut across the cultural and economic barriers that had often separated highbrow and vernacular, vulgar and genteel, and had demarcated between wit and humour. And, in the 1820s and 1830s at least, a major consequence of the widespread adoption of the wood engraving as a mechanism for making and printing graphic images was the miniaturisation of the image, a shrinking that acknowledged both the shape and form of the boxwood block and the ability of the wood engraving to be printed as part of a typeset page surrounded, if required, by print.

The use of the term 'caricature magazine' was not new in the 1820s and 1830s. There had been publications called *The Caricature Magazine* published in the first two decades of the nineteenth century, most notably Thomas Tegg's massive reprinting project that assembled caricatures by the likes of Woodward, Rowlandson and the Cruikshanks into volume form with separate title pages.[1] But in these instances 'magazine' was used more in its military sense of a depot, repository or storehouse than as a declaration of periodicity. By the 1820s caricaturists had begun extensively to use small images to fill larger plates with panels of thematically related or, increasingly, gatherings of miscellaneous jokes and jottings, much of which was directed at the widening market for graphic scraps to fill albums or cover screens. Additionally, many caricaturists began to use short series (usually six-, eight- or twelve-plates) of oblong folio sheets, published in paper covers and usually focused round a single theme, as a method of publication rather than adhering to the single comic idea that usually structured late-eighteenth-century political caricature. All these formal developments can be understood as an acknowledgement of a changing market-place, and a recognition that caricature needed to be reinvented in order to remain commercially successful.

Additionally, there were magazines that drew on precedents from other areas of print culture to suggest how larger etched or engraved images might be integrated into serial forms. Perhaps the most persuasive example of ways in which traditional caricature used the central mechanism for such integration – the folding plate – comes from *The Attic Miscellany*, a periodical that was published between 1789 and 1792.[2] Each issue was prefaced by a folded engraved caricature by Samuel Collings to augment the smaller, separate-page copper engravings, usually of theatrical subjects, that were laid into the text of the magazine. Yet even here, where the caricature maintained something of its traditional size and shape, Collings's caricatures were in fact produced for earlier separate publication, and re-used to give panache and visual complexity to *The Attic Miscellany*, thus losing in the process something of their immediacy and satirical purpose.

---

1 *The Caricature Magazine, or Hudibrastic Mirror* 5 vols. (London, 1808–1809).

2 *The Attic Miscellany; and Characteristic Mirror of Men and Things* (London, 1789–1792). The use of 'mirror' in the title is an interesting foretaste of the widespread use of this term in later caricature magazines to suggest the ways in which caricature reflected back human folly to its consumers.

Nonetheless the use of folding plates which retained at least a remnant of the scale and impact of traditional caricature, as well as sustaining the etched or engraved reprographic mode that prohibited integration into the typeset page, proved a widespread mechanism for offering the visual appeal of large scale comic images. It was used across a wide range of relatively downmarket print genres, most notably comic annuals, song-books (many of which were first published in serial form and then re-published as volumes with the addition attraction of a multi-panelled, coloured frontispiece) and as books for children. Publishers of popular anthologies of songs like Oliver Hodgson or John Fairburn were especially active in commissioning engraved and coloured plates that were structured to include a number of images illustrating the miscellaneous contents of the volume they accompanied. By the mid-1830s even the tiniest 'Little Warbler' meanly produced by a provincial publisher might attempt some level of grandeur through a vivid, folding frontispiece, however crudely drawn (Illustration 1). Within these kinds of print genres, which sought wide popularity and which cut across distinctions between genteel and vernacular modes, visual hybridity in response to a widening market was frequently a defining characteristic. The widespread use of fold-out, engraved frontispieces, often brightly coloured, as a mechanism for providing small-sized volumes with a large and glamorous form of illustration, suggests that wily publishers were well aware of the traditional appeal and elevated status of the large-scale engraving, and remained keen through the 1820s and 1830s, just at the moment when the single-plate caricature tradition was stumbling, to bind in such plates to even extremely modest publications.

John Atkinson's plates for James Beresford's much reprinted *The Miseries of Human Life*, a key publication in founding a long tradition of comic anthologies of urban irritations and inconveniences, provides an interesting and complex example of the ways in which traditional caricature might be sustained and marketed through association with a printed text.[3] The first edition of Beresford's book was published in 1806 with a fold-out engraved frontispiece in a familiar late-eighteenth-century caricature idiom. The book was so successful that Beresford added a second volume in 1807, published again by William Miller as a two-volume set that replaced the fold-out frontispiece from the original edition with a prefatory stipple engraving in each volume, which, together with occasional diagrammatical, wood-engraved illustrations dropped into the text and engraved title pages, suggested an increasing encroachment of the visual, in a wide variety of reprographic forms, into the text. The continuing commercial potential of traditional caricature aimed at relatively wealthy collectors and connoisseurs was further and rapidly exploited by Beresford's publisher, William Miller, who brought out a paper-bound portfolio of *Sixteen Scenes Taken from the Miseries of*

3 James Beresford, The Miseries of Human Life (London, 1806). By 1807 the Miseries had been reprinted seven times, and enjoyed a new lease of life when later editions were published to accompany a second volume. These two volumes made up The Miseries of Human Life; or the Groans of Samuel Sensitive, and Timothy Testy; with a few supplementary sighs from Mrs. Testy.

Illustration 1: The Little Warbler, or Comic and English Song Book (Derby, n.d.). Engraved fold out frontispiece and title page. From the author's own collection

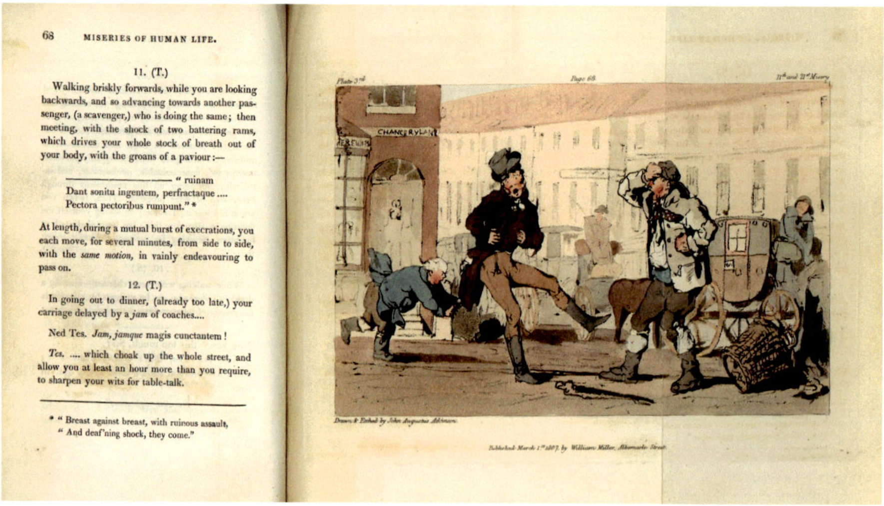

Illustration 2: A fold out etched illustration by J. A. Atkinson bound into an 1807 edition of J. D. Beresford's Miseries of Human Life. From the author's own collection

Human Life in 1807.[4] The textual visualisations were in this case in the form of etchings that could be hand-coloured for more extravagant purchasers, and later editions of the *Miseries* often bound in Atkinson's illustrations (Illustration 2).

These appropriations of traditional caricature formats and idioms to support serial publications nonetheless fall well short of anything that might properly be called a 'caricature magazine'. It was only in the early 1820s that the potentiality of a maga-

4 John Augustus Atkinson, Sixteen Scenes Taken from the Miseries of Human Life (London, 1807). Each of Atkinson's plates is accompanied by a page printing an appropriate 'Misery' and contains page references to the two volumes of Miseries, thus insisting on the textual origins of the 'miseries' idea.

zine in the modern sense that centred on satirical images began to be fully explored. *Duncombe's Miniature Caricature Magazine,* which began publication in 1821, offers a good starting place for discussion, although in the event the publication proves to be, in the tradition of Tegg's *Caricature Magazine,* less a magazine than a series of caricatures first issued as single plates. Duncombe's list at this time was an assemblage of inventive uses of the emergent genres of mass-circulation publishing, with an especial interest in small-scale 'songsters' or anthologies of popular songs, children's books and primers, and serialised song books illustrated with wood-engraved vignettes or fold-out engraved frontispieces. *Duncombe's Miniature Caricature Magazine* lasted for at least forty-nine issues, thus offering evidence for a continuing fondness for engraved single-plate images that offered complex and sometimes trenchant commentary on passing political and social events drawn using the traditional graphic vocabulary and comic tropes of eighteenth-century caricature. Nonetheless, like the *Caricature Magazine* it is an assembly or repository, published on an occasional or topical basis rather than as a regular serial.

There are, however, two significant elements of *Duncombe's Miniature Caricature Magazine* that suggest a movement towards more sustained serialisation. The first is the use of the word 'miniature' in Duncombe's title for the series, which suggests that the publisher recognised that the scale and expense of traditional caricature needed to be re-thought for a new, less genteel, less wealthy audience. In practice the level of miniaturisation involved was relatively modest – the prints in the *Miniature Caricature Magazine* are by no means tiny even if they represent a significant re-thinking of the caricature form and visual impact. Perhaps more significant was the way in which Duncombe, largely a publisher of song-books, play-texts and childrens' literature, marketed his 'magazine'. Here is an advertisement taken from volume 6 of *The Portfolio,* one of many weekly miscellanies form the 1820s that used simple wood engravings by way of illustration.

> SMALL CARICATURES
> Elegantly coloured, adapted for Scrap-Books, Comic Illustrations or Screens,
> DUNCOMBE'S MINIATURE CARICATURE MAGAZINE.
> N.B. This work is printed on fine, thick, drawing royal paper, and highly coloured in the best style: the size is nine inches long and eight wide: they are numbered, and so contrived, as to bind together in a volume, thus forming a never-ending fund of amusement, at a lower price than ever before offered to the public, and comprising one of the best collections of Caricatures ever published.
> Published in Parts at 1s. each in a neat printed wrapper, or in single numbers at 3d. each. Part 9 is just out.[5]

5 The Portfolio VI (London, 1828), p. 384.

It is interesting to see Duncombe here covering every possible market for his publications and especially the potential re-use of caricatures as scraps or decoration on furniture. But the important issue for my argument is his recognition of this publication as both cheap and as forming a *series* which might be bound into a sustained if not necessarily coherent volume. The use of multi-format issues is also important in suggesting a movement towards what might be called 'serial consciousness', in which a single issue, part issue and volume might all prove to be mechanisms for extending consumption and establishing temporal expectations, and the rhythm of serial consumption, in the consumers.

Despite these formal experiments in bringing together the caricature and pre-existing forms of print culture, the first recognisable caricature magazine is generally agreed to have been the seventeen folio issues of *The Glasgow Looking Glass* which became *The Northern Looking Glass* after five issues, and which was published in Glasgow between 1825 and 1826 (Illustration 3).[6] The artist was William Heath, a relatively well established comic draughtsman, and the magazine was produced lithographically, thus allowing freehand text to be drawn on the stone alongside or even around graphic content. The Glasgow University web-site notes 'each issue is laid out to imitate the make up and contents of a contemporary newspaper. The usual elements – such as advertisements and regular features, including digests of domestic and foreign news – are pictorially and punningly illustrated'. Yet the effect is more one of pastiche or even travesty rather than imitation of a newspaper. By this time in the mid-1820s, the nature and forms of comic image-making had been rapidly overtaken and indeed transformed by the availability of lithography and wood engraving as reprographic modes, and a major shift towards serialisation as a method of publishing was well underway. So it is hardly surprising that Heath used lithography to structure the large page of the *Northern Looking Glass. The Glasgow Looking Glass* was clearly a hybrid venture, more newspaper than magazine, more local than national, more socio-cultural than political, and comprised as much of comic illustrations as something that is recognisably a caricature. Of particular interest is the way that Heath used the characteristics of lithography to allow himself to combine freehand script, rather than typeset text, with illustration, thus permitting the construction of a complex page in which images of differing size and scale could be assimilated into the overall design. While the venture was short-lived and limited by its localness, nonetheless, the *Northern Looking Glass* pointed the way forward for cultural entrepreneurs and speculators in London who were increasingly aware of the periodical as a powerful attraction to its widening group of customers.

Inevitably it was a London entrepreneur, Thomas McLean, who found a way to translate the experimentation of the *Northern Looking Glass,* which had been expen-

---

6 The University of Glasgow Library has mounted an extremely useful web-site that offers a detailed account of *The Glasgow Looking Glass* and shows a good number of illustrations taken from the journal. See special.lib.gla.ac.uk/exhibns/month/june2005/html.

Illustration 3: The first issue of *Glasgow Looking Glass* (1825) illustrated in lithography by William Heath. By permission of University of Glasgow Library, Special Collections

sive and localised, into something approaching a sustainable commercial venture. Retaining the artist, (William Heath), most of the title *(The Looking Glass)*, and the reprographic mode (lithography), McLean's *Looking Glass* was launched in 1830 (Illustration 4).[7] It ran as a monthly until 1836, Heath giving way to Robert Seymour, and Seymour to Henry Heath as the magazine's artist.[8] Unlike its Glasgow predecessor, *The Looking Glass* showed relatively litle interest in combining text and image, and insisted on a close allegiance to the visual iconography and the gestural vocabulary of political caricature. Both of the large pages that formed each issue were built entirely out of visual material with only the speech bubbles and captions of traditional caricature by way of textual accompaniment. What was new about *The Looking Glass* was a recognition that the continuation of the political caricature tradition was dependent on its further developing its alliance with images that were more centrally concerned with social conduct, manners and the class pretensions and assumptions of the emergent middle classes. This is not to say, of course, that caricature had previously ignored socio-cultural topics, but rather that the juxtaposition of politics and manners as subjects for graphic comedy was in this instance rendered abrupt and visually confrontational through occupancy of the same issue or even page of the periodical.

But perhaps the key figure in the development of periodical formats for lithographed comic images, and indeed wood-engraved caricature as well, was the shadowy and perhaps politically radical Charles Jameson Grant, whose work may be characterised by relentless experimentation, feverish productivity and a willingness to work in any medium, mode or format that might enable him to become a force in the market-place.[9] There is no space to go into detail about Grant's considerable output of periodical illustrations here, nor is it easy to be clear about the extent of work produced by any particular draughtsmen for comic periodicals in this period. Many illustrations were published without an artist's or an engraver's signature. Magazines and their publishers made false claims about who their artists actually were, especially invoking the prestige associated with having 'Cruikshank' on the title page, or else hiding behind the generic contributions of 'leading artists'. A considerable number of projected illustrated comic magazines lasted for only a few, or even a single, issue. A considerable number of titles that can be found in publishers' advertisements during this period no longer exist in any known copy.[10] Accordingly, research in this area is never likely to be anything other than speculative about the range of comic publications available at any particular historical moment, although the confused mass

7 For an excellent, detailed and well informed study of the development of lithographed comic journals in the 1830s see Richard Pound's unpublished 2002 University of London Ph.D. thesis, Serial Journalism and the Transformation of English Graphic Satire 1830–36.

8 Ibid., pp. 126–140.

9 Richard Pound (ed.), C.J. Grant's Political Drama: A Radical Satirist Rediscovered (London, 1998).

10 See Joel Wiener, A Descriptive Finding List of Unstamped British Periodicals (London, 1970) for a major listing of periodicals, which includes the title of many periodicals with 'no known copy' available in libraries.

Illustration 4: Issue 15 of *The Looking Glass* (1st March 1831). From the author's own collection

of surviving magazines does provide evidence of a restlessly productive and market-driven explosion of interest in issuing humorous periodicals.

It is possible to say, however, that Grant was responsible for the bulk of the illustrations in at least the following serials: *The Caricaturist* (1831), *Clark's Weekly Dispatch* (1841), *Cleave's Picture Gallery of Grant's Comicalities* (1836), *Cockney Adventures and Tales of London Life* (1838), *Dawson's Magic* (1834), *Everybody's Album and Caricature Magazine* (1834–35), *Grant's Oddities* (1834), *John Bull's Picture Gallery* (1832), *Laughing Made Easy* (1832), *Lloyd's Political Jokes* (1836), *The Penny Satirist* (1836), *The Political Drama* (1833–35), *The Weekly Show-Up* (1832), *The Pickwick Songster* (1836–7), *The Penny Comic Magazine* (1837?) and *Whim-Whams* (1835).[11] For the reasons given above, this list is certainly incomplete. These publications cut across all kinds of mechanisms for publishing satirical images in serial form – unrelated single caricatures published within a regular series, large-page lithographed magazines comprising only or largely visual elements organised on to a complex, large-page, small-scale wood engravings subsumed with circumambient text, large-scale wood engravings drawn as crude outline woodcuts, and much else. But Grant's management of the lithograph as a key element in a caricature magazine is perhaps his most original contribution to the development of the illustrated periodical. *Everybody's Album* (Illustration 5) used a crowded page incorporating elements as diverse as tiny silhouettes and comic doodlings alongside large-scale satirical comment, in this issue a comic denunciation of the fashionable craze for smoking.[12] This large image retains the scale of traditional caricature within its framed border, yet the crowded content and range of targets suggests an ebullience that related to the energy of contemporary London streets. The use of a grid of four images that construct a rudimentary comic strip across the bottom of the page as well as the main image stand in obvious formal contrast to the free-floating images that occupy the centre of the page, images that make use of lithography's ability to fade the image into the page without the need for framing. Grant's lithographed work is especially notable for his interest in panelled sheets that use grid-like rules to structure and contain the mass of small images. *The Caricaturist* was in a very similar mode to *Everybody's Album* (Illustration 6) except in the use of larger-scaled images which, despite a deliberately simple and aesthetically negligent linear mode of construction, were aimed at making considerable visual impact more in the tradition of broadside images than sophisticated caricature. The main image illustrated here forms a damning critique of the cruelty of discipline in the navy.[13]

11 This list is based on Pound's research with additions drawn mainly from advertisements found in other magazines published at this time.

12 *Everybody's Album and Caricature Magazine*, first published by Kendrick and then Dawson, ran fortnightly for nearly forty issues, beginning on 1st January 1834.

13 *The Caricaturist*, 1st August 1832.

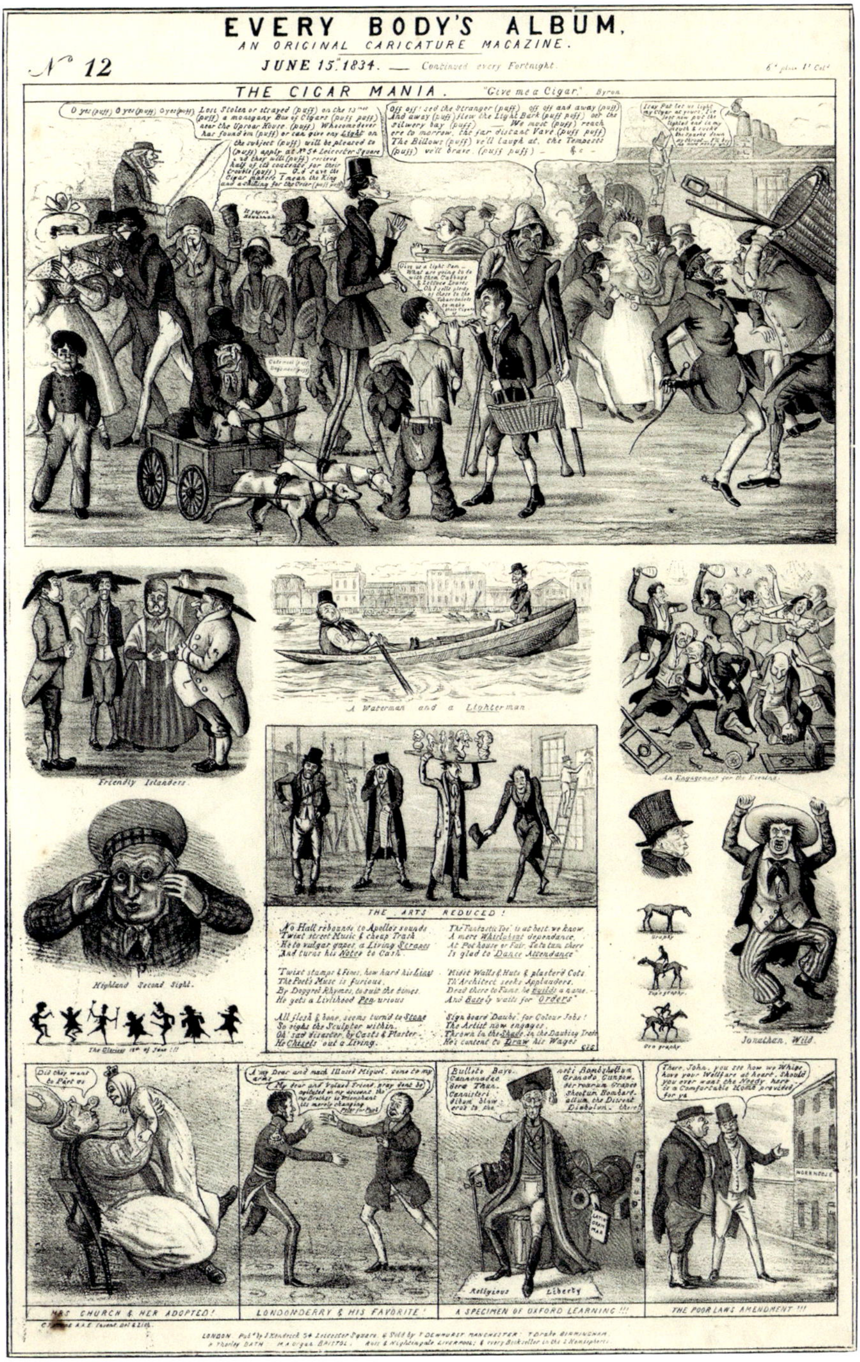

Illustration 5: Charles Jameson Grant, *Everybody's Album* 12 (London, 1st June 1834), lithograph. From the author's own collection

Illustration 6: Charles Jameson Grant, *The Caricaturist* 13 (London, 1st August 1832), lithograph. From the author's own collection

It is possible to regard these large-page, multi-panelled, lithographed and seemingly miscellaneous caricature magazines of the early 1830s as essentially deriving from a wish to preserve as much of a tradition of political caricature as possible while at the same time acknowledging the changed circumstances of the market for comic visual culture. Such acknowledgement came in the recognition of the growth of a strong market for small-scale scraps, in the awareness that social satire and the comedy of manners had an increasing appeal to consumers, and through growing exploitation of the characteristics of lithography (speed of production, the ability to inscribe plates with a written text, an ability to accommodate both large- and small-scale images of any shape).

The evolution of wood engraving in the early 1830s into what would quickly become the dominant mechanism for illustrating humorous periodicals derives from quite different sources, and foregrounds subversion of the demotic and vernacular into something more genteel as well as a recognition of the role that wood engraving, especially in comic form, was playing in the commercially and culturally successful development of other genres of illustrated serial publication. These genres comprised not just those cultural formations that bridged between the vernacular and the genteel – song-books, play texts, and children's literature most obviously – but also newer ones more closely associated with the 'march of intellect' and the transformation of the social structure through mass literacy. One such genre was the 'jeux d'esprit' – the reprinting of a short classic text, usually in verse, in small size pamphlet form illustrated with sophisticated, full–page, comic wood engravings by the likes of Robert Cruikshank, Thomas Jones and Robert Seymour.[14] Another comprised the mass of cheap, weekly 'information' magazines that arose in the 1820s, each issue illustrated on its front page with a wood-engraved vignette that, while most frequently informative rather than diversionary, increasingly made use of comic images to lighten its didactic purposes.[15] One obvious example is *The Casket,* published in the late-1820s by Benjamin Steill and making extensive use of comic images by artists such as Seymour and Robert Cruikshank, images often drawn from other publications and not evidently relevant to the text of the magazine, to attract potential customers.[16] A third was the increasing range

14 See Brian Maidment, Comedy Caricature and the Social order 1820–1850 (Manchester, 2013), pp. 73–74 for an account of this print sub-genre. The notorious publisher William Kidd, who was less than honest about who had illustrated his publications, was a leading figure in developing this format.

15 For overviews of the 'information miscellanies' see Jonathan R. Topham, 'The Mirror of Literature, Amusement and Instruction and cheap miscellanies in early nineteenth-century Britain' in: *Science in the Nineteenth Century Periodical:* Reading the Magazine of Nature, ed. Geoffrey Cantor (Cambridge, 2004), pp. 67–90 and Brian Maidment 'Dinners or Desserts? – Miscellaneity, Knowledge and Illustration in Magazines of the 1820s and 1830s', *Victorian Periodicals Review* 43, no. 4 (Winter 2010), pp. 353–387.

16 The publishing history of *The Casket* is confusing in ways characteristic of illustrated magazines at this time.

of texts which offered a kind of proto-realist social investigation through the form of urban sketches, again produced in small formats appropriate to the full-page vignette wood engraving, and built up of short literary and visual forays into the picaresque metropolis. Yet such publications were not innocent of political content, and often contained something beyond the picturesque in their depiction of the urban lower classes. George Cruikshank was especially adept at combining finely conceived and executed comic wood engravings with a compassionate awareness of the energy and visual interest of the everyday life of urban streets. *Mornings in Bow Street* and *Sunday in London,* both collections of verbal and graphic sketches of the lower reaches of London life, provide obvious examples of his superbly finished and densely linear work in this mode.[17]

The assimilation of these new sources and influences, none immediately or specifically derived from political caricature, into a wide variety of wood-engraved illustrated comic periodical literature in the early 1830s is a fascinating subject of study. To suggest some of the variety of approaches possible for the artist, publisher and editor by this time, it is worth looking briefly at a couple of solutions offered by the indefatigably inventive C.J. Grant. In *The Penny Satirist* (Illustration 7) a relatively small image using the graphic codes of traditional caricature adapted for the cruder if vigorous linearity of wood engraving has been inscribed into a large multi-columned page that speaks of the newspaper on the one hand and the vernacular broadside on the other. In a different mode, Grant's extensive series of 'Political Dramas', published by G. Drake in 1834 and 1835 (Illustration 8), made a spectacular subversion of the wood engraving from tinyness into hugeness, and drew on long traditions of images aimed at public display to put across Grant's extended critique of 'old corruption'. Frequently associated with the radical press Grant's politics remain nonetheless difficult to assess, with his continuing hatred of manifestations of state oppression to some extent compromised by his equally sustained distaste for the mass of the people. Grant's wood-engraved political commentary contained within periodicals did to some extent rework this reprographic medium in the direct tradition of political caricature, as did Robert Seymour's celebrated vignette illustrations for a range of publications such as, most famously, *Figaro in London* but also for a wide range of topical political periodicals and ephemera issued by progressive publishers like William Strange, Benjamin Steill and Effingham Wilson.[18] Much work remains to be done on this interconnected group of politically engaged publishers.

---

17 John Wight's Mornings at Bow Street (London, 1824) was a collection of short narratives derived from some of the more picturesque cases that came before the magistrates at Bow Street, which suggested the variety as well as the hardships of lower class urban life. The same author's Sunday in London (London, 1833) was a polemical pamphlet written to oppose sabbatarian attacks on the freedoms of working people to enjoy themselves.

18 *Figaro* in London, initially edited by Gilbert à Beckett and published by William Strange, ran from 1832 to 1839 and formed an obvious predecessor to the forms of illustration developed by Punch in the early 1840s.

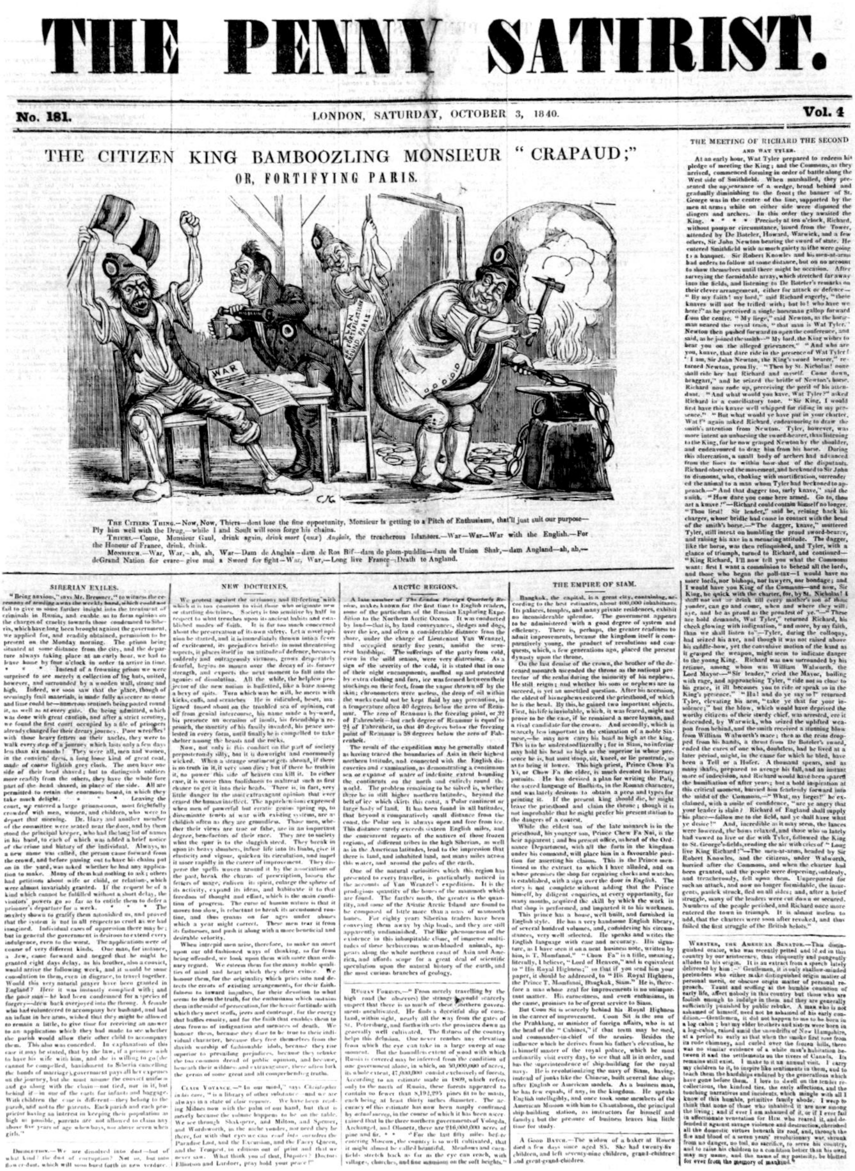

THE PENNY SATIRIST.

No. 181. LONDON, SATURDAY, OCTOBER 3, 1840. Vol. 4

THE CITIZEN KING BAMBOOZLING MONSIEUR "CRAPAUD;"

OR, FORTIFYING PARIS.

The Citizen Thing.—Now, Now, Thiers—dont lose the fine opportunity, Monsieur is getting to a Pitch of Enthusiasm, that'll just suit our purpose—Ply him well with the Drug,—while I and Soult will soon forge his chains.

Thiers.—Come, Monsieur Gaul, drink again, drink *mort* (*aux*) *Anglais*, the treacherous Islanders.—War—War—War with the English.—For the Honour of France, drink, drink.

Monsieur.—War, War,—ah, ah, War—Dam de Anglais—dam de Ros Bif—dam de plom-puddin—dam de Union Shak,—dam Angland—ah, ah,—deGrand Nation for evare—give moi a Sword for fight—War, War,—Long live France—Death to Angland.

SIBERIAN EXILES.

NEW DOCTRINES.

ARCTIC REGIONS.

THE EMPIRE OF SIAM.

THE MEETING OF RICHARD THE SECOND AND WAT TYLER.

Illustration 7: Charles Jameson Grant, wood engraved illustration to *The Penny Satirist* vol. 4, no. 181 (London 3rd October 1840). From the author's own collection

But even politically aware satirists like Grant were aware that socio-cultural subjects were by the early 1830s rapidly displacing the specifically political as the focus of interest for the wider circulation of satirical images, and that the relatively small

Illustration 8: Charles Jameson Grant, The Political Drama No. 128 (London: G. Drake c. 1833–34), wood engraving. From the author's own collection

vignette wood engraving located within or alongside the typeset page had to a large extent ousted the single-plate, topical, engraved, etched or even lithographed caricature, and was evidently more suited to the demands of frequent, serial publication. It is at this moment, too, that artists who had their strong initial training as wood engravers began to appear widely as comic draughtsmen, thus challenging with their expertise the productions of artists like George Cruikshank who had had to adapt to wood engraving later in their careers. Robert Seymour offers an interesting example of a jobbing wood engraver who served a long apprenticeship in that medium throughout the late-1820s with the publishers Knight and Lacey, a firm that specialised in the publication of the new 'information' journals and miscellaneous gatherings of anecdotes.[19] This new generation of artists – Kenny Meadows, John Leech and Seymour among them – were gathered together by the sporting weekly journal *Bell's Life in London* between 1827 and 1832 (Illustration 9) to produce comic images of urban types and metropolitan street encounters, images that were dropped into large newspaper-type sheets and which form an important predecessor for traditions of urban investigation largely expressed as 'sketches', that emerged in the 1840s and 1850s.

19 Maidment, op. cit. (2013), chap. 5.

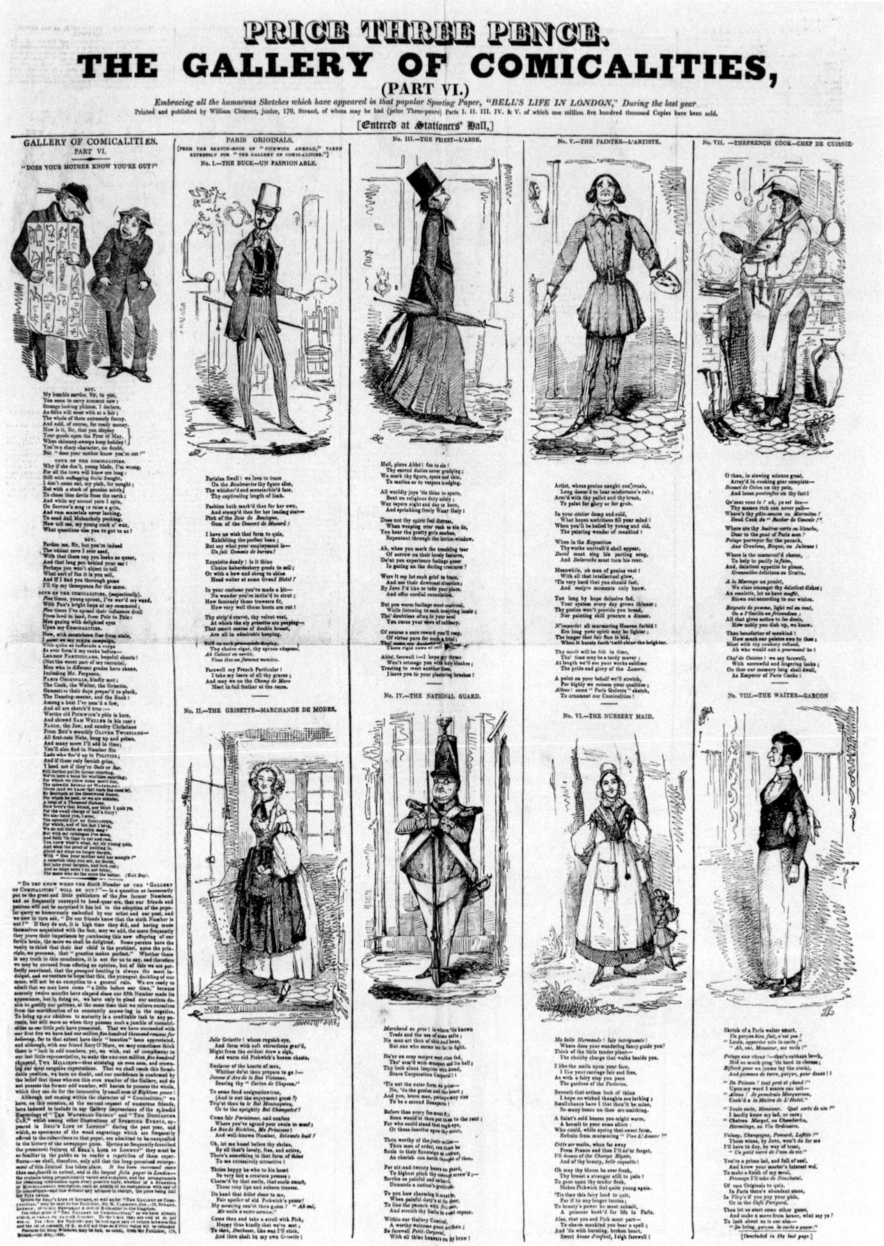

PRICE THREE PENCE.

THE GALLERY OF COMICALITIES,

(PART VI.)

Embracing all the humorous Sketches which have appeared in that popular Sporting Paper, "BELL'S LIFE IN LONDON," During the last year.

[Entered at Stationers' Hall.]

GALLERY OF COMICALITIES. PART VI.

"DOES YOUR MOTHER KNOW YOU'RE OUT?"

PARIS ORIGINALS.

No. I.—THE BUCK—UN FASHIONABLE.

No. II.—THE GRISETTE—MARCHANDE DE MODES.

No. III.—THE PRIEST—L'ABBE.

No. IV.—THE NATIONAL GUARD.

No. V.—THE PAINTER—L'ARTISTE.

No. VI.—THE NURSERY MAID.

No. VII.—THE FRENCH COOK—CHEF DE CUISINE.

No. VIII.—THE WAITER—GARCON

Illustration 9: The Gallery of Comicalities, *a re-published gathering of illustrations and articles taken from Bell's Life in London* (c. 1836). From the author's own collection

The extent to which such small-scale, rapidly drawn, wood-engraved comic images depicting day-to-day social intercourse had come to dominate the market for humorous graphic publications can be gauged from the knowledge that no less than five magazines of this kind bearing the title of 'comic magazine' appeared in 1832 alone. William Marshall was producing a weekly *New Comic Magazine* with 'numerous original comic engravings', the title page claimed, by 'R.Seymour' (Illustration 10). At some point this magazine seemed to have become *The Comic Magazine,* although by this time the illustrations were claimed to have originated from 'R.Cruickshank & c.', and the text from 'the most popular comic writers of the day'. Marshall relaunched this format, in an extremely debased form, with *The Penny Comic Magazine* in 1837. Lower still in the market was *The Penny Comic Magazine of an Amorous, Clamorous, Uproarious, and Glorious Society, for the Diffusion of Grins,* which seemed unable to sustain the entertaining satirical critique of *The Penny Magazine* much beyond its title. Little better could be expected from the ever energetic publisher of penny-issue fiction Edward Lloyd, whose short-lived 1d. weekly, *The Weekly Penny Comic Magazine; or, Repertory of Wit and Humour* may have been edited by T.P. Prest. Then there was the much more expensive 6d. weekly periodical called *The Original Comic Magazine* issued by the prolific publisher of song books, play texts and other downmarket serials, John Duncombe. The extent of the publishers' battle to annexe a single title suggests something of the frantic competition to serve up graphic humour in a cheap periodical form in the early eighteen thirties.

The activities of Gilbert à Beckett, the editor of the most sustained and literary *Comic Magazine* which ran to four volumes published between 1831 and 1834 and was illustrated by wood engravings by Robert Seymour, gives a further sense of the frantic energy, endless inventiveness and low success rate of illustrated comic magazines in the early 1830s. À Beckett was famously hyperactive but, with the possible exception of *Figaro in London,* seldom successful progenitor of periodicals of every kind. Although hardly fair or objective, Alfred Bunn's famous diatribe, the 1847 *A Word with Punch,* contained a withering critique of a Beckett's editorial career. Characterising à Beckett as 'Mr. Sleekhead' and citing his 1834 bankruptcy petition, Bunn concluded: Editor of thirteen periodicals and lessee of a theatre into the bargain! And all total failures! Poetry, prose, wit, humour, conceit, slander, sarcasm, and every order of ribaldry going for nothing! Where *has* been the public taste? – the people ought really to be ashamed of themselves for persisting in not buying so much genuine genius!…What? *The Wag! The Thief! The Ghost! The Lover!* Nay, even *The 'Terrific' Penny Magazine!* and *Poor Richard's Journal!* all passed over by the cold and disgraceful hand of neglect!![20]

While Bunn's list contains several more journals at least as obscure as those cited here, he fails to mention *The Comic Magazine* among them. Almost equally reticent is Arthur William à Beckett's biographical memoir, *The à Becketts of 'Punch',* noting

20 Alfred Bunn, A Word with Punch (London, 1847), p. 6.

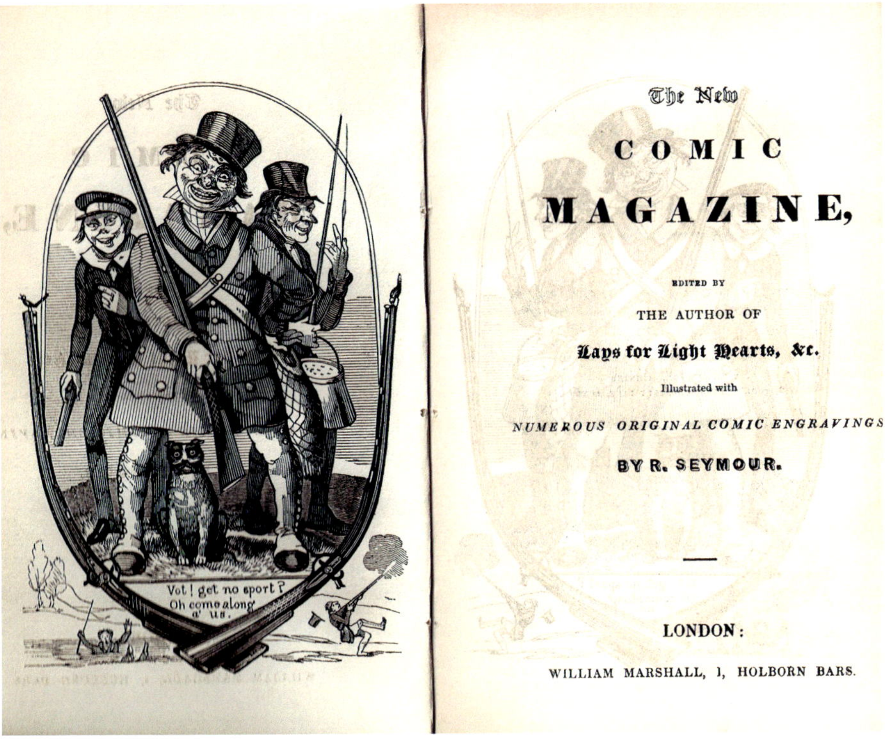

Illustration 10: Robert Seymour?, wood engraved frontispiece to *The New Comic Magazine* (London, n.d.). From the author's own collection

only that 'during the three years of my father's connection with *Figaro in London* he was continually starting other papers. He produced the *Wag* and the *Comic Magazine*.'[21] And even his three-year editorship of *Figaro in London,* without doubt à Beckett's most ambitious and successful magazine and the one most capable of sustaining the caricature tradition in its wood-engraved illustrations by Seymour, ended disastrously in 1834 when à Beckett fell into financial difficulties.

By 1834, however, it is probably fair to say that the concept of a magazine principally devoted to, or structured by, the publication of caricature had run its course. Certainly by 1841 *Punch* had begun to transform graphic satire by introducing the wood-engraved 'big cuts', which seem in hindsight the inevitable outcome of a shift from the caricature to the cartoon as the obvious medium for political graphic satire. Yet I am reluctant to suggest that there is a simple, clear line of development or moment of sudden transformation when the political caricature as understood by Gillray, Rowlandson and George Cruikshank is re-invoked – or even re-invented – by

21 Arthur William à Beckett, The à Becketts of 'Punch'. Memories of Father and Sons (Westminster, 1903), p. 46.

the full-paged wood engravings that formed one of the central elements of *Punch*. The intense experimentation of the 1820s and 1830s had shown that traditional caricature lent itself very poorly to the periodical idea as it emerged into Victorian consciousness. Single-plate engraved satire, and even lithographic prints, were to a large extent inimical to the visual interests of an early Victorian periodical press eager to exploit the wood engraving as a versatile and easily produced reprographic medium capable of being assimilated into a typeset page without difficulty. *Punch,* with its adaptable squarish double-columned page, made immediate use of many forms of comic illustration that had been developed by the humorous magazines of the 1820s and 1830s as well as the full-page political cartoon. Tiny silhouettes, autonomous vignettes set within the columns of type, and embellished capital letters all helped to construct the journal, and were especially apparent in the teeming pages of the *Punch Almanack*. The sometimes sorry comic publications of the 1820s and 1830s frequently suggest an evident degeneration of the caricature tradition into crudely drawn if vigorous publications, in which wit has been reduced to coarse humour and a sharp political vision into a slapstick version of human failings and grotesquerie. But in their energy, inventiveness and engagement with the serial idea, these magazines brought life to a caricature tradition that was increasingly unable to sustain its commercial and artistic presence in the rapidly changing market place for visual culture in the 1830s and developed the wood-engraved comic image to the point where it could form a central and cherished element in Victorian periodical culture.

Sune Erik Schlitte

Beyond the Image. Practices of Caricature in the Artistic Field

Der Nexus zwischen schriftlicher und bildlicher Satire wurde im 18. Jahrhundert häufig durch das gemeinsame Abdrucken beider Medien befördert. Diese Verbindung wird im vorliegenden Text anhand der Verssatiren John Wolcots untersucht, der als einer der bekanntesten Satiriker seiner Zeit von der Forschung bisher nur wenig Aufmerksamkeit bekam. Wolcot begann seine Karriere als Kunstkritiker und verlegte sein Engagement schon bald auf die Politsatire, was die enge Verbindung dieser Felder im Bereich der Publizistik veranschaulicht und eine weitere Kernthese dieses Beitrags darstellt. Weiterhin sind seine Texte ein Beleg dafür, dass in Text und Bild der Satire des späten 18. Jahrhunderts Gesellschaft sowohl abgebildet als auch produziert wurde.

In the late eighteenth century – the so-called 'Golden Age of caricature' – visual and textual satire were often published together.[1] One aim of the following paper is the analysis of connections between these two genres Those producing such works often laid claim to such congruities: 'Quote from my work as much as you please', a phrase of John Wolcot (1738–1819) – better known by the pseudonym Peter Pindar – was not only a piece of advice for his readers, it was his working method.[2] Wolcot quoted other texts and often illustrated his works. This opening phrase, asking the reader for a critical interaction with the text, is written in one of Wolcot's satirical pamphlets to the exhibition of the Royal Academy of Art. This fact brings us to one of the main ideas of the satire and caricature of that time: A written piece of satire does not often stand alone. It is always in a state of interaction and cross-communication with its audience, the critics and the visualized characters of the same period. It is also in exchange with the visual caricature of the time and shares with it some of the most important topics. Indeed, they were often presented together when published side by side. Analysis is shown to be necessary, and Wolcot as one of the outstanding characters of his time proves to be a good example for such an analysis.

The interaction mentioned above is one of the main ideas of the 'visual turn', to quote just one of the many names to which this cultural paradigm has given rise. In

1 Diana Donald, The golden age of caricature. Satirical prints in the age of George III (New Haven, 1996).

2 The Works of Peter Pindar Esq. To which are prefixed Memoirs of the Authors Life, A new edition, Revised and corrected, With copius index, Five volumes Vol.I., (London, 1812), p. 9.

accordance with the requirements of this turn, describing and interpreting an individual picture is not sufficient; the picture needs to be understood in its context and the discourse to be investigated within the visual and textual regime of that particular time.[3] Thus, the message conveyed in caricatures by James Gillray, Thomas Rowlandson, John Wolcot and other protagonists were part of a wider discourse.[4]

The purpose of this paper is to analyze the interaction between textual and visual satire. There is much evidence that these were interlinked and were understood in this way.[5] In the following John Wolcot's work is used as a means of analyzing these interrelations. One of the reasons for this understanding is the fact that his textual satires were published together with visual caricatures. Other reasons are to be found in theoretical discussions of aesthetics of the time with regard to the art forms of poetry and painting, which were held in similar esteem. This contemporary understanding of 'art' was derived from Horace's *Ars Poetica* and the phrase 'ut pictura poesis'.[6]

The second aim of this paper is to consider to what extent John Wolcot and other satirists were critics of the ruling class in the late eighteenth century. Such interrogations have so far given rise to very diverse conclusions: some see the satire of John Wolcot as advice designed to bring about better governance on the part of George III, who had lost his way in the sphere of day-to-day governance.[7] Others see Pindar as

---

3 Tom Holert, Regimewechsel, Visual Studies, Politik, Kritik, in: Klaus Sachs-Hombach (ed.), Bildtheorien. Anthropologische und kulturelle Grundlagen des Visualistic Turn, p. 334; Bernd Roeck, Visual turn? Kulturgeschichte und die Bilder, in: *Geschichte und Gesellschaft*, Zeitschrift für historische Sozialwissenschaft 29 (2003), pp. 294–315; Christian Kruse, Positionen der Kunstwissenschaft als historische Bildwissenschaft, in: Jan Kusber (ed.), Historische Kulturwissenschaften, Positionen, Praktiken und Perspektiven (Bielefeld, 2010), pp. 81–104; W.J.T Mitchell, 'The Pictorial Turn', in: Artforum, No. 30, 1992, pp. 89–94.

4 Bernd Roeck, Das historische Auge, Kunstwerke als Zeugen ihrer Zeit, Von der Renaissance zur Revolution, Göttingen 2004, pp. 73–77; Arline Meyer, Parnassus from the foothills, the Royal Academy viewed by Thomas Rowlandson and John Wolcot (Peter Pindar), in: *The British Art Journal* 2002, pp. 32–43.

5 Critics and artists of the 18th century often took burlesque and mock heroic poems from Homer or Virgil as role models. One famous example is Alexander Pope's satirical and critical writings (Emmanuel Schwartz, Satire unmasked by reading; in: Elizabeth C. Mansfield [ed.], Seeing satire in the eighteenth century (Oxford, 2013), pp. 15–39, esp. pp. 15–16.); the most influential theory for satire at the time was probably John Dryden's 'Discourse concerning the Original and Progress of Satire' (Dustin Griffin, A critical reintroduction (Louisville, 1994), pp. 14–24). Satire is not necessarily found in written text it is although find in pictures, music and performances (George Austin Test, Satire, Spirit and Art (Gainsville, 1991), p. 8)

6 Udo Kultermann, Geschichte der Kunstgeschichte (Munich, 1996), pp. 50; Henry Markiewicz, Uliana Gabara, Ut pictura poesis: A history of a topos and the problem, in: *New Literary History*, Vol.18,3 (1987), pp. 535–558; Meyer, op.cit., p. 33.

7 Robert Vales, Peter Pindar (John Wolcot) (New York, 1973), p. 122.

standing in clear opposition to George III and as an admirer of Thomas Paine's *Rights of Man.*[8]

In order to show affinities between text and picture in the satire of the time, a contextualization of John Wolcot is necessary. Afterwards, two case studies will lead to an analysis of the interaction between text and picture. The first one will deal with the early work of Wolcot as art critic. Wolcot's first successful work on the London publishing market was *Lyric Odes to the Royal Academicians* in 1782.[9] This early work, which earned him a name as a critic on the London art scene, will provide the first case study for the analysis of Wolcot's style of critique and the interaction between text and picture.

The second case study will examine Wolcot's work as political critique in his text *The Lousiad,* which argued against the repression of the people as a consequence of royal power.[10] As a successful author of the London publishing scene Wolcot had both his supporters and opponents. His anti-Royalist position created a lot of enemies. The outlook shows some of the debates Wolcot took part in, which were often connected to the political scene.

To the English public of the late eighteenth century, John Wolcot was better known by the pseudonym Peter Pindar. Before becoming a satirist Wolcot worked as a surgeon, doctor and clergyman. During his apprenticeship as a surgeon he wrote his first verses and spent a year in France to learn the language. In 1767 he was awarded a medical degree from the University of Aberdeen. In 1768 Wolcot travelled to Jamaica as the physician to the Governor of Jamaica, William Trelawney. After Trelawney died in 1772 Wolcot left his position and returned to England.[11]

It was during his time as a physician in Truro, where he established a medical practice, that he developed the habit of writing satirical pamphlets about some of the town's well-known people. This caused many problems, which may well have led to Wolcot's decision to leave Truro. In 1781, at the age of 42, he decided to move to London, taking with him the young artist John Opie. He had discovered Opie's talent some time before in Truro and together they decided to embark on a joint venture. Wolcot would support the young artist with his critiques which would make Opie better known to a wider audience.[12] This sort of collaboration between artist and critic

8 Klaus Finger, Volkstümliche Satire der Industriellen Revolution, John Wolcot ('Peter Pindar') und seine Nachfolger (Frankfurt/M., 1984), pp. 104–170; Johannes Dobai, Die Kunstliteratur des Klassizismus und der Romantik in England (Bern, 1974), Vol. 2, pp 1162–1164.

9 Peter Pindar, Lyric odes, to the Royal Academicians, a distant relation to the poet of Thebes (London, 1782).

10 Peter Pindar, The Lousiad a heroic-comic poem, Canto I. (London, 1785).

11 http://www.oxforddnb.com/view/article/29828 (last accessed 10th August 2013).

12 R. Polwhele, Traditions and Recollections, Vol. 1, Domestic, Clerical and Literary (London, 1826), pp. 77–80.

was not rare in the eighteenth-century art scene.[13] In the late eighteenth century, the world of art criticism was not highly developed and apart from Wolcot's work there had been just a few critiques published in newspapers such as the Morning Post and the Daily Advertiser. These alternated between sophisticated connoisseur's critiques, which reported on Jonathan Richardson's essay *The Art of Criticism;* and, at the other end of the spectrum, pieces that were concerned with the Royal Academy of Arts and its involvement with and symbolism of political power.[14] It was in this context that Wolcot had to draw attention to his work, while he still had the chance to establish himself as an author in this fast-moving scene. The development of the London art market with the establishment of the Royal Academy of Arts, the growing auction market and the rising sales of prints created many career opportunities.[15]

Starting in 1782, Wolcot published satires for over twenty years, opening with the highly successful 'Lyric Odes, to the Royal Academicians', and later on often came to refer to such topics as the politics of the day and the Royal Family.[16] His odes, ballads, epigrams, heroic couplets, songs and verse epistles published in quarto size ran to amongst 12 and 50 pages in length and sold for one to three shillings.[17] They were widely published and often pirated. The rise in price from one to three shillings could well have been a particular catalyst for this copying, as evidenced in the cheaper issues which appeared in his name from 1788. From 1800, Wolcot's sight was poor and his publishing activities came to a halt. But many epigones followed in his footsteps using similar names – for example Polly Pindar – or even his own name.[18] In addition to his satirical texts, Wolcot published in a couple of other genres such as that of his tragedy *The Fall of Portugal* or *The Royal Exile,* but these rarely met with much success.[19]

As a downside to any relative success, the satirist had to cope with several drawbacks associated with the genre. One example was the poor reputation of a satirist in

13 Other artists like Nathaniel Hone even took a shortcut and wrote the critique themselves (Royal Academy of Arts Archive RAA/SEC/1/80); Mark Hallett, 'The Business of Criticism', The Press and the Royal Academy Exhibition in Eighteenth-Century London, in: Solkin, David (ed.), Art on the line. The Royal Academy exhibitions at Somerset House, 1780–1836 (New Haven, CT, 2001), pp. 65–76; esp. pp. 68–69.

14 Hallett, op.cit, pp. 65; Meyer, op.cit., pp. 36–37, Holger Hoock, The King's Artist. The Royal Academy of Arts and the Politics of British Culture 1760–1840, New York 2003, S. 134–135.

15 Oskar Bätschmann, Ausstellungskünstler, Kult und Karriere im modernen Kunstsystem (Cologne, 1997); John Brewer, The pleasures of the imagination. English culture in the eighteenth century (London, 1997); Holger Hoock, op. cit.; Thomas Bayer, John Page. The development of the art market in England, money as a muse, 1730–1900 (London, 2011).

16 Peter Pindar, Out at last, or the fallen minister, an invective against W. Pitt (London, 1801); Peter Pindar, More money, or, odes of instruction to Mr. Pitt, with a variety of other choice matters (London, 1792); Peter Pindar, Sir Joseph Banks and the Emperor of Morocco (London, 1788); Peter Pindar, The Rights of Kings, or loyal odes to disloyal Academicians (London, 1791).

17 H.J. Jackson, England's populist Pindars, in: *The Electronic British Library Journal* 2002, Art. 4, pp. 1–18.

18 Jackson, op.cit., pp. 3–4.

19 http://www.oxforddnb.com/view/article/29828 (last accessed 30th July 2013).

society. The satirical text and the satirical picture held a similar status as a popular art.[20] Taking into account the fact that the work offended famous personalities such as William Pitt the Younger or the royal dynasty, this bad reputation is not surprising. Indeed, in comparison to other satirists and caricaturists Wolcot's standing is not exceptional. James Gillray, Thomas Rowlandson or John Williams shared a reputation as heavy drinkers and arrogant 'falstaffs' for whom personal benefit was the only aim. Caricaturists were generally not included in the early dictionaries of artists, and the death of a famous caricaturist such as Gillray was not even commented on in the press. Their art had the reputation of being ephemeral and little more than commodity literature.[21] This social stigma is a further correlation between caricature and satire which might have led to the fact that those producing such works in these genres often shared groups of friends, such as John Wolcot and Thomas Rowlandson, who both belonged to the circle of the engraver and publisher John Raphael Smith.[22]

It has often been argued that the English satirical picture was strongly influenced by the *English gentleman,* who came to know this type of art during his Grand Tour on the Continent. They developed an affection for this piece of art during their tour on the continent and introduced it as a gentlemanlike habit to London circles, from where it spread out and developed into the highly elaborated satire of the late eighteenth century. Another reason for the development of the satirical picture that should be cited is the stable situation in Parliament at the time. In this context, the Wilkesite Riots, the French Revolution or the American Revolutionary War encouraged the development of the art form.[23] But a role model often overlooked for the satirical picture may have been its textual equivalent. The satirical text addressed individual people in an aggressive manner from very early on.[24] Thus, it is possible to say that the transition in visual caricature of the late eighteenth century was partly affected by textual satires.[25]

20 Christina Oberstebrink, Karikatur und Poetik, James Gillray 1756–1815 (Berlin, 2005), pp. 51–61, Louis I. Bredvold, A note in defence of satire, in: Bernhard Fabian (ed.), Satvra, Ein Kompendium moderner Studien zur Satire (Hildesheim and New York, 1975), pp. 83–94.

21 David Alexander, Richard Newton and English caricature in the 1790s (New York, 1998), pp. 55–56; Diana Donald, The Age of Caricature (New Haven, 1996), pp. 22–27.

22 Meyer, op.cit., p. 37.

23 Amelia Rauser, Caricatures unmasked. Irony, authenticity, and individualism in eighteenth-century English prints (Newark, 2008), pp. 17–19; Werner Busch, Das sentimentalische Bild, die Krise der Kunst im 18. Jahrhundert und die Geburt der Moderne (Munich, 1993), pp. 459–460; Tamara Hunt, Defining John Bull. Political caricature and national identity in late Georgian England (Aldershot, 2003), pp. 89–96.

24 The discussion about the quality and use of literary wit was held among philosophers, clerics, scientists, pamphleteers and jurists early in the 18th century. Well known authors like Alexander Pope or John Dryden made some of their greatest achievements in satiric verse (Roger D. Lund, Ridicule, Religion and the Politics of Wit in Augustan England (Surrey, 2012), pp. 1–11.).

25 Matthew Hodgart, Satire, Origins and Principles (New Brunswick, 1969), pp. 7–14.

Before delving into satire and its interaction with politics, we must take a brief look at Pindar's art criticism and his satirical texts. He made his debut on the London scene with one such piece, which combined art criticism and satire, the satirical text *Lyric Odes, to the Royal Academicians.*[26] Wolcot's writing about the Royal Academy of Arts stood in relation to his task to establish his friend John Opie, 'The Cornish Rembrandt', as a figure on the London art scene.[27] This plan turned out to be very successful: after just one year, Opie had five pictures at the annual exhibition of the Royal Academy.[28] This may have been the source of the friction between Opie and Wolcot, which marked the end of their collaboration. Whether it was the recent marriage of Opie or the painter's newfound higher income which had to be shared with Wolcot is hard to say.[29] But what is certain is that this enterprise ended in a dispute between the two.

Wolcot's first text on the exhibition of the Royal Academy takes the reader on an imaginative stroll through the exhibition, starting in front of the building with a short critique of architectural style before commanding the reader to go inside: 'Now let us see what this rare dome contains.'[30] Citing simply the names of the artists rather than the pictures themselves, even the contemporary reader would have needed some additional information, or would have needed to have visited the exhibition himself.[31] Wolcot's main targets were established artists like Benjamin West:

> O West, what hath thy pencil done?
> Why, painted God Almighty's Son
> Like and Old-clothes-Man about London street!
> Place in his hand a rusty bag,
> To hold each sweet collected rag [...]. [32]

Using a simple rhyme scheme Wolcot attacked West, criticizing him mainly because of his status as an established artist who had gained a lot of royal patronage. Nevertheless, Wolcot's texts were highly successful and his comments on the need for a reform of the Royal Academy of Arts played a part in the art-discussions.[33]

His later satirical works, however, show that his main interests were in the sphere of politics or at least its interaction with the field of arts. In his satire *A celebration, or the academic procession to St. James* he described the members of the Royal Acad-

26 Peter Pindar, Lyric op. cit.
27 Dobai, op.cit., pp. 1160–1163.
28 Meyer, op.cit., p. 34.
29 Ada Earland, John Opie and his circle (London, 1911), p. 45.
30 Wolcot, Works, op.cit., p. 16
31 Holger Hoock, op. cit., pp. 206–27.
32 Wolcot, Works, op.cit., pp. 17; The picture is probably a sketch from the ascension that is in the Tate Gallery in London today.
33 Dobai, op.cit., pp. 1160–1163.

emy as puppets of the King. This criticism to artist is repeated in other works and is an indication of his main objective:[34]

> Were I to write thy epitaph, I'd say
> 'Here lies below a painter's clay
> Who work'd awy most furiously for Kings
> And prov'd that the fire of inclination
> For pleasing the great Ruler of a Nation
> And fire of genius, are two diff'rent things.'[35]

In his judgment the Royal Academy of Arts was not a free institution but rather the King's political weapon. Even when Wolcot is standing in the focus of the text he is representing a type of satirist, who was publishing their texts in a wider cultural scope in which they were referring for example on the regime of the Academy over the artistic field.[36] Other pamphleteers like John Williams (1761–1818) alias Anthony Pasquin held similar ideas about the Royal Academy of Arts, and conflicts between the Academy and the British Institution for Promoting Fine Arts in the United Kingdom showed that the Royal Academy was not the unquestioned leading institution of the London art scene.[37]

Peter Pindar's satire *The Lousiad* refers to an incident that took place in the royal household. The story told was that when the king sat down for dinner with several members of his family, he found a louse on his plate. Guessing that it came from the one of the kitchen staff, he ordered that all the servants have their heads shaved.[38] In Thomas Rowlandson's picture print we see George III, the queen and three princesses seated at a small dinner table (Illustration 1).[39] The king is holding a plate with the louse on it and is turning around to address his cook in a furious manner. The two servants behind the King's chair appear anxious. A viewer of the picture may have the impression of an untidy kitchen. However the reader who recognized the picture whilst reading the attached story would have been able to discern a tale with political impact.

The story was published in five cantos over a period of ten years. It is a didactic play about ruling, opposition and justice. Beside these crucial topics, the reader is

34 Peter Pindar, Celebration, Or, the academic procession to St. James's; an ode (London, 1794).
35 Peter Pindar, Subjects for painters (London, 1789), p. 5.
36 Holert, op.cit., p. 340.
37 Anthony Pasquin, Memoirs of the Royal Academicians, being an attempt to improve the national taste, Vol. 1. H.D. (Symonds, 1796); The establishment of the British Institution established new connoisseurs of art in the London art scene which lead to frictions between the *Institution* and the *Academy* (Peter, Funnell, Die Londoner Kunstwelt und ihre Institutionen, in: Celina Fox [ed.], Metropole London, Macht und Glanz einer Weltstadt 1800–1840 (Recklinghausen, 1992), pp. 154–156, esp. pp. 160–161.)
38 Pindar, Lousiad, op.cit., S. 171–172.
39 http://www.britishmuseum.org, BM Satires 7186.

Illustration 1: Thomas Rowlandson, is this, your louse (London, 1787), etching, BM 1868,0808.5668 © Trustees of the British Museum

privy to much mocking of George III, as one can read in the first meeting of the king and the louse:

> Paint heavenly Muse, the look, the very look
> That a Sovereign's face possession took
> When he first saw the Louse in solemn state
> Grave as a Spaniard, march across his plate
> Yet could a Louse a British King surprise
> And like a pair of Saucers stretch his Eyes?
> The little tenant of a mortal head
> Shake the great Ruler of Three Realms with dread?[40]

The rhetorical question is mocking the authority and power of George III. It is hard to find a smaller living creature than a louse but it frightens the king nonetheless. Here, Wolcot is taking the king's fear to another level, with a comparison drawn from political life: 'Not with more horror did his eyes behold/Charles Fox, that cun-

40 Wolcot, Works, op.cit. p. 177.

ning enemy of old.'[41] Charles James Fox was one of the worst enemies of George III in the disputes surrounding the American Revolutionary War, the East India Company and the French Revolution and should undoubtedly have scared George more than a louse.[42] As a result, the king is portrayed as not being able to separate real risk from a mere bagatelle. After several pages of being mocked, the king shows a delayed rejection with the interjection:

> 'How, how? What, what? what's that, what's that?' he cries,
> With rapid accent, and with staring eyes:
> 'Look there, look there; what's got into my house?
> A Louse, God bless us! Louse, louse, louse, louse, louse.'[43]

The repetition of the words 'what' and 'louse' gives a picture of a babbling king who is terrified by a microscopic animal. The king's lack of linguistic dexterity was well known to the contemporary English public and Wolcot is exaggerating it with his hyperbole. After this eruption, George III tries to find the original carrier of the Louse, whom he believes is one of the cooks. He orders that their heads be shaved and that they wear wigs. However, the cooks, insisting on their rights, threaten a minor uprising: 'Then pray, Sir, listen to your faithful Cooks/Nor in the Palace breed a Civil War:'[44] The intended message for the reader here is undoubtedly that a king who cannot control his kitchen staff will never be the right man to contain a civil war on the other side of the world, in the American colonies. As the story continues and the rebellion worsens the cooks receive assistance from their wives, who join them in their struggle against royal injustice. They go on to denounce the reason behind their king's harsh reaction as lying in their social standing: 'Any thing's good enough for a humble folk / Shored here and there, forsooth; call'd Dog and Bitch / (God bless us well) because we are not rich.'[45] But all the pleading and denouncements are to no avail. The cooks' heads are shaved. As a final injustice, they do not even get the wigs that they were promised. At the end of the text, the Louse gets the power of speech and tells his story. Born on a page's lock, he was one day knocked off and fell into the hair of a dairymaid from which he crawled into that of the king.[46] In the age of the revolution *The Lousiad* found many readers in all classes. The main reason for the conflict in the story was the overreaction of a king who is revealed as being to blame for his own untidiness. But how was this mock heroic poem received in English soci-

41 Wolcot, Works op. cit. p. 177.

42 http://www.oxforddnb.com/view/article/10024?docPos=1 (last accessed 9th August 2013); Brendan Simms, An odd question enough'. Charles James Fox, the crown and British policy during the Hanoverian crisis of 1806, in: *The Historical Journal* 38,3 (1995), pp. 567–596.

43 Wolcot, Works op. cit. p. 184.

44 Wolcot, Works op. cit. p. 240.

45 Wolcot, Works op. cit. p. 282.

46 Wolcot, Works op. cit. pp. 304–315.

Illustration 2: Charles Knight, after John Boyne, *Comic Readings* (London, 1791), hand-coloured etching and stipple, BM 1870,0514.2850 © Trustees of the British Museum

ety? Who were the readers of satire at the time? Was it simply the case that everyone read them at home, alone? The caricature *Comic Reading* by John Boyne provides us with an idea of the contemporary consumption of satire. An old man with a monocle stands at a lectern reading a text to a crowd of nearly seventy people. On the side of the lectern is written: 'Select Poems from | Peter Pindar | Don Quixote & | Tristram Shandy.'[47] Apparently, satire was a public event which attracted a substantial group of people, with an interest in political matters (Illustration 2). In this case, one could even argue that the public power of the general government was met with opposition in the form of the power of the growing bourgeoisie.[48]

47 http://www.britishmuseum.org, BM Satires 8278.

48 There is a lot of evidence that the satire was often performed in public: 'After dinner, the following song, written by Peter Pindar, Esq. and set to Music by Mr. Shield, for the occasion was sung by Mr. Wigstead, one of their Highness tradesmen.' (Morning Chronicle [London, 31th October 1792]). Hence satire was not just consumed in solitude, it was also listened to in a social way and it was a part of the public sphere of London (Andre Krischer, Politische Kommunikation und Öffentlichkeit in London. Zur Entwicklung einer Großstadt im 17. Jahrhundert in mediengeschichtlicher

As one might expect, the reaction of the press and public to Peter Pindar was mixed. Some publications, such as *The English Review,* saw Peter Pindar as being of the ilk of well-known and established authors:

> There are a number of scribblers, who, having no merit of their own, [...] Thus Sterne was imitated by those who had pretentions neither to humour nor sentiment; and thus our friend Peter Pindar is unmercifully lashed by many, whose only talent at satire is scurrility and calling names.[49]

One of Wolcot's principal antagonists was William Gifford (1756–1826).[50] He was the editor of the *Antijacobin, or Weekly Examiner,* which was sponsored by William Pitt's Tory government. He was well-known for several satires such as *The Baviad* which attacked Whiggism and Jacobinism.[51] His pamphlets confronted John Wolcot directly:

> This man certainly possesses a species of humour; but it is exhausted by a repetition of the same manner, and nearly the same ideas even to disgust. [...] Thus obscure man has contrived, by these qualifications, to thrust himself upon the public notice, and become the scorn of every man of character and virtue.[52]

As mentioned before the reputation of caricaturists and satirists was very poor. One reason is their doubtful influence on society and their art which is supposed to be ephemeral. Giffords arguments brought forth against the satirist can therefore be seen as a general critique. However, the fight between the two got more individual. Wolcot was not willing to accept the very criticisms that he himself launched against others. The conflict was taken from the pamphlets to the London newspapers:

> A rencontre took place yesterday in the shop of Mr. Wright, the bookseller, between the celebrated Peter Pindar and Mr. Gifford, author of the Baviad. We need not inform our literary readers that in reply to the many sarcasms thrown out by Peter Pindar against the author of the Baviad and other Poems, Mr. Gifford lately published a severe and keen satire against

Perspektive, in: Irmgard Ch. Becker (ed.), Die Stadt als Kommunikationsraum. Reden, Schreiben und Schauen in Großstädten des Mittelalters und der Neuzeit, Sigmaringen 2011, pp. 55–87, esp. pp. 56–57; Hannah Barker, England, 1760–1815, in: Simon Burrows (ed.), Press, politics and the public sphere in Europe and North America, 1760–1820, Cambridge 2002, pp. 93–112, esp. pp. 93–95; Jürgen Habermas, Strukturwandel der Öffentlichkeit [Berlin, 1971]).

49 *The English Review, or an Abstract of the English and Foreign literature* (London, 1783), p. 495.

50 http://www.oxforddnb.com/view/article/10669?docPos=2; Gifford was not just an enemy of Wolcot, he also attacked John Williams so strongly in his satire 'the Baviad' that Williams took him to court. (Courier and Evening Gazette [London, 1st October 1800]).

51 Roy Benjamin Clark, William Gifford Tory Satirist, Critic, and Editor (New York, 1931), http://www.oxforddnb.com/view/article/10669?docPos=2 (last accessed 20th July 2013).

52 William Gifford, Epistle to Peter Pindar by the author of the Baviad (London, 1800), pp. 5–6.

> Peter. […] This literary combat yesterday produced blows. Dr. Wolcot went into the shop of Mr. Wright, where Mr. Gifford was seated reading a newspaper. […] Upon which the Dr. aimed a blow at his brother poet with a cane.[53]

In this case, the literary fight was taken to a more physical level and was widely published in London newspapers. Wolcot's aggressive reaction shows that the satirist of the late eighteenth century was a person of public interest. His reaction was widely published and often shared in the London public sphere. The fact that 'low-brow' art was read in the highest of London's circles shows the attention Wolcot's texts got from the Prince Regent. Many have claimed that the Prince Regent benefitted from Pindar's publishing, because Pindar mocked his father, and it was even said that the prince might have paid Pindar. As the following article shows, some of the rumours were discussed in public:

> The town are in daily expectation of the new Eclogue announced by Peter Pindar: and a certain critic […], has been heard to say, in the true spirit of old Shandy, 'Were I despotic Prince, I would oblige this Peter, *nolens volens,* to write me such a one every week.'[54]

George III probably did pay Wolcot a pension. Many reasons for this have been suggested. In Thomas Rowlandson's caricature *Peter's Pension,* we find a visualization of one of these ideas (Illustration 3). The king is standing on the right-hand side of the picture. He is shown in profile to the left and is holding out to Peter a rolled document inscribed with the word 'Pension'. Peter, a thin, elderly man, turns away, holding out both hands to ward off the gift. A paper inscribed 'Odes' is peeking from his pocket. Both are wearing wigs and old-fashioned clothes. The King is carrying a sword. Beneath the design is engraved: 'Ah! let me Sire refuse it – I implore – I ought not to be rich whilst You are poor.'[55] This royal desire to grant Wolcot a pension shows that the power of satire was greater than one might think. Even Wolcot himself used the pension story and published a satire entitled *Peter's pension, a solemn Epistle to a sublime Personage,* which might have been published to boost his own standing by fuelling the rumour of a public pension.[56] Many authors discussed the rumours that Wolcot might have been the recipient of a pension from the crown in the years 1788–89 to stop him publishing attacks on the royal manner of governance. Moreover, he refused to write pamphlets in support of the Crown and apparently did not accept further payments of the pension after a short period.[57]

---

53 General Evening Post (London, 19th August 1800).

54 Public Advertiser (London, 12th April 1786).

55 http://www.britishmuseum.org, BM Satires 7399.

56 Peter Pindar, Peter's pension, A solemn epistle to a sublime personage, With an engraving by an eminent artist (London, 1788).

57 William Jerdan, The Autobiography of William Jerdan. With His Literary, Political and Social Reminiscences and Correspondence During the Last Fifty Years (London, 1853), pp. 262–270; Finger,

Illustration 3: Thomas Rowlandson, *[Peter's pension]* (London, 1788), etching, BM 1868,0808.5812 © Trustees of the British Museum

There was great pressure for parliamentary reform from some radicals during the 1790s. When reading Peter Pindars satire the growing power of Parliament under William Pitt the Younger and the illness induced absences of George III must be kept in mind. Furthermore, one must consider the fact that the freedom of press was established in 1695 but was restricted in the times of the French Revolution. The *treason trials* of 1794, the *seditious meeting act* and the *treason act* of 1795 show that the government was willing to eliminate the radical movement.[58] In this specific situation of political suppression, satire was one of the few ways to express radical ideas because it was not widely censured.

It is within this context that Pindar's pamphlets should be read. In *Liberty's last squeak,* he is fighting against the newly issued laws which defined argument against

op.cit., pp. 163–164; Theodor Reitterer, Leben und Werke Peter Pindars (Dr. John Wolcot) (Vienna, 1900), p. 23.

58 John Dinwiddy, Conceptions of Revolution in the English Radicalism of the 1790s, in: Eckart Hellmuth (ed.), Transformation of political culture, England Germany in the late Eighteenth century (Oxford, 1990), pp. 535–560; pp. 538–542; Rachel Rogers, Censorhsip and Creativity, The Case of Sampson Perry, Radical Editor in 1790s Paris and London, in: *lisa* (revue LISA/LSA e-journal) 11,1 (2013)

the king as high treason.[59] His works were not only attacking the king, they were also fighting the law as well as being a commitment to the freedom of speech.[60] Along these lines further research on the works of Peter Pindar and his many epigones would be fruitful in order to gain new insights into the history of the public sphere.

Satire and caricature of the time interacted with one another through the genres' proponents and their products. Contact between textual satire and visual caricature was achieved in many ways: their shared political topics were a source of collaboration. Similar stylistic devices such as the hyperbole also supported this interaction in many ways. One such interaction was the publishing of a picture and a text together, which made it possible to tell a story on different levels, as *The Lousiad* shows. The possibility to express criticism marks a turning point in the late eighteenth century which made possible a gradual change of language in text and picture, but was not necessarily followed by a change of political practice. The works of Peter Pindar and other satirists were read by a wide public which was interested in the debates and fights between satirists like John Wolcot and William Gifford. The rumours about the pension paid to Peter Pindar demonstrate that satirists had sustainable power in the political world of the late eighteenth century. Finally, the example of Peter Pindar manifests the overlap between the functions of literary criticism, art criticism and political criticism in the late eighteenth century. The growing art market during that time showed interrelations with high politics in terms of patronage and the founding of academies and institutions. These interlinks made the combination of art critic and political critic possible, as in Peter's *Lyric odes, to the Royal Academicians* and indicates the attraction that other satires such as *The Lousiad* could have to a wider audience.

59 Dinwiddy, op.cit., pp. 535–560; Michael Lobban, Treason, Sedition and the Radical Movement in the Age of the French Revolution, in: *Liverpool Law Press* 22 (2000), pp. 205–210.

60 Finger, op. cit., p. 139.

The Contributors

James Baker
is a digital curator at the British Library. His research interests include satirical printing, the manufacture of visual culture in eighteenth and nineteenth century Britain, urban protest, spatial analysis, representations of authority, and the digital humanities.

Werner Busch
was professor of art history at the Department of Art History at the Free University of Berlin. From 2003 to 2009, he chaired the collaborative research cluster 'Ästhetische Erfahrung im Zeichen der Entgrenzung der Künste'.

Timothy Clayton
is an associate fellow of Warwick University. He has published widely on British prints and the international print trade and is currently engaged on a book about the battle of Waterloo and an exhibition, 'Bonaparte and the British', for the British Museum.

Karl Janke
is a freelance author and curator. He studied art history, archaeology, and philosophy in Hamburg. He has published several books on art of the nineteenth and twentieth century, in particular for the Wilhelm Busch – Deutsches Museum für Karikatur und Zeichenkunst in Hanover, Germany.

Brian Maidment
is professor of the history of print culture within the department of English at Liverpool John Moores University. He has particular research interests in nineteenth-century periodicals, the literature produced by labouring class authors, and visual culture – especially caricature and satirical prints.

Christina Oberstebrink
is an independent art historian and translator living in Berlin. She specializes in eighteenth century art theory and caricature, the reception of Aristotle's Poetics in eighteenth century English art theory and its impact on concepts of genres, and historiography of artistic biography.

Sheila O'Connell
is curator of British prints before 1900 at the British Museum. Her main interests are satirical and popular prints. She and Tim Clayton are currently planning an exhibition on 'Bonaparte and the British' to be held at the British Museum in 2015.

Temitope Odumosu
is an art historian with a research focus on the imaging of African people in Western visual culture. She is interested in how popular visual media influences and participates in identity politics. She is currently the Marie Curie Postdoctoral Fellow for EUROTAST – a training network researching the transatlantic slave trade through history, bio-archaeology, social anthropology, and genetics.

Sune Schlitte
studied history and German at the University of Göttingen. He is currently working on the project 'The Politics of Art. The Emergence of a Market in the Long Eighteenth Century' as a member of the Ph.D.-research group on the Personal Union between England and Hanover at the University of Göttingen.

The Editors

Anorthe Kremers
As Vice Head of the Conferences & Symposia Unit at the Volkswagen Foundation in Hanover, Germany, she is responsible for the contents of the foundation's conferences, symposia, and lecture series in the humanities and social sciences. She studied history and French at the universities of Tübingen and Grenoble.

Elisabeth Reich
As Scientific Assistant at the Wilhelm Busch – Deutsches Museum für Karikatur und Zeichenkunst in Hanover, Germany, she is responsible for the archive of the British cartoonist Ronald Searle whose estate is hosted by the museum. She studied history and Scandinavian languages at the universities of Erlangen, Uppsala, and Kiel.